Life Skill Education and Curriculum

Life Skill Education and Curriculum

Gracious Thomas

SHIPRA

(2010, revised and enlarged edition of 'HIV Education and Prevention published first in 2001in cloth binding.)

Rs. 250; US$ 10

ISBN: 978-81-7541-253-8

2020 Impression

Life Skill Education and Curriculum

Published by:
SHIPRA PUBLICATIONS
LG 18-19, Pankaj Central Market,
I.P. Ext., Patparganj, Delhi 110092, India
Ph.: +91 11 22235152/6152, 9650028065
Email: info@shiprapublication.com
Website: www.shiprapublication.com

To
Late Professor Maria Faustina
with Gratitude

Acknowledgements

Many people from various walks of life urged me to prepare this document. The work on this book extended over a long period of time and drew diverse sources of intellectual and financial support. Obligations thus involved in the preparation of this book have been many. It is impossible to adequately express the debt that is owed to the many persons and associations, who made this work possible. It is, however, a distinct pleasure to record my gratitude and appreciation to those who have contributed to the development of this volume.

I express my profound gratitude to Prof. H.P. Dikshit, Vice-Chancellor, Indira Gandhi National Open University (IGNOU), New Delhi, and Prof. S.C. Garg, Pro-Vice Chancellor, IGNOU for their constant cooperation and encouragement in my endeavours to fight the HIV/AIDS epidemic particularly, through academic pursuits such as curriculum development, awareness campaigns through teleconferencing sessions, interactive radio counseling and organization of state and national level seminars.

I am highly obliged to my numerous HIV infected clients and their families who were a source of inspiration for me to put on record the anxieties and concern expressed by them. Their confidence in me and their acceptance of me have helped me along the way in gaining lot of experience in HIV counselling which have reflection in this book.

I place on record my special gratitude to my colleagues at IGNOU for their moral support and help in many ways. I am deeply grateful to Prof. A.K. Agarwal, Dr. R.P. Singh, Dr. Gurchain Singh, Dr. S.K. Palit, Ms. Santosh Tanwar, Mr. Joseph Varghese and Mr. Ram Kishan from IGNOU for their constant support and encouragement.

I owe a special debt of gratitude to the numerous persons: physicians, para-medicals, school and University teachers, NGO and donor agency functionaries, and the participants who attended various seminars, conferences and workshops on HIV/AIDS organized by IGNOU for their comments, suggestions and sharing of views on various issues.

My wife Lay and our two children Edwin and Elvis deserve my profound gratitude for their abiding interest, concern and support to me in my involvement in the area of HIV/AIDS.

Many thanks are due to Ms. Maya Kumari and Mr. Balwant Singh who provided me secretarial assistance to compile this manuscript.

New Delhi **Gracious Thomas**

Preface

To the young people in our educational system HIV is not anything new. Most of them were born into a world where HIV was already present. Since the detection of HIV in 1981, much has been done to create awareness and educate people on the what, why and how of HIV/AIDS. The spread of HIV across the globe has a devastating effect. Advancements made in the area of economic development and human potential have been challenged. Millions have lost their lives. Hundreds of thousands have become orphans. Some of the village communities have been completely wiped out. Many households have been left with only grandparents and grandchildren.

HIV has also affected human relationships and life styles. Although the world has made progress in all aspects of life, no satisfactory progress has been made to prevent and control the spread of HIV/AIDS. HIV has not spared any nation or people. While it has infected millions across the world, many more millions have been affected: economically, socially and emotionally.

The world community has initiated numerous activities and projects to prevent and control the spread of HIV. However, the results have not been encouraging. Most of the initiatives so far were to contain the spread of the virus through mechanisms which created hurdles in human relations. Such initiatives have not shown encouraging results. Many advocates of HIV/AIDS prevention focused on preserving and supporting certain unethical and immoral behaviours which in fact cause the spread of HIV. When people prefer to adopt lifestyles which are away from natural and social norms they should also be prepared to face the consequences of such actions. The Indian community is a society which has a rich value system. Values are mainly derived from three sources: religious teachings, guidance from parents and guidance from teachers. Theses three sources provide moral guidance for a healthy and decent living. HIV infections are mostly caused by certain lifestyles such as sex outside marriage, injecting drugs into one's own body and unhygienic practices by health care providers. If people choose to opt behaviours and practices which are away from the prescribed norms, they are challenged by life threatening illnesses.

Under these circumstances, what we need is an intervention which is culture specific, academically sound and socially acceptable. Interventions during the past two decades were based on strategies, materials and messages similar to those developed for the western society. Most of the interventions originated from world bodies such as UNAIDS, WHO and other international donor agencies. India too followed the suit. The results were not encouraging: neither the parents nor the teachers were comfortable in addressing the issues in the way they were presented.

It is therefore apt that we evolve a set of strategies, objectives and methods which are culture specific. The present volume is an effort to discuss some of the issues associated with the HIV/AIDS prevention and control in India. Apart from examining the intervention strategies of the national government, an effort has been made to develop a draft proposal for HIV/AIDS prevention and control along with a curriculum on the subject.

The seven chapters presented in this book are unique in that they are the first attempt by a professional social work academic who has been involved with HIV/AIDS work for over a decade in India to apply academic oriented social analysis to the issues associated with the prevention and control of HIV/AIDS.

Chapter one is an introductory chapter presenting information about some of the basic facts about HIV infection and AIDS. Chapter two is on the role of teachers in HIV/AIDS and life skill education. Chapter three deals with a detailed description about the global and national scenario of HIV/AIDS. Chapter four talks about the vulnerable population in India who are at risk of HIV infection. The main discussion in chapter five is about the strategies of the National AIDS control programme by the Government of India and their implications in the prevention and control of HIV/AIDS.

One of the major outcomes of the present work is to evolve a viable plan of action for the prevention and control of HIV/AIDS in India which has been presented in chapter six. Another major objective of the present volume is to develop a curriculum on HIV/AIDS and Life Skill Education which may be adopted by the educational system at various levels. Chapter seven provides the course structure and syllabus comprising as many as 15 courses in detail and suggestions for about 18 electives in areas related to HIV/AIDS.

In addition to the above, this book also provides the National AIDS Prevention and Control Policy, National Blood Policy, and Bibliography of print materials on HIV/AIDS and life skill education.

It is hoped that this volume will be of immense use to policy makers, academics, NGOs, HIV counselors and those involved in the fight against HIV/AIDS.

Gracious Thomas

Contents

1
A Profile of HIV/AIDS

Recent conventions on HIV/AIDS across the country indicate that infection with Human Immunodeficiency Virus (HIV), the virus that causes Acquired Immuno Deficiency Syndrome (AIDS) has made its way into all strata of Indian society. This killer disease is spreading with unprecedented rapidity, and has emerged as a serious socio-economic and public health problem. AIDS seems to be the most dreaded disease in human history. The tragedy of AIDS in the worst affected countries of Africa and the West is likely to repeat itself in India as we step into the new millennium unless measures are taken in time to counter it. While offering curative care and rehabilitation to the HIV infected patients seems to be a distant reality in India in the absence of a vaccine and affordable drugs for treatment, evolving various strategies to prevent and control the unabated spread of this pandemic is desirable and possible. For this immediate and effective response in new programming areas such as "attitudinal and behavioural change, community-based care and support initiative 'through teaching, research and extension' and the maintenance of human development in the face of an increasing rate of illness and death is required".[1] It is in this context that the medical, University and school system of education assume importance.

An attempt has been made in this book to apply academic oriented social analysis to the problem of the prevention and control of HIV/AIDS in India. The eight chapters provide the reader with the basic facts about HIV, the profile of the research, global and national scenario of HIV, high-risk groups in India, strategies of the Government of India for the prevention and control of HIV, proposals and suggestions for action plan and a curriculum on AIDS, sex and family life education.

The HIV/AIDS Disease

HIV is a very small, fragile virus which cannot survive for long outside the human body. Therefore it is not contagious and cannot be passed from person to person easily like the flue virus, or by ordinary social contacts. It is a member of a group of viruses called retroviruses. Retroviruses are simple microscopic organisms dependent on a host for reproduction. These microscopic organisms lack an independent metabolism and cannot grow without energy and nutrients supplied by a host cell.

An individual infected with HIV may lead a normal life perfectly well with no physical symptoms i.e. HIV non-symptomatic. As the disease progresses, that person will begin to have different illnesses and physical symptoms i.e. HIV symptomatic. The term AIDS is used when the disease has progressed and the individual develops one or more serious infections or conditions.

HIV is a deadly virus, which can remain in the body for several years before causing damage to the immune defense system. So far in all cases the development of HIV in the human body leading to AIDS has proved to be fatal. Till date no vaccine has been developed to protect people carrying HIV. Strictly speaking AIDS is the last or the fatal stage of HIV infection - also called "full-blown AIDS".

AIDS is an acronym made up of the first letter of the words Acquired Immune Deficiency Syndrome. The word acquired was conveniently chosen because the illness was acquired during a period of normal life. It was in 1981 that unusual opportunistic infections were identified in a number of people in the United States of America. These people ultimately died as the infections did not respond positively to any therapy.

Testing Facilities

The most widely used tests for HIV are known as ELISA (enzyme-linked immune sorbent assay) and Western Blot. To ensure the highest degree of accuracy, blood samples which test positive for antibodies to HIV, using the ELISA test, are usually subjected to the confirmatory test, namely, the Western Blot test. Although the cost of ELISA test is comparatively lower, the Western Blot test can be a heavy burden, particularly for most

Indians as it costs several times more than the ELISA test. Other tests or combination of tests may also be used, depending upon new developments in this field. While all the testing centres in India use the ELISA test, very few centres have the facilities for the Western Blot test. A list of government approved HIV testing centres in the country are given in Appendix-I.

ELISA Test

In ELISA, blood and other body fluids are tested with indicator solutions that detect the presence of antibodies directed against HIV. Tiny volumes of solutions are required for the ELISA test. It is usually automated to yield accurate results and therefore the chances of any type of error is minimised. However, it is possible that at any time inaccurate results can also be obtained. It is, nevertheless, estimated that careful performance of the ELISA test and appropriate use of confirmatory procedures make over 99 per cent cases accurate.

The ELISA test can indicate whether antibodies against HIV are present or not. If antibodies are found to be present, then it is all the more necessary to find whether the antibodies are caused by infection with HIV or the test has found antibodies that are corective with HIV antibodies without the presence of HIV. This is possible only by using a more sophisticated test, namely, the Western Blot test. It may be noted that the Western Blot test should be made mandatory in all cases of ELISA positive results to confirm the fact whether one is HIV positive or not. This is all the more necessary in India and other developing countries since large number of HIV testing kits imported from abroad were found to be defective.

Western Blot Test

The Western Blot is a less sensitive test than the ELISA. It follows a slightly different approach than the ELISA test. A negative ELISA does not require further testing. However, sufficient time gap should be allowed for the production of antibodies — between time of infection and the time of testing for HIV. Further, if subsequent exposure to HIV takes place after the test, ELISA test will have to be repeated. In short we may say that negative

Western Blot test rules out HIV infection while a positive Western Blot test confirms HIV infection.

Voluntary Testing

Massive awareness programme at all levels with accurate and complete information and pre-test counselling services are required to motivate potential target groups for voluntary testing. Voluntary testing is recommended for the following groups in India:

- Past and present intravenous drug users and their sexual partners;
- Sex workers, devadasis and their sexual partners;
- Homosexual and bisexual men and women and their sexual partners;
- Lesbians and their partners;
- Individuals donating blood, organs, tissues, semen and milk;
- Recipients of blood not tested for HIV;
- Recipients of organs, tissues, milk and semen from donors who are not subjected to HIV test;
- Eunuchs involved in sexual activities particularly with homosexual men;
- Prison inmates involved in homosexual/lesbian activities within the jails;
- Persons involved in extra-marital and pre-marital sex;
- Persons having more than one sexual partner;
- Persons having symptoms of HIV/AIDS;
- Children of sex workers;
- Street children involved in sex and drug abuse;
- Police and defense personnel involved in homosexual and lesbian activities;
- Truck drivers who involve in sexual activities on the highways;
- Defense personnel returning from foreign assignments if they were engaged in extra-marital sexual activities abroad or if they have received donated blood or human organs;

- Persons who got their whole or parts of the body tattooed;
- Children of HIV positive women;
- Tribal women who practice prostitution as their traditional profession and their partners;
- Physicians and para-medical personnel who frequently get hurt while performing surgery or administering injection particularly if they have a fear of contracting HIV;
- Hemophiliacs who have received blood clotting factors;
- Sexual partners of HIV infected people or of people in the preceding groups; and
- Thalassemia patients.

Indigenously Developed Kit

Dr. Pradeep Seth and Dr. Mohammed Najeet Siddiqi from the All India Institute of Medical Sciences (AIIMS) have indigenously developed an AIDS test kit. This can be effectively used to verify whether an HIV test is positive or negative — for which India has been spending precious foreign exchange to import over a million kits annually.[2] The Government of India has been importing HIV testing kits under the World Health Organisation (WHO) scheme of life saving drugs. The import cost has been substantially brought down from Rs. 30 to about Rs.18 per kit. As mentioned earlier, a number of kits imported had to be withdrawn from the market as they gave faulty diagnosis. Further, these kits could hardly diagnose some of the HIV types peculiar to India.

It is expected that the indigenously developed kits will further bring down the cost of ELISA test to about seven rupees per test kit. The newly developed kit has undergone rigorous field tests on one thousand (1000) laboratory and five hundred (500) field trials taken at random from different blood banks. These tests have provided absolutely accurate results. According to Dr. Seth[3], the kit will have hundred per cent sensitivity and specificity. It would be able to detect all the virus sub-types present in India while, the imported kits often failed to recognize some of the strains found in this country.

Care and Treatment

As on date no therapy is available for the treatment and cure of HIV infection. Medical practitioners across the world are making all out effort to develop drugs, and many drugs are already under trial. No doubt, treatment is improving and consists mainly of fighting the symptoms of the "opportunistic" infections which take advantage of the victim's damaged system: pneumonia, fungal infection, tuberculosis, cancer, diarrhoea etc. But when the treatment stops, the same or a different infection eventually returns. A substance which eliminated the virus without poisoning the patient, would be the ideal drug for treating AIDS, but even this would not be a cure if the virus had already destroyed part of the person's immune system. In this case, curing the patient would require repairing the damage and restoring immune functioning to normal[4].

Alternative treatments differ from the conventional treatment using drugs. There are number of indigenous treatments existing in various cultures. Homoeopathy treatment, for example, involves the use of minute doses of drugs in the process of treatment. Homoeopathic physicians around the world are certainly involved in research and treatment of HIV/AIDS patients with the hope of finding adequate and result oriented treatment to fight the HIV virus.

Efforts through Ayurvedic Treatment

At the Amala Hospital in Trichur, Kerala, two eminent Ayurvedic Physicians are involved in the treatment of HIV/AIDS patients. In this research institute about 200 HIV infected patients are receiving treatment through Ayurvedic preparation. Although these humble and dedicated physicians do not claim any cure for the HIV/AIDS disease, their treatment does yield results – probably results which may even match the treatment involving Zidovudine (ZDV or AZT), didanosine (DDI) and Zalcitabine (DDC), and perhaps the protease inhibitor developed by the Abbott laboratories. One can find large number of HIV infected persons not only from various parts of the country but also from abroad (particularly from gulf countries) visiting the Amala Hospital's Ayurvedic department. Let us be proud that there is at least one hospital where an HIV infected can go with some sort of hope, where he/she is welcomed.

Dr. Kesavan and Dr. Rajagopalan are providing wonderful services to the hapless victims of HIV/AIDS in a country where high profile institutions and internationally famous physicians dare not touch an HIV/AIDS victim. It is unfortunate that they receive hardly any appreciation from medical forum within the country. Then what to talk of financial support? They are not invited to national and international conferences; exposure visits, and are not included in any of the decision making or advisory committees and panels for HIV/AIDS in the country.

At the same time some other Ayurvedic practitioners from the country claim to have cured AIDS patients. They regularly advertise in local and national newspapers and periodicals about their success in fighting the HIV virus. However, till date no confirmed AIDS cure case is available for quoting. One Ayurvedic practitioner, Dr. T.A. Majeed claims that he has cured a couple of AIDS patients with Ayurvedic treatment using "Immune cure".[5] Although the AIDS patients named are still alive, they have not subjected themselves for AIDS test after having undergone the treatment. It may be true that Ayurvedic treatment can be effective in controlling certain symptoms of HIV/AIDS infection. However, there is no evidence to their claim to treat AIDS patients and cure them within a period of "hundred days".

Reliability of Alternative Treatment

AIDS being a dreaded disease with no known vaccine available to save the life of a person if infected, compels an individual to look for alternative treatments. Given such a situation, it is but natural that scores of quacks appear time and again to deceive the victims of HIV/AIDS. It is therefore appropriate that certain important points are borne in mind by the HIV infected persons as well as their counsellors while planning for alternative treatment. Let us briefly list out some of these important points.

1. If one is infected with the HIV virus, it is necessary that he/she approach a competent person for counselling and guidance. This is very essential particularly in the case of HIV/AIDS. The competent person may be his/her family

doctor; a professional social worker, a psychologist or an agency involved in AIDS related work. They can provide emotional support as well as proper guidance regarding treatment and care. It is appropriate for the HIV infected to seek their opinion about the various possibilities of treatment and care instead of depending on incomplete and inaccurate information from other sources.

2. HIV/AIDS being a topic of concern for every nation and community, any breakthrough in research to fight the virus will receive wide publicity within and outside the country. The various media all over the world will carry any such information for the benefit of the millions infected with the virus. This will be supportive evidence about the effectiveness of any treatment whether they are traditional, conventional or other indigenous treatment.
3. Any authentic study and the break-through made are to be published in reputed medical journals that are peer-reviewed. All scientifically valued studies are published by journals on supplying adequate information and supportive evidence.
4. Any advertisement to promote the use of a particular treatment should be crosschecked. Even a couple of personal testimonies should not become the base for accepting and adopting treatment. The motive behind the advertisements should also be studied. Popularity and profit may become part or sole motive behind such publicity.
5. In the past there were several instances in which promoters of a particular treatment claimed of having achieved positive results. At the same time they were not willing to disclose the ingredients used in the production of such compounds. One cannot and should not accept such arguments because patents that protect the owner of the drug are easily obtained. For example, AIIMS has now applied for a patent of the indigenously developed kit both in India and abroad.
6. With the advancement of science and technology, improvement in international economy and trade and

healthy bilateral cooperation's there is no need for any HIV/AIDS patient to travel abroad for treatment. Any new treatment if found effective can easily be imported from one country to another. Therefore do not be lured away by such mediators and agents without examining the reasons involved for not importing any such treatment. Further, world bodies like the UNAIDS will step in to help the poor nations to tide over the crisis.

7. It is always essential to verify the credentials of a treatment promoter. One should not hesitate to make interaction with such persons before taking a decision to accept treatment. It is all the more important to be careful and vigilant about therapies that are claimed to treat different diseases simultaneously. Further, if one is already under the treatment of a physician from the conventional medical system, he/she must seek his/her opinion and guidance before switching over to any other option.

IMPACT OF HIV ON ECONOMY

One of the emerging challenges of HIV/AIDS is the threat posed by it to the economy of a nation. HIV has become a development issue not only to the third world countries, but also to the developed nations. It has shattered lives of many promising individuals- sports persons, film personalities, musicians, politicians, bureaucrats and even physicians; it has shattered scores of families; it has wiped out human lives from several villages; it has claimed the lives of people in their productive age; it has generated poverty; it has deepened misery; and it has eroded the economy and social services in many countries.

John McCallum, Chief Economist of the Royal Bank of Canada says that AIDS strikes at our stock of human capital just as surely as it strikes at the immune system. AIDS snatches earnings and spending power from the economy. He explains that the people afflicted are in the prime of life, spending money on all sorts of goods and services and that if not for AIDS, they would have continued to be productive workers, taxpayers, consumers and savers. According to his calculation, the medical cost from the time of diagnosis to death per person totals about US $ 100,000. He projects that AIDS would cost the Canadian economy $ 8 billion in 1996. He also estimates that the Canadian economy would lose $ 30 billion by 2010 when the number of AIDS cases is projected to increase to 60,000.[6]

The impact of AIDS is great on a country's economy. It has to equip itself with adequate infrastructural facilities for screening blood, providing counselling services, medical care, home care, institutional care, undertake research to develop treatments, conduct surveys to study the high-risk groups as well as behaviour patterns, train health care providers and those in social and social service sector, undertake massive awareness programme and education at all levels. A developing country like India, which is trying to improve its economic status, seems to have consciously avoided to take up the cause of AIDS with required seriousness. What is alarming is that the scores of international agencies operating in the country and the media too seem to have faithfully fallen in line with the thinking of the policy makers.

Estimates of the economic impact of the first 10,000 American AIDS patients are telling. These patients average period of stay in the hospital was 166 days and the medical cost was about $140,000 per patient. An average of $19,000 of income was lost during the 360 days these patients remained away from their work on account of AIDS and future earnings lost averaged $ 460,000 per patient. The overall economic impact of these 10,000 patients, excluding research funding and educational costs, was about $ 6.3 billion with only $ 1.4 billion from direct medical expenses.[7]

In India treatment opportunities are very limited. There is hardly any initiative from the government side to offer treatment to the HIV infected. We are still in the stage of setting up testing centers across the country. The achievements made so far are not worth mentioning. State governments have not utilized the funds year marked for AIDS prevention activities. Even in the best of hospitals in the country, one cannot get treatment for AIDS. If this is the situation in the national capital and metros, what to talk of the treatment facilities in the rest of the country. Studies conducted show that even at the premier medical institute of the country (AIIMS), patients and health care workers run a risk of HIV transmission: infection control measures are inadequate, precautions are not enough and awareness of HIV/AIDS is not sufficient even among the physicians.[8]

To date there are a couple of health care centers, which take care of the AIDS patients. They include the St. John's Medical College Hospital, Bangalore, Christian Medical College Hospital, Vellore, Snehadaan Bangalore, AIDS Research and Control Center (ARCON) at Mumbai, the National Chest Institute at Gautam Nagar, New Delhi, Center for AIDS Research and Education, Madras, Amala Cancer Hospital, Trichur in Kerala etc. While many infected persons turn up for care and treatment, these hospitals run with non-governmental assistance find hard to meet the costs of treatment. For example Dr. Hira of ARCON says that treatment options are available only to those who can afford it. At ARCON, the treatment per person costs Rs. 20,000 a month. The viral load tests cost Rs. 4,200 per test per person. They are conducted by the Polymerize Chain Reaction (PCR) thermocycler, which measures the amount of virus present per milliliter of blood.[9] It is the first, and possibly only center in the country prescribing and monitoring the combination therapy treatment. However, at the Amala Cancer Hospital, treatment to HIV positive patients are provided with indigenously developed Ayurvedic medicines. The Homoeopathic department at this hospital also provides treatment although no claim is made so far about its success rate. The two Medical College Hospitals mentioned above are the only ones in the country till date to admit HIV infected along with other patients for treatment without discrimination.

For one or the other reasons the political will has conveniently chosen to avoid any debate on the impact of AIDS on the economy of the nation. This is primarily because the existing political system hangs in the air and everyone is bothered about clinging on to the chair as long as one can manage. Time has come for a national awakening during this new millennium to free the masses from the clutches of the corrupt politicians and bureaucrats and the hundreds of thousands perpetuating the same culture.

COMMUNICATION ROUTES OF HIV/AIDS DISEASE

The AIDS virus can pass on to an individual through three routes namely, sexual exposures, contact with contaminated blood and blood products and from a mother to her child through pregnancy and birth. It is essential to know the routes of HIV transmission for attempts to contain the further spread of the virus. Some infected people may be efficient transmitters of HIV than others and this transmission efficiency may vary according to the stage of illness. Individuals infected with the virus can pass on the same to those who are not infected even though they may not exhibit the symptoms of HIV/AIDS. Because most people with HIV are currently not sick, most transmission occurs from those without symptoms. Understanding how HIV spreads is important in order to draw up a strategy for the prevention and control of HIV/AIDS in any society.

Although HIV has been isolated from a number of bodily fluids and tissues, including blood, saliva, tears and breast milk, the virus can only be transmitted in certain well-known ways. It may be noted that HIV is not transmissible through normal day-to-day contact. It is most commonly transmitted through sexual contact: from women to men, from men to women, between men and between women. HIV is also transmitted through infected blood, blood products, human tissues and organs. People have become infected via blood transfusions, infected blood products including donated organs and via the sharing of syringes and hypodermic needles. In several developed countries, donated blood is now routinely screened for antibodies to HIV, making this form of transmission rare. For example in UK, USA and Australia every unit of blood is screened for HIV before transfusion. However, in places where blood is not systematically tested and where many people are infected with the virus, transmission in this way may still be common. There have also been a few cases of transmission in medical environments, usually involving needles. In other cases, the virus has been transmitted by recycling needles that have not been properly sterilised.

HIV can also be passed from an infected mother to her baby, before or during birth-this is known as pre-natal transmission.

Before birth, HIV may be transmitted across the placenta to the developing fetus. During birth, the virus may be transmitted via the mother's blood or bidily secretions.

A small number of cases of transmission through breast milk have been recorded but it is believed that these were typical occurrences in which mothers had received infected blood during transfurions immediately after giving birth[16]. Conclusive evidence demonstrating that the mother's milk was the only possible route by which a baby became infected has not been found. The World Health Organization (WHO) has specifically recommended that whether or not they are carrying the virus all mothers from developing countries should breast feed their own children[10]. HIV can also pass on to an infanct from an infected mother's cracked nipples during breast-feeding through small volumes of blood. Various known sources of HIV infection in India recorded by NACO is given in TAble 1.1.

Table 1.1
Risk /Transmission Categories In India

	No. of cases	Percentage
Sexual	89064	85.76
Perinatal transmission	3713	3.58
Blood and blood products	2113	2.03
Injectable Drug users	2649	2.55
Others (not specified)	6318	6.08
Total	**103857**	**100.00**

Source: NACO, MHFW, Govt. of India, April 2005

Communication Via Sexual Exposure

HIV transmission from men to women and from women to men is well known and well documented. The semen of men who are infected do contain HIV virus. During heterosexual genital intercourse

HIV enters a woman through the small breaks in the lining of the vagina. Unlike the penis the vagina is known to have many potential entry sites. This is so because the vagina is exposed to a greater volume of infectious material than is the penis. In the case of men, genital ulcers serve the same function as breaks in the lining of the vagina by providing the virus a direct passage to the blood stream. It may be noted that there are several confirmed cases of HIV transmission through artificial insemination with semen of men not known to be infected. Therefore it has become necessary for screening sperm donors for HIV.

The AIDS virus is primarily transmitted through sexual contact. There are two key scientific factors which allow us to understand its spread: the likelihood that an infected person will transmit the virus to a partner during sexual intercourse; and the frequency with which individuals acquire new sexual partners[11]. HIV is carried in seminal and vaginal fluids and in cervical secretions, as well as in blood. Any exchange of fluids during intercourse can result in transmission of the virus across the porous membranes of the vagina, penis, mouth or anal canal into the blood streams. The fact that seminal fluid transmits the virus is confirmed by the studies of artificial insemination. Women have even been infected by a single exposure to infected semen during artificial insemination[12].

Much of the information about the heterosexual transmission of HIV comes from studies which compare men and women who have remained HIV negative with those who have become HIV positive during the sexual relationship with an HIV positive partner. These studies have tried to assess why some people acquire the virus and others do not. They examine the risks associated with unprotected sexual intercourse as well as the influence of additional "co-factors" such as sexually transmitted diseases (STDs) which increase both vulnerability in acquiring the virus and the likelihood that an infected person will transmit the virus[13].

HIV and Substance Abuse

Intravenous drug use is one of the routes because the drug users frequently share the needles to inject drugs. Contaminated blood particles are found to remain inside the previously used needles and syringes thereby providing opportunities for the HIV virus to transmit to the subsequent users of the same needle and syringe. According to the information available, in 1990 an estimated 1.1 million Americans used to inject illicit drugs. Among them more than 80 per cent were believed to have been sharing their needles and syringes[14].

In India, the transmission of HIV through intravenous drug use (IDU) has been reported particularly from the north-east.[15] the detection of HIV-positive cases in Manipur has been documented since 1989. Conservative estimates put the number of drug users in this state at 30,000 of whom 20,000 are IDUs. Frequent sharing of syringes and needles has facilitated the transmission of HIV. The infection is believed to be as high as 73 per cent in this section of the population. Available literature and statistics of the IDU population have sometimes originated from studies stressing HIV testing and awareness creation among drug addicts resulting in their stigmatization and increased isolation, even to the extent of criminalisation.

The main reason for the spread of the virus in Manipur is said to be the close proximity of the former kingdom to the poppy growing areas in Myanmar. HIV positive cases have been found to be highest in places such as Moreh and Churachandpur, both of which are believed to be the transit routes through which drugs are smuggled out of Myanmar.[16] Frustration among the youth, unemployment, underdevelopment and a long-standing unstable policy have been major contributors to the widespread societal stress leading to the unabated abuse of substance in this part of the country.

Frumkin and Leonard[17] say that because of the early widespread arrival of HIV among the intravenous drug users in New York City, this population (the drug users) has served as a model for transmission of HIV through drug use. Studies conducted in New York found that up to 88 per cent of infected drug users admitted to routinely sharing needles with other drug users. As many as 74 per cent of New York city intravenous drug users also claimed to frequent shooting galleries, sites where needles are passed widely among anonymous drug users. Many that does not attend shooting galleries often used drug injected equipment provided by the drug dealer, who then also lent the same equipment to others. About one-half of New York City drug-users who acquired HIV earlier knew that they had shared needles with homosexual men. Reports such as this imply a substantial introduction of HIV from male homosexual into the population of the drug users. Because the majority of the drug users are heterosexual, these people may have further spread the virus into groups who may never have had contact with male homosexuals.

One should not lose sight of the fact that all over the world intravenous drug users inject drugs using needles and syringes, which are also being shared largely. Although studies pertaining to the extent of the spread of HIV through sharing needles are not many, we have enough documented cases from various countries which confirm the rapid transmission of the virus through this route. As reported earlier, India is not an exception to this.

In Europe and in the United States along with the free condom distribution, free and confidential needle exchange programme has been launched with a view to help drug users to avoid contaminated blood while injecting drugs. The author had the opportunity of visiting number of such needle exchange and condom distribution centers in the UK and USA. One can see drug users and those interested in collecting condoms visiting such centers from early morning to late into the night. In these two countries there is widespread awareness about the need for the prevention and control of AIDS. With massive AIDS education programmes along with adequate facilities provided to meet the various needs of the high risk groups, people in these countries demonstrate a sense of maturity and responsibility. One may say that India is still seventeen years behind these countries in planning and implementing appropriate measures for the prevention and control of AIDS.

It is a fact that due to lack of proper information, drug users very seldom take adequate measures to use sterilized needles and syringes for injecting. Frumkin and Leonard[18] say that public health measures explored in different locales have reduced the risk of HIV infection to varying degrees. The efforts to reduce HIV transmission in drug users include implementing educational programmes that explain the risks inherent in using contaminated equipment, exchanging "clean" for "used" syringes, legalizing syringe sales, providing antiseptics to treat needles before their use, implementing methadone maintenance programmes, and providing primary drug treatment to the individual from his or her habit. No single approach is so far uniformly effective and the relative values of each of these different procedures are under evaluation.

Communication via Blood

With the advent of HIV in India, the health professionals as well as the Government of India were forced into action to prevent and control the spread of this dreaded virus. Several action plans were drawn up and implemented. Some were positive and encouraging while some others were met with world wide criticism: One such positive action plan of the Ministry of Health and Family Welfare, Government of India in 1989 was to engage the services of M/s A.F. Ferguson and Company to study the status of the blood bank programme in India.

The Ferguson study reported that there were a total of 1018 blood banks operating in India in the public and private sector. It also reported that a total of 1.95 million units of blood were collected by these banks annually. Some of the major observations made by the Ferguson study were: [19] (a) an overall shortage of blood, specially from voluntary donors; (b) blood from professional donors was most unsafe; (c) testing of donated blood for HIV and Hepatitis B was limited and erratic; (d) the blood component production, availability and utilization was extremely limited; and (e) a shortage of health care professionals and specialists in the blood transfusion services.

Official statistics (DGHS) show that in all there are about 5,96,203 hospital beds in India. According to the WHO recommendation the average blood requirement per hospital bed per annum comes to about 11 units. This would mean that the annual requirement of blood for the existing hospitals is about 6 million units[20]. It is a matter of great concern to imagine where the rest of the blood came from when the number of blood units collected is estimated to be about 1.95 million as reported earlier by the Ferguson & Co. study.

According to the report published by the National AIDS Control Organisation (NACO) the blood banks in the country have been licensed by the relevant authorities. It is a matter of concern to note that among the 485 government managed blood banks in the country, only 391 have been licensed as on 30th April, 1997 while among the 565 private blood banks 427 are licensed[21]. They say ..."charity begins at home". Although the first AIDS case in India was reported in May 1986, till date the authorities have not realised the urgency of licensing the blood banks which would make the screening of blood for HIV mandatory. Here it would be unfair to talk about any other effort for the prevention and control of AIDS within the country. Everyone concerned about the AIDS problem should express their displeasure on such negligence where human lives are taken for a ride. The Supreme Court of India has recently banned professional blood donation.

Near about 90 per cent of the pregnant women in India are anaemic requiring blood transfusion. As reported earlier when the blood requirement in the country is about 6 million units per annum while the actual collection is only 1.95 million, where does the rest of the required blood come from? Further, the estimate arrived at is based on the number of hospital beds. In the country where nearly 75 per cent of the people live in rural areas while more than eighty per cent of the hospital beds are located in urban areas, what is the logic in calculating blood requirements in terms of hospital beds? What, otherwise, one may like to clarify is that there is a greater demand for blood donation and transfusion in rural India, which is under-reported. This requirement is certainly met from local resources (i.e. local blood donation). But how many such locally collected blood units are tested for HIV?

It has been reported by NACO[22] that 94 per cent of blood units collected by commercial blood banks come from professional blood donors. Based on the National Policy framework developed by the Central Council of Health in 1982, eight objectives were developed in the strategic plan for the prevention and control of AIDS in India. The objectives are:

i) strengthening the National Blood Transfusion Services;

ii) ensuring an adequate supply of blood to all blood centers;
iii) ensuring the safety of blood and blood products;
iv) developing facilities for the production of components;
v) developing and strengthening facilities for plasma fractionation;
vi) strengthening external quality control of blood and blood products;
vii) undertaking research on blood transfusion service operations to improve safety, efficacy and supply;
viii) developing and strengthening effective management, monitoring and evaluation of blood transfusion services.

The government of India's schedule F XII-B provides the necessary legal framework as per the Drug and Cosmetic Act. The existing rules specify licensing for physical facilities of equipments, staff accommodation, labeling etc. With the advent of AIDS into the country amendment has been introduced to add few more provisions to the existing rules, which include:

a) Testing procedures of blood and blood products; quality control of reagents; specified qualification and experience requirements for blood bank personnel;
b) Preservation for specimen samples of each unit of blood in pilot tube for 72 hours. after transfusion;
c) Maintenance of complete and accurate records;
d) Mandatory testing to ensure the freedom of blood and blood products from HIV antibodies;
e) Approval of license by the Central License Approving Authority (which means the Drug Controller of India) prior to the granting of a license;
f) Whole human blood and components shall conform the standards as prescribed under the Indian Pharmacopoeia.

It is a known fact that HIV reproduces in CD4 lymphocytes, which circulate in the blood and other human fluids. It is not only associated with the cells in which HIV grows, but it is also present in blood associated with cells. Therefore, while transferring blood from an infected person to an uninfected person small numbers of lymphocytes also will pass along to the blood stream of the recipient. Any contaminated blood transferred into an individual's bloodstream is a potential route of HIV transmission.

Blood contaminating equipment's like needles and syringes, scalpels, glass vessels containing blood that break and pierce the skin, needles used for piercing ears and nose for using ornaments, needles and indigenous equipment's used for tattooing and circumcision-both male and female circumcision are all possible routes by which HIV can infect a person.

Risk Involved in Blood Donation

We have lot of information about the spread of HIV through blood and blood products. It is therefore suggested that the following groups may refrain from donation of blood, human tissues and organs in order to reduce the risks involved:

- People who have tested positive for HIV.
- Men who have had sexual contact with a sex worker or involved in extra-marital sex and their partners.
- Man who had sex with another man.
- Persons involved in prostitution.
- Eunuchs involved in sexual activities with men and women and their partners.
- Truck drivers and their sexual partners.
- Intravenous drug users.
- Recipients of transfusion of blood, semen, human organs or tissues.
- Persons stuck with a needle from a health care center after 1986 for tetanus injection, acupuncture or for any other medical purpose.
- People who got their ears or nose pierced, or any part of the body tattooed.
- Women involved in lesbian activities with several partners.
- Rape victims and their partners.

Communication via Mother to a Child

One of the three known routes of HIV transmission from one person to another is the transmission from a mother to her child. However, children are also susceptible to HIV infection through any of the other two routes discussed earlier, either through sexual activity or drug use.

There is widespread belief among several communities in India that sexual intercourse with a virgin would rid an individual of STDs. Often we come across reports in media about sexual exploitation of girlchildren by STD/HIV infected persons from various parts of the country. Although in most of the cases, murder do not take place, but transmission of STDs/AIDS to innocent girl children is a possible factor.

The estimated 60 million street children that the Indian cities shelter, involve in sexual activities before the age of ten. Drug abuse is very common among them. These children are potentially at risk for the transmission of HIV through sexual activities and drug abuse. HIV infection in a young child raises possible doubts of child abuse if his/her mother is not HIV infected and if the child has not been exposed to the route of blood transmission.

Medical practitioners estimate the risk of HIV transmission through breast milk at 29 per cent for mothers who are postnuptially infected. In the cases of women who are presently infected, risk of transmission is higher. The WHO has recommended bottle-feeding for the children of HIV infected mothers in Europe and in the United States. However, for developing countries, the WHO still recommends that HIV infected mothers should continue to breast-feed their children because of the higher risk involved in bottle-feeding children in third world countries. Given the way the AIDS virus is spreading in developing countries, particularly countries like India and Thailand, the WHO may reconsider such recommendations because at least half of the population in some of these countries have people living above poverty line while many of them also fall into the category of the rich in the world.

There are several known ways by which a child gets HIV infected. Most of the children worldwide are known to be infected by HIV by their mothers while in the uterus or during delivery.

Research has proved that not all infants born to HIV-infected women become infected with the virus. However, about 25 to 30 per cent children born to HIV positive mothers are found to be developing HIV/AIDS.

Other groups of children regularly being exposed to HIV include the Thalassemic and hemophiliac patients who require blood transfusion and use of clotting factor frequently. Much has been reported about how frequently children are being given blood transfusion by HIV contaminated blood supplied from not only unlicensed blood banks but also from the Red Cross Society of India in Delhi, Bombay, Calcutta and other parts of the country. The only reason is purposeful negligence by the authorities, bureaucrats and policy makers.

SUMMARY

Understanding facts about HIV/AIDS, HIV testing facilities, existing care and treatment options for the AIDS disease, reliability of alternative treatment, impact of HIV on economy and routes of HIV transmission alone will not serve the purpose unless and until individuals, experts, and social and health organisations take adequate steps to prevent and control the spread of this disease. The existing treatment facilities mentioned above are practically out of reach for an ordinary Indian. Further our medical experts are not either trained to treat AIDS patients or are not interested in leaving their areas of specialization to involve in AIDS treatment. There is much need for an open and frank approach to the problems caused by AIDS, which can be materialized through appropriate policy measures. This is possible only through social action, community organization and empirical research on delicate issues like the sexual behavioural pattern.

REFERENCES

1. David E. Bloom and Joyce V. Lyons(eds), *Economic Implications of AIDS in Asia*, UNDP, New Delhi, 1993.
2. Rakesh Puri, *A reliable detection device* Rashtriya Sahara, New Delhi, October 1997.
3. *Ibid.*

4. Panos Dossier, *AIDS and the Third World*. The Panos Institute, London, 1988.
5. Mathew, P.C. Report on AIDS *Majeedinat Marunnu Thattippennu Vidagthan* In Malayalam daily, Kalakaumudi, Bombay, 16 Oct 1994.
6. Ann Gibbon, *AIDS could cost billions in lost productivity: Economist - disease wrests both earnings and spending power from economy*, The Globe and Mail, July 11, 1996.
7. Lyn Frumkin and John Leonard, *Questions and Answers on AIDS*, PMIC, Los Angeles, 1994, P. 135.
8. Kalpana Jain, AIIMS Staff runs high risk of HIV infection, TOI, New Delhi, 27 July 1997.
9. Sameera Khan, interview with Dr. Subhash Hira of Mūmbai-based AIDS Research & Control Center (ARCON), *Three epidemics and a doctor*, TOI 13, July 1997.
10. International Baby-Food Action Network Statement reproduced in Echo, Dakar, 1989, No. 11.
11. R. Anderson and R. May *Plotting the Spread of AIDS*. New Scientist, March 1987 Volume 26.
12. M. A1-Nozha and others, correspondence, *Female-to-Male: An Efficient Mode of Transmission of Human Immunodeficiency Virus (HIV)*. Journal of Acquired Immune Deficiency Syndrome, February 1990, Vol.3, No.2, PP 193-194. (Quoted by Panes).
13. Panos Dossier: *Triple Jeopardy-Women & AIDS*. The Panos Institute, London, 1990.
14. Information shared during the sixth Annual Conference on Social Work Response to HIV/AIDS at New Orleans, USA, May-June 1994. The author was a participant in this conference.
15. Namaram Kishalaya, *Manipur - the battle against AIDS*, Nexus, New Delhi, April-May 1996.
16. Nirmalya Banerjee, *Manipur leads north eastern states in HIV cases*, TOI, 13 October 1997.
17. Frumkin, Lyn and Leonard, John *Questions & Answers on AIDS* (Second Edition). PMIC, Los Angeles, California, 1994.
18. *Ibid.*
19. NACO, National AIDS Control Programme, (NACP), India, Country Scenario, an update. April 1993, pp. 61-65.
20. NACO, National AIDS Control Programme, India: Country Scenario-an update, December 1996, NACO, New Delhi, 1997.
21. *Ibid.*
22. NACO, NACP, update April 1993, op.cit.

2

Role of Teachers in Life Skill Education

Introduction

The human race on this planet have been living with HIV/AIDS for over a quarter century now. Young people in our classrooms were born into a world where HIV was already present. However, very few are aware of its magnitude and its impact on the future of mankind. We do not know how exactly deadly illnesses such as heart attack and cancer spread. Nonetheless, we know exactly how HIV spread from one person to another. It is a life style problem which can be prevented through education and behaviour modification. Statistics from across the globe indicate that most of those infected with HIV are in their productive and reproductive age group of 15-50 years. This trend is true for India as well where nearly 90 percent of the infected belong to this age category.

National and international bodies and governments across the world have been fighting the battle against HIV/AIDS for almost three decades. Much money, time and energy have been spent in this battle. However, the results are far from encouraging particularly in a developing country like India. With the advent of satellite communication network, market economy, consumerism and globalization process, drastic changes are taking place in the society leading to adaptation to new and risky life styles especially among the adolescents and young adults. Much of the media messages offer more harm than protection to the young people. There is much resistance among the young to follow traditional practices and advice of parents and elders. The tendency among them is to confide in the peer group.

Educational institutions continue to have greater influence on the young mind than parents and religion. Considerable amount of time have been spent in the schools and colleges by the youth. Therefore teachers and educational institutions have a greater say in imparting accurate and adequate information on sensitive issues such as HIV/AIDS which has much association with facts of life that are personal and private in nature. In order to impart correct information, one must educate oneself and evolve appropriate strategies, objectives and methods.

Why to Introduce HIV and Life Skill Education

There are several reasons for introducing 'HIV and life skill education' in the school and higher education system in the country. Some of them include:

- There is an alarming increase in the rate of HIV infection in the country—5.1 million at the beginning of 2005.
- Most of the infections occur among young people in their productive and reproductive age group of 15 to 50—about 90 per cent.
- The annual new incidence of sexually transmitted infections (STIs) in India is estimated to be around 14 million.
- The infections of both HIV and STIs have spread from specific high risk target groups to general population both in rural and urban areas.
- There is no vaccine for prevention of HIV as on date.
- There is no drugs which can cure HIV/AIDS infection.
- There are too many myths and misconceptions regarding HIV/AIDS, sex and sexuality among people from various walks of life.
- Most of the awareness programmes and their contents are based on packages which were developed in the West for permissive and promiscuous society. Parents and teachers in India often find discomfort in handling most of these sensitive topics.
- Any reasonable intervention to be effective require that the subject contents are socially acceptable and academically sound.
- Most parents find discomfort in discussing matters pertaining to facts of life and life skill, with their children.
- Issues pertaining to HIV/AIDS can be discussed only in the context of sex and sexuality since most of the infection in India (over 90 per cent) occur through heterosexual contacts.

- There is a dearth of well prepared text books on HIV and life skill education in India.
- There is a need for trained teachers and trainers of trainees (ToTs) on HIV and life skill education.
- There is stigma attached to HIV/AIDS. Infected people and their close relatives continue to face discrimination.
- There is a need to provide value education based on respect for parents and elders, moral and religious teachings.
- There is a trend among young people to listen to and accept what a teacher teaches than those that are imparted by parents.

The above mentioned points speak volumes about the need for incorporating HIV/AIDS and life skill education in the curriculum of our schools and higher education system.

Life Skill Education (Sexual Health Education)

There is much resistance to teaching and/or discussing on sensitive topics that are associated with sex and sexuality which are taboo subjects. Policy makers and academicians have tried to invent more palatable words to replace terminologies such as reproductive health education and sexual health education. In our discussion in this chapter we use the term 'life skill education' to mean sexual health education which also include family life education.

'Life skill education' in the context of HIV/AIDS is aimed at enabling teachers and students to discuss about issues pertaining to topics associated with the prevention and control of HIV/AIDS through behaviour modification.

Objectives

Some of the objectives of HIV/AIDS and life skill education include the following:

- To provide accurate and complete information on the what, why and how of HIV/AIDS, its prevention and methods for its control.
- To provide correct information about facts of life (process of growing up) from physiological, moral and emotional aspects.
- To enable the learner to acquire necessary skills in dealing with issues associated with sex and sexuality.

- To enable the learner in mastering skills in avoiding high risk behaviour such as sex outside marriage, injecting drugs and unhealthy and unhygienic practices in personal and professional lives.
- To enable service providers to have accurate information and knowledge on HIV/AIDS and related topics which will enable them to perform their duties effectively.
- To enable teachers and ToTs to provide meaningful counselling services and guidance to young people.

Strategies

Considering the social and behaviour modification aspects of HIV/AIDS prevention and control, there is a need to define some of the essential strategies for appropriate educational intervention. These strategies could include:

Avoid Fear Campaign

In the initial stages of the outbreak of the HIV/AIDS epidemic, fear campaign was one of the popular strategies adopted by various agencies, governments and activists. Even today many who are not well aware of the extent of the phenomena associated with HIV/AIDS, tend to propose fear campaign to turn away people from high risk behaviour. Experience from across the globe clearly indicate that fear campaign often turn out to produce negative impact. This has in fact become counter-productive by creating panic among those not involved in high risk behaviour, by creating stigma and discrimination against those infected or associated with the infected and forcing those infected to hide their status and/or go underground.

Adoption of Positive Attitudes

As a result of wide spread infection across the country, we can observe a middle reaction from the ordinary public and service providers. Children are discriminated against in schools, patients are refused treatment, care and support from health care institutions and HIV infected from village communities continue to be ostracized even after two decades of intervention to create awareness and education of people from various walks of life. There is so much of stigmatization and discrimination that people have been turned out of jobs, not allowed in places of worship and forced to leave from their places of residence.

There is a need to adopt positive attitude to people living with HIV. All of us live with and move about in public—places market-place, transport, places of worship, entertainment spots, restaurants etc.—alongwith HIV infected. We fail to recognize them. By looking at an infected, one cannot know whether that person is infected. Only an HIV test can confirm the HIV status of a person. Because of our negative attitude, we tend to force the infected to remain underground. For fear of stigma and discrimination most infected would not disclose their HIV status. Thus as a society we create a situation in which the infected are unable to seek medical intervention and emotional support. Above all, many infected would continue to spread the virus to their spouses and/or sexual partners bringing about a more serious problem to the society.

Therefore there is an urgent need to create a conducive environment which will enable the infected to disclose their HIV status. An HIV infected can continue to live normal life for several years and contribute to the family, community and the society. If the society can accept and extend necessary care and support to the infected, they will be able to live much more meaningful lives. Every education and awareness programmes should aim at enabling the learners and beneficiaries to adopt positive attitudes of acceptance, love and compassion to the infected. Such interventions will only become successful in a democratic society.

Life Style Based Interventions

HIV/AIDS is a life style disease. Pre-marital sex and extra-marital sex are certain immoral life style practices which are also high risk activities. Similarly intravenous drug use is a life style being practiced by many young people for one or another reason. Unhygienic practices by health care providers too is a form of life style behaviour. Not following universal precautions while treating patients can be highly risky. Use of gloves while examining a patient and performing surgery and precautions while administering an injection are essential guidelines. When health care providers prefer to challenge such hygienic practices, they are adopting a life style that is different from the normal and exposing oneself to risk of getting infected. It is, therefore, essential that any educational intervention on HIV/AIDS should be addressing issues pertaining to life styles.

Value Based Intervention

Dignity of human beings must have priority over all other consideration while embarking on any educational programme. Infection with HIV should not be a consideration to isolate the infected or to discriminate those who are associated with or related to an infected. The infected need care and support. They have every right to live their full lives as any other human beings. Many of those who get infected are innocents. There is no rationale to refuse care, support, love and compassion to the innocent victims.

An appropriate educational intervention for prevention and control of HIV should be value based which will have regard for the dignity of every individual. Importance of the values of human life are embodied in the teachings of various religions, lessons taught by teachers in educational institutions and the guidance provided by parents. If one is taught to adhere to the teachings of parents, teachers and religion, human dignity can be preserved and a meaningful and result oriented intervention can be made.

Promotion of a Culture of Life

HIV/AIDS and life skill education must follow a strategy that will promote a 'culture of life' than a 'culture of death'. With liberalization and globalization, the tendency to look for materialistic gains and ego satisfaction is rampant. The national census 2001 show the ever increasing gap in the male-female ratio-933 females for 1000 males. Sex determination tests and selected abortion of female fetus have become common. One of the estimates show that over 100,000 abortions take place in India every day (there is no authentic estimate). If there are five members in a family on an average, this practice of killing the unborn is directly affecting 500,000 people in a day. To put it more emphatically, the degradation of value for human life keep on increasing day by day. Time has come when a female child is not even safe in its mother's womb.

Euthanasia is another practice which is gaining momentum in many societies. Those on life support system and the elderly are victims of this practice. With the increase in HIV/AIDS cases, there are also reports of selected elimination of human lives—especially of those infected. The number of dowry related deaths in the country is on the rise. There is also a tendency to suggest abortion of the unborn child of the infected woman. Similarly, most pregnancy out of wedlock too end up in abortion. Honour killings is also a matter of concern when we talk about 'culture of life'. All these are a matter of the "culture of death' rather than a 'culture of life'.

In 'life skill education' it is important that we promote a culture of life than a culture of death. Teachers and ToTs have a greater role to play in this form of education which is very much a part of family life education.

Moral Education

The initial cases of HIV were found among the homosexuals. Even today nearly 90 percent of the infection in India occurs through sexual route as a result of promiscuity. Therefore much of the interventions for prevention depend on adopting mechanistic strategies based on immediate and short term goals. Most of the campaigns for this strategy have the support of international bodies and foreign governments who do not have priority for moral and value based intervention where dignity of individuals are given priority. As a result, most programmes do not have scope for promoting moral values and religious teachings.

India being a land of religions, there is a need to put in place a culture specific strategy for educating the learners on sensitive topics which will have public support. None of the religions promote immorality and extramarital or same sex relationships. Well over 95 percent of all marriages in India take place in places of worship through religious rituals and traditions. Therefore it is but natural for the majority to welcome an intervention strategy, which is based on moral grounds. One important aspect to be kept in mind by teachers and ToTs is that hardly any one talks about a strategy that is founded on 'morality'. It is also true that no one strategy can solve the problem. We need to apply various strategies—all of which will have some impact. However, for the target groups in educational institutions a value based and morally founded programme would be an ideal one.

Promotion of Abstinence

Although HIV/AIDS prevention programmes are in place for over two decades, there is hardly any abstinence programme in India. Even a country like the United States of America have gone out of its way to promote abstinence programme in all its fifty States. There are over 700 abstinence programmes being promoted by the Bush Administration. Apart from this several faith based organizations also promote abstinence programme among the youth, particularly through educational institution.

Through abstinence programme the adolescents and youth are motivated to wait until marriage to have sex. Young people are encouraged to sign 'sex within marriage only' (Virginity until marriage) pledges and millions are reported to be joining such programmes. Teenage pregnancies are reported to be declining. Many US youth are being flown to the UK to campaign among the youth in that country to promote abstinence programmes. The results have been very encouraging.

The trend in pre-marital sex in India is just the reverse of what is happening in most western countries. While 60 to 80 percent of teens are reported be engaging in sex before they are twenty, in India their percentage is between 16 to 20. This alone show that our young people are still within reach. Value system, obedience to religious teachings, adherence to the guidance of teachers and parents are very much in place for most young people in India. It is therefore apt that we encourage the good practices and age old rich value system of our country. It will be convenient for teachers to promote abstinence among school children which will have overwhelming support from most—if not all—parents.

Strengthening Social Values

Certain behaviour patterns are supported by social frames and cultural norm.[1] Although much progress has taken place in the area of civilization and social reforms unhealthy certain practices continue without any change. For example, female genital mutilation is being practiced in about 30 countries in Africa. Initiatives in the area of women empowerment have not made much headway in those countries. Honour killing is yet another practice which is being condemned by every civilized nation. Among certain tribes in India sex before marriage is permitted and in some cases the girl has to prove that she is able to conceive. In case if she conceives, the boy must marry her. Devadasi system is another practice which continue to exist in certain parts of the country.

While it is appropriate that we regard and respect certain cultural practices and traditions, the snowballing increase in the spread of HIV/AIDS which has much to do with certain forms of practices associated with sex and sexuality may need to be discouraged and even be stopped in the wider interest and survival of a particular community.

It is true that while certain social norms which determine behaviour patterns may tend to be negative, there are also certain other social norms which are positive. Some of the studies in American population have shown that people who are devoted to religious practices and following religious teachings (irrespective of which religion) become sexually active at a later stage (at an older age) and prefer to perform their marriage in their respective places of worship. The divorce rate among such people are found to be much less and most of the couple are found to be living in monogamous relationship.

The above discussion only support the view that positive values and social norms need to be reinforced and re-introduced in the curriculum which will go a long way creating a responsible community for a positive living.

Common Good over Individual Interest

In a world of consumerism, ego satisfaction gains predominance over all other considerations. Collective action for common good gets less preference. We live in an age when the young are motivated to achieve maximum pleasures and glamour of the physical senses and that becomes the prominent aim in their lives. The means to achieve this aim is seen as a commodity. In this process social responsibility and social relationships become low priority. In fact, responsible social behaviour at individual and societal levels become less and less important. As a result sexual relationships are seen as means for individual's satisfaction and not for mutual gains stable and relationships. When individual satisfaction becomes priority in sexual relationships, mutual responsibility will tend to decrease. Subsequently, regard and respect for the partner and his/her body will have no consideration. Eventually the partner will be seen only as a commodity for achieving the pleasures of the physical senses. The consequences of such actions can lead to high risk behaviour which will expose the person to infection with HIV.

It is therefore desirable that HIV/AIDS and life skill education follow such strategies which will have the support of a responsible society (like the Indian Society) where the majority follows social norms and values which are aimed at common good.

Let us not under-estimate the young. Very often there is a tendency to under-estimate the young people. It is not true that the youth cannot change their life styles. There are numerous examples to show that life-styles can be changed for better. Better educational opportunities have transformed the life and living standards of people in many societies. Young people have determination to accept challenges and transform themselves. It is unfair to under-estimate them. Proper education and guidance will go a long way in enabling the youth to take right decisions for the betterment of their personal lives and subsequently that of their community. It is therefore desirable that the youth are exposed to all options so that they can make their own choices for living an HIV free life.

Planning for HIV/AIDS and Life Skill Education

HIV/AIDS has threatened the society as a whole as it undermines the educational base of future generations. There are several instances across the country when children are refused admission in schools or are forced to take school leaving certificates because of their HIV infected status and/or of their relatives HIV status. The only response to such negative attitudes is to offer a well planned programme of study which will provide accurate and complete information on the what, why and how of HIV/AIDS, how it spreads, how prevention and control can be brought about, how stigma and discrimination can be challenged, how love, care and support can be extended to every infected and affected and how to motivate the society to have a compassionate approach to those infected.

The basic right to education should be guaranteed to all, as it is the prime condition to ensure guarantee the livelihood of future generations. In the context of HIV/AIDS, education on health and gender, sexuality and reproduction should provide young people with essential and potentially life saving knowledge and skills.[2]

Children are active, creative change gents and not just dependants. Children should have a meaningful participation in HIV/AIDS related activities through support to their own organizational bodies like youth organizations and student clubs. New prevention strategies should be based on experiences with previous programmes and take into account people's realities for them to be effective.[3]

In the Indian context, for an effective educational intervention, we need to implement an HIV and life skill education programme which is culture specific. Too much of dependence on materials produced for a promiscuous society where sexual freedom is the norm of the day would not be of much use. Indian experience on HIV related intervention in educational system during the last two decades was not encouraging. Neither the teachers nor the parents are comfortable with the approach and the suggested contents. It is therefore apt that we design and develop a curriculum which is indigenous. Some of the actions proposed to be taken towards imparting HIV and life skill education in the Indian context would be as follows:

Assessment of the Existing Realities

There is a need to assess the existing scenario of HIV/AIDS in the country. In some places the spread of HIV may be faster and concentrated on a particular group like the sex workers in Mumbai and the drug addicts in some of the states particularly in the North-east. In some states the estimates may be very high while in some other states, the number of cases reported may be too little. This need not necessarily be true. The kind of health delivery system, counselling and testing facilities, proper reporting system are responsible for reasonable estimation. We do not have an effective and uniform system across the country.

Extent of correct knowledge about HIV/AIDS and related topics is another parameter. Similarly, it is essential that the teacher examines various types of materials that are available for HIV and life skill education. In the education system, we need to use materials which provide accurate and complete information developed by responsible agencies which have the approval of competent authorities from education sector.

Training and Refresher Programmes

Being a teacher does not mean that one is competent to teach any subject. HIV and life skill education is a sensitive and delicate topic. It is not a fun subject. To be effective, one needs to study the subject and acquire adequate knowledge as well as skills in handling the topic. It is not desirable that a teacher depends on only one book or a set of materials. It is essential that views of various writers are understood in the right perspective. There is also a need to co-relate the subject to local situations and culture. Every teacher should undergo a formal training programme of reasonable duration either in a face to face situation or through distance learning mode. It is also essential that those who already had one or another form of training should undergo refresher courses which will enable them to update themselves with the latest that is happening in the area of HIV/AIDS, new developments, research results and best practices.

Analysis of Target Group

The extent to which one should involve, how the subject should be treated, how much of inputs should be provided, how much of information can be expected from the students etc. will depend on various aspects such as rural and urban situations, whether the institution is only for boys, only for girls or co-educational, gender of the teacher, and private or government owned institution. Based on the target group and their extend of exposure, a teacher must prepare herself/himself to make one's intervention. There are also differences of opinion about who should teach about HIV and life skill education. Gender and one's subject of specialization should not become hurdles. What is required is commitment and devotion to duty. A student friendly approach is certainly of great importance. It is certainly difficult for many untrained teachers to talk on HIV/AIDS and related issues such as sex and sexuality. Proper short-term training programmes, personal reading and participation in discussion in formal and informal settings would certainly eliminate much of the difficulties.

Programme Objectives

It is essential that specific programme objectives are identified. This will enable the teacher and the students to focus on specific goals. The aim should be to provide accurate and complete information on all topics taken up for discussion. Content clarification is an essential component. It is certain that introvert students may not take courage and/or feel free to raise questions. Some of the topics associated with the issue are taboo subjects and therefore different strategies must be adopted in dealing with the subject. Question box is a common method for enabling students to ask questions and seek correct answers. Education objectives and extent of content that would be discussed will depend on the kind of target group and their exposure. A teacher should have an open mind which will enable the students to be serious as well as frank in discussing various issues. This is necessary in order to achieve the desired objectives.

Interactive Sessions

It is essential that teachers and ToTs must plan the lessons to be proportionately interactive in nature. Although various strategies can be adopted to make the teaching learning process interactive and interesting, focus on the subject of discussion should have priority over all other considerations. It is necessary that the teacher choose a specific topic for discussion, provide adequate input on the subject matter, describe various and relevant aspects pertaining to the topic such as its historical aspects (if applicable), statistics (latest data, if applicable), experiences, model and/or innovative initiatives, profile of institutions, stories of the infected and/or affected etc. Followed by the presentation of the teacher, discussion can be initiated for clarification, suggestions and sharing of views. The whole idea is that the classroom environment must be made learner friendly. Once the students understand the importance of the subject, communication will become easier. Apart from direct teaching and classroom interaction, students can also learn by way of organizing extracurricular activities such as essay writing, poetry, role play, development of poster, slogan writing, exhibition, visits to certain agencies associated with the subject matter etc.

Enrichment Programme

There are a number of short term courses being conducted by NGOs and some University departments on HIV/AIDS and related areas like counselling, research etc. Two of the most comprehensive programmes are being offered by the Indira Gandhi National Open University, New Delhi through distance learning.

Certificate in HIV and Family Education (CAFÉ)

CAFÉ is a six months programme. This is available both in English and Hindi. The fee for this programme is less than nine hundred rupees. Entry qualification is 10 + 2. The programme can be completed within a maximum period of two years which would mean that a student can appear four times in the term end examination to clear the certificate programme comprising four courses of four credits each. The print materials are well prepared and is being updated frequently by the University.

School and college teachers from any part of the country can register for this programme. Programme details are available with IGNOU study centres, IGNOU Regional Centres and IGNOU website at: ignou.ac.in

Diploma in HIV and Family Education (DAFE)

DAFE is a one year programme. One gets up to four years to complete this programme and as many as eight chances to appear for term-end examination. There are seven courses—six courses of four credits each and the seventh course is an eight credit dissertation (project work). This Diploma programme is primarily meant for teachers, NGO functionaries and those interested in the subject. It is available both in English and Hindi. The progrmme fees is less than one thousand eight hundred rupees. The entry qualification is 10+2.

This distance learning programme has an excellent set of printed materials which will be given to each student registering for the programme. A wide variety of topics pertaining to HIV/AIDS, family life education, life skill education, alcohol and drug addiction, communication and counselling have been covered in this package. The University also provides facility for face to face classroom teaching (optional), teleconferencing facilities and interactive radio programme.

The above mentioned CAFÉ and DAFE programmes are the best comprehensive programme available as on date which has the approval of higher education system in the country. One of the important aspects of this programme is that it is indigeneously developed by the best of experts and institutions within India.

PRINT MATERIALS ON HIV/AIDS

In this section on print materials, an attempt has been made to provide a brief write up of about some of the books on HIV/AIDS and related topics in circulation. Since lots of books are now available, the author has chosen only a very few books that are available easily in the country.

HIV/AIDS: A Handbook for Young People

"HIV/AIDS: A handbook for young people"[4] by Gracious Thomas is one of the latest books meant for youth and young people. It is in fact the first text book promoting 'abstinence' among young people in the country. In all there are 18 chapters dealing with relevant topics about HIV/AIDS. The chapters also include exercises for students. There are also some illustrations.

Chapter one is an introduction to HIV and AIDS. It deals with the basics of HIV/AIDS. In Chapter two HIV/AIDS has been presented as a special disease particularly, because of its special nature as a life style disease. Chapter three discusses about the history of HIV/AIDS. The seriousness of an epidemic can be known only if we know the extent of its spread. In Chapter four details about the extent of the spread of HIV around the globe as well as within India have been discussed. Chapter six focuses on vulnerable population in India to HIV infection. This chapter is titled "people at risk of HIV infection".

Unlike other life threatening diseases like heart attack and cancer, here is an illness about which we have adequate information particularly, about its mode of transmission. Chapter five deliberates about how HIV spread from one person to another. HIV/AIDS creates panic among people because of the taboo attached with it. Misconceptions and misinformation is the main cause forcing people to hide their HIV status. Chapter seven deals with the various aspects pertaining to misconceptions about HIV/AIDS. Alongwith misconceptions, we also need to understand stigma, discrimination and human rights violations which have be explained in chapter eight. Details about HIV testing and issues associated with it are described in chapter nine. Some of the most vulnerable population groups who need most care and support are the women and children. Issues pertaining to these two groups have been examined in chapter ten. One of the important aspects of HIV is that it is a Sexually Transmitted Disease (STD). Chapter eleven describes some of the commonly found STDs. One of the routes of HIV transmission is through the practice of sharing needles by injecting drug users. Chapter twelve discusses the issue of alcohol and drug addiction in relation to HIV/AIDS. Many people are dismissed from service if they are found to be HIV positive. Some agencies also test people for HIV before providing employment. In chapter thirteen the author describes HIV as an issue in employment.

In Chapter fourteen an attempt has been made to examine the need and importance of prevention and control of HIV/AIDS. Chapter fifteen deliberates on the care and support to HIV patients. Palliative care of HIV/AIDS patients is an important aspect which has been discussed in chapter sixteen. Helping a dying AIDS patient is another aspect which has been explained in chapter seventeen.

The last chapter has tried to redefine the words AIDS to convey the message "Abstinence in Definitely Safe". In fact the last chapter has beautifully summarized the core message of the book—that the young people must be motivated to adopt decent life styles to prevent and control HIV/AIDS.

Economic Implications of AIDS in Asia

Economic Implications of AIDS in Asia[5] edited by David E. Bloom and Joyce V. Lyons is a direct outgrowth of a United Nations Development Programme—Sponsored Regional Consultation on Economic Implication of HIV/AIDS in Asia and the Pacific, held at Bangalore from May 25-28, 1992.

The book starts with an introduction by one of the editors Joyce V. Lyons. Chapter two contains the seminal work of Mechai Viravaidya,

Stasia A. Obremskey, and Charles Myers which was not presented at the Bangalore consultation. The other papers included in this volume are the economic impact of AIDS on the Republic of Korea, the economic impact of AIDS on Malaysia, the economic impact on the Thailand's transport sector, the implications of AIDS for the Agricultural sector in Lao PDR, economic consequences of the HIV/AIDS in the Philippines, the economic implications of AIDS in Southeast Asia and a chapter by David E. Bloom and Sherry Glied on who is bearing the cost of the AIDS epidemic in Asia?

The nine chapters according to the editors are unique in that they are the first attempt by economists to apply economic analysis to the problem of the HIV and AIDS in Asia. These chapters fall into three broad groups. The first group of chapters namely, chapters 2, 3 and 4 consists of country studies on the cost of medical care and the costs of foregone output associated with the epidemic. The second group of chapters namely, chapters 5, 6 and 7 departs from studying countrywide cost impacts and focuses instead on specific economic sectors. The third group of chapters, namely, chapters 8 and 9 concentrates on distributional issues associated with the effects of the AIDS epidemic.

This volume convey three messages: first the AIDS epidemic is not simply a health problem; it is also a problem that has economic roots, consequences, and solutions. Second, the epidemic imposes large costs on inidividuals and their families; and third, the massive future costs can be averted by the immediate development and implementation of AIDS prevention strategies.

Law, Ethics and HIV

Law, Ethics and HIV[6] edited by Robert A. Glick contains the papers presented at the United Nations Development Programme sponsored Intercountry Consultation on Law, Ethics and HIV held in Cebu, Philippines between 3-6 May, 1993.

This book reflects both the research undertaken in advance of the Intercountry Consultation as well as much of the documentation introduced at the meeting itself. This volume has been presented in three parts. Section one consists of issue papers, commissioned by UNDP which served as working documents for the Intercountry Consultation. The topics discussed include law and HIV/AIDS at the work place, information law and privacy, family law, law and customs, and women and HIV/AIDS. Section two has the country papers from Thailand, Malaysia, India, Papua New Guinea, Singapore,

Philippines, Indonesia, Sri Lanka, Mangolia and China. Section three presents the policy or strategy papers. They include HIV epidemic as a development issue, Global epidemiology of HIV/AIDS, strategies for ethical and effective policy, public health Vs. individual rights, health law Vs. individual rights in developing countries and criminal law and HIV. It may be noted that many of the papers appear only in much shortened form from their original texts.

The papers indicate that the Asia-Pacific region with the highest concentration of population on our planet could become the major battle ground of HIV/AIDS in the decades ahead. The authors have not been content to explain the difficulties. They have gone to make recommendations for the legal changes and the social reforms that are necessary for an effective response to HIV/AIDS. These reach down into quite detailed ideas which are worth reflecting upon. In the absence of a vaccine or cure for HIV/AIDS the only weapon available at the moment is behaviour modification. Therefore lawyers, ethicists and public policy-makers have to play a vital role in this epidemic.

The AIDS Handbook

The AIDS Handbook—A guide to the understanding of AIDS and HIV[7] is a co-authored handbook by John Hubley, Shankar Chowdhury and V. Chandramouli and published by Popular Prakashan, Bombay. This book has seven chapters running into 140 pages.

The introduction chapter deals with what is AIDS, history of AIDS and the Indian and global scenario of AIDS. Chapter two describes the biology of the HIV virus, the immune system, testing for HIV and the four theories of HIV. Chapter three is on the symptoms and disease. It deals with the WHO care definition of AIDS, AIDS in children, and the treatment and outcome. Chapter four concentrates on transmission of HIV. It provides information on sexual transmission, sexually transmitted diseases, transmission via blood transfusions and intravenous drug injections, risks to health workers and risks to families of AIDS patients. Chapter five is on prevention of AIDS. In this chapter the authors have outlined the prospects for development of a vaccine, changes in sexual life styles, prevention of sexually-transmitted diseases, making blood transfusion services safe, prevention of transmission from mother to child, safeguards regarding injections and skin piercing procedures, promoting safe practices by health workers, public health measures, ethical issues and human rights, role of non-governmental organisations and the national AIDS control programmes. Chapter six is about counselling and services for persons infected with HIV or ill with AIDS. Chapter seven provides an action plan for AIDS education by choosing target audience, involving the community, choosing appropriate messages, planning programmes for priority groups, reaching young people out of school, reaching men and women, sex workers, promoting condoms, using effective communication methods and evaluating educational activities.

The effort made by the authors is timely and most required. They have made an attempt to discuss on various issues relating to HIV/AIDS, its transmission and action plan for prevention as well as counselling services. Discussion on some of the topics like masturbation, homosexuality, menstruation etc. could have been useful had the authors taken little more interest in providing adequate information in the light of the cultural background and the psychological factors involved in such phenomena. No doubt, this book is handy, prepared in simple language understandable to ordinary people who have command over the English language. If the desired goal is to disseminate knowledge, such a book should have been priced low may be through some financial assistance from donor agencies or the State.

AIDS in India: Myth and Reality

AIDS in India: Myth and Reality[8] by Gracious Thomas explains in simple language the concept and origin of HIV/AIDS, its means of transmission, the target groups likely to be easily infected, experiences of HIV/AIDS victims, and some of the behavioural patterns prevalent in India, particularly homosexuality and promiscuity. Some measures for the prevention and control of the disease are also discussed. The information given in this book will be highly useful not only to the health workers and NGOs but also to academics, social workers and almost anyone in the street.

There are eight chapters and an AIDS glossary in this book. Chapter one deals in brief about the potential target groups in India who are likely to be infected by HIV as well as transmit the virus to others. Chapter two explains in simple language about the disease AIDS, symptoms of HIV infection, HIV tests and the treatment options. Chapter three presents the history of the origin of AIDS, while chapter four describes the various means of HIV transmission. In chapter five some of the experiences of the victims of AIDS from within and outside the country are narrated. While chapter six concentrates on promiscuity, chapter seven examines the practice of homosexuality in India. In chapter eight, the reader is provided with some information about the extent of the spread of AIDS in various parts of the country. Apart from this, certain measures regarding the prevention and control of AIDS are also discussed in this chapter. The AIDS glossary given in appendix explains several terms concerned with the disease AIDS.

This is one of the first books on AIDS brought out for open sale in the market written by a non-medical person involved in counselling HIV/AIDS patients as a professionally trained social worker.

AIDS, Social Work and Law

AIDS, Social Work and Law[9] by Gracious Thomas, N.P. Sinha and Johnson Thomas K has seven chapters, two appendices and a glossary on AIDS and Law. The chapters are: (*i*) what is AIDS; (*ii*) Sexually transmitted diseases; (*iii*) AIDS and social work; (*iv*) skills and abilities of an HIV/AIDS social work counsellor; (*v*) AIDS, social reality and law; (*vi*) AIDS and international law; and (*vii*) AIDS and national law.

The book has described some basic facts about HIV/AIDS, types of common STDs, treatment options and prevention, role of medical social worker in the care of HIV patients, and the skills and abilities of an HIV/AIDS social work counsellor. The three chapters on AIDS and the law provide adequate legal information on the legal issues surrounding HIV/AIDS. The book also includes two highly informative appendices: (*i*) The dentists (code of ethics) Regulations 1976, and (*ii*) Code of medical ethics: medical council of India—Declaration.

The authors have taken interest to present adequate information on all three aspects, namely, issues on HIV/AIDS, Social Work and Law in simple language understandable to an ordinary reader. This book can be used as a reference text for training programme's as well as for other academic purposes.

AIDS and Family Education

AIDS and family education[10] by Gracious Thomas presents eight chapters on HIV/AIDS, counselling and guidance, social work intervention and on family life education in relation to HIV/AIDS. Dr. K.R. Narayanan, the Vice-President of India in his foreword has expressed confidence that this volume will join the corpus of literature on AIDS in awakening people against this deadly infection.

Chapter one deals with the meaning of AIDS, signs and symptoms of HIV infection, HIV tests and treatment possibilities. Chapter two presents a detailed account of the routes of HIV transmission, while chapter three deals with the history of AIDS development. In chapter four, the basic aspects of counselling and guidance are briefly explained while in chapter five, AIDS situation in India based on the latest data available on the subject from various states and union territories is discussed. In this chapter, a brief discussion about the need for social work intervention is also incorporated. In chapter six the need, importance and objectives of family life education has been presented, while chapter seven describes the facts of life by explaining the male and female sexual anatomy with the help of diagrams. There are several common concerns of young people in matters of sex and AIDS. These have been discussed in chapter eight. There is also a glossary on AIDS and sex which will help the reader to understand the discussion better.

The volume will be of immense use to AIDS educators and teachers and parents interested in helping young people to learn actual facts about human reproductive system and related issues from the Indian point of view.

National AIDS Control Programme India

National AIDS control programme India: country scenario update[11] is an annual publication of the National AIDS Control Organization, Ministry of Health and Family Welfare, Government of India.

It is a well prepared document presenting briefly the HIV/AIDS scenario in the country giving official statistics based on the data received from various states and Union territories. It has six section—A, B, C, D, E and F.

Section A deals with the challenge where it describes what is AIDS, how it is spread, strategies for prevention and control and the situation of AIDS in Asia and India. Section B discusses briefly the international response and national response and talks about the prevention and control programme and about research and development.

In section C the national AIDS control programme is being presented. It reviews the programme management, inter-sectoral collaboration, HIV/AIDS surveillance, sexually transmitted diseases, condom programming, targeted interventions, components of blood safety, the information, education and communication (IEC) component and the reduction of impact. Section D provides financing strategies while section E gives five annexes on global developments, HIV testing centres for surveillance, HIV reference centres, zonal blood testing centres and training. Section F gives the list of the members of NACO.

This volume (1995) gives a comprehensive picture, both of the current HIV/AIDS situation, and of the components which form the National AIDS Control Programme. It provides knowledge about the disease and its prevention, as well as deals on the range of activities taking place under NACO's initiative. It is in fact the only authentic record of the government's policies, strategies and programmes as far as HIV/AIDS in India is concerned.

Multimedia Self-Study Kit

Multimedia self-study kit for professionals who counsel people living with HIV/AIDS[12] is produced by NCM publishers, Inc. New York. The leader's guide which is being reviewed contains a transcript of the video, graphics and a listing of supplementary resource materials. Earlier on February 26, 1994, the 1994 National HIV Frontline Forum Video Teleconference was presented via satellite to 33 cities in the United States, Canada and Puerto Rico. There is also a video tape which has three hours of presentation, discussion and live question and answer sessions.

The Leader's guide provide transcript of six presentations. They are: (*i*) guiding clients through treatment by Mark L. Illeman; (*ii*) Substance Abuse by A. Billy S. Jones; (*iii*) Cultural competency by Lana Kaopua; (*iv*) Women and HIV by Susan M. Gallego; (*v*) Psychosocial aspects of counselling by Robert H. Ramien and (*vi*) Grief, multiple loss and burn out by Judy Pollastek.

These presentations provide excellent material on the topics discussed with the latest upto date information on the subject. The discussion and question and answer sessions following the presentation and the listing of supplementary resource materials is of immense use to the readers. Viewing a videotape can certainly create immediate impressions. However, print materials provide an easy access to knowledge and information depending upon situation. Further, one has freedom to pick and choose what one wants. It is also easy to read again and again a point until one is fully satisfied.

AIDS and Substance Abuse

AIDS and substance abuse[13] edited by Larry Siegel comprise about 13 papers on AIDS and chemical dependency and related topics contributed by experts in the field.

The paper on The impact of AIDS on the Chemical Dependency field by Robert G. Ninen provides an overview of the effects AIDS epidemic might have on the provision of services to alcohol and other drug dependent or abusing persons. Barry Stimmel in the paper 'To test or not to test: The value of routine testing for antibodies to the human immunodeficiency virus' says that, of all controversies in medicine, none has aroused more emotion, than the subject of routine testing for infection with the human immunodeficiency Virus. Donald I. Abrams has reviewed the 'current knowledge about the empdemiology, virology, and clinical manifestations of HIV infection and AIDS' in his paper on AIDS update—1987.

Other interesting papers in this volume include 'Alcohol and Drugs as co-factors for AIDS' by Rob Roy MacGregor,'The prevention of HIV infection associated with drug and alcohol use during sexual activity' by Ron Stall, Heterosexual contacts of intravenous drug abusers: Implications for the next spread of the AIDS epidemic by Debra L. Murphy, 'Sterile needles and the epidemic of Acquired Immunodeficiency Syndrome: Issues for drug abuse treatment and public health' by Peter A. Selwyn, 'Neurocognitive impairment in alcoholics: review and comparison with cognitive impairment due to AIDS', by Melvin I. Pohl,' The response of state agencies to AIDS, addiction and alcoholism' by Chauncey L. Veatch III,'Treatment of substance abuse in patients with HIV infection' by Barbara G. Faltz and Scott Madover; 'Current and future trends in AIDS in New York city' by Stephen C. Joseph and 'the role of substance abuse professional in the AIDS epidemic' by David E. Smith. These papers provide lot of information on AIDS and substance Abuse particularly with regard to the United States of America.

Questions and Answers on AIDS

Questions and Answers on AIDS[14] by Lyn Frumkin, M.D. and John Leonard, M.D. is a publication designed to offer basic and practical information on a variety of issues relating to HIV/AIDS.

In all there are eight chapters dealing with topics such as the cause of AIDS, the manifestations of HIV infection, opportunistic infection, transmission of HIV, diagnosis of HIV infection, epidemiology of AIDS, treatment of HIV infection and HIV and public policy. The authors have taken pain to provide carefully researched and accurate and complete information on various topics by way of answering as many as 133 questions. Apart from this, there is also a glossary and list of references.

Chapter one has provided information on the causes of AIDS, immunity, retroviruses etc. by answering ten questions on various aspects of the disease. Chapter two has answered questions from 11 to 26 on topics like the definition and history of AIDS, incubation period, symptoms, wasting syndrome, HIV infection in women and children etc. Chapter three dealt with the various aspects of opportunistic infections by answering questions from 27 to 43. It has touched upon various terminolgies like pneumocystis carinii, Kaposi's Sarcoma, candidiasis, zoster, leukoplakia, cervical dysplasia etc.

Chapter four has described various issues relating to the transmision of HIV by answering questions from 44 to 81. It has covered topics like the routes of HIV transmission; risks faced by haemophiliacs, prisoners, homosexuals, health care workers etc.

Chapter five has narration about the diagnosis of HIV infection by answering questions from 82 to 95. It has dealt with HIV testing in great detail. Chapter six speaks about the epidemiology of AIDS through questions 96 to 102. Special reference has been given to HIV in underdeveloped countries as well as USA in this chapter. Chapter seven discusses the issues relating to treatment of HIV infection by answering questions from 103 to 123. It talks about the various strategies used to treat HIV infection, development of vaccine, life expectancy of patients, experimental approaches, research, clinical studies, evaluation of alternative treatment etc. Chapter eight has concentrated discussion on HIV and public policy while dealing with questions from 124 to 133. It has dealt with topics such as role of quarantine, guidelines for schools, economic impact in USA, insurance, legal issues etc.

This book is written in an objective and understanding fashion. It will be of immense use to all those who are interested in reading about HIV/AIDS. Further, this book may fill in the gap of knowledge for the NGOs, health workers and school teachers.

NGO Responses to HIV/AIDS in Asia

NGO Responses to HIV/AIDS in Asia—case studies[15] edited by Jenny Huddart and Joyce V. Lyons contains case studies developed during two case development workshops held in India and Thailand during 1991 and 1992, organised and supported by the UNDP Regional Project, "Development Implications of HIV/AIDS". Some of the cases were field tested during the UNDP—sponsored workshop "Developing NGO—Business Partnerships", held in Hua Hin, Thailand in June 1992.

The collection of cases included in this volume provides an opportunity to share the experiences of a number of NGOs within the Asia Region as they developed and implemented their HIV/AIDS programmes. The organisations selected for inclusion in this case book represent a cross-section of the types of programmes and organisational responses that are emerging from the non-governmental sector throughout Asia. The cases are intended to help NGOs that are not yet involved in HIV/AIDS interventions to reflect upon and plan for such programmes. The cases are also intended for those NGOs already involved in HIV/AIDS programmes to think critically about their own programmes and organisations, and to identify new strategies and approaches that could be used to effect improvement.

This book is divided into two major sections. Section I contains the six cases, together with the associated learning objectives for each case. With each case a set of "Discussion Questions" are included which are intended to encourage readers to focus their thinking on specific issues and problems. Some suggestions on how readers should approach the case materials are provided at the front of the materials relating to each case.

Section II of this book contains some notes on each of the cases, called "Facilitators' Notes", which are intended to help course facilitators to prepare their own analysis of the case. These notes are not intended to be the "right answers" or the only answers to the questions posed; there are no single right answers to the situations faced by the organisations described. The notes are, however, meant to help readers to focus on what the authors found to be key issues. Readers may disagree with the ideas suggested in the notes and hold firmly to their own analysis and interpretations.

The themes in this case book include: how NGOs can reach out into the community; the integration of HIV/AIDS interventions into existing programmes; planning and initiating programmes; finding and sustaining funding support; organising and developing the NGO's human resources; working with volunteers; and monitoring and evaluation. These cases can be used for individual self-study, self-directed group study and for classroom use.

AIDS/HIV Treatment Directory

AIDS/HIV treatment directory[16] compiled and published by medical editors: Donald Abrams, Deborah Cotton and Kenneth Mayer reproduces guidelines for the use of antiretroviral drugs in HIV infection, as published in the Journal of the American Medical Association. This text summarizes the proceedings and conclusions of a state-of-the-art conference convened by the National Institute of Allergy and Infections Disease of the National Institutes of Health. The state-of-the-art conference was held amid the uncertainty generated by the results of the concorde study of AZT in asymptomatic HIV infection. The uncertainty is reflected in the final guidelines, which often describes a set of rational treatment options for particular patients, rather than dictate a single treatment. The panel allows physicians considerable flexibility in the treatment of HIV infection, and stresses that clinicians must constantly integrate current scientific advancement into their practices.

You Can Do Something About AIDS

You can do something about AIDS[17] edited by Sasha Alyson is the result of a cooperative effort by the publishing community to volunteer its resources in the fight against AIDS. This book is one way of responding to the impending disaster that AIDS would bring about in the near future. Several companies, fashion, entertainment and other industries have all cooperated in the publication process of this book which provides a variety of ways in which people from various walks of life have spoken about what and how things can be done to reach out to the masses in educating about AIDS and caring for people with HIV/AIDS.

Promoting NGO/Business Sector Partnership for AIDS Prevention

Promoting NGO/Business Sector Partnerships for AIDS prevention: consultation proceedings and manual[18] edited by Joyce V. Lyons and Karen Y. Morita contains valuable insights and ideas which were contributed by the participants. It also documents the structure, the process and the content of the meeting so as to provide a model for others.

The consultation meetings were held from 22-25 June, 1992 at the Royal Garden Village Hotel in Hua Hin, Thailand. The participants included representatives of business and NGO partners, government and UN organizations. The meeting was organised and supported by UNDP Regional Project, with assistance from WHO.

On the first day the meeting focussed on defining NGO/Business partnerships, while, on the second day the entire time was devoted to discussion on 'promoting partnerships: shaping Business Responses to HIV'. During the day long deliberation on the third day, the participants conncentrated on discussing 'Developing NGO partnership skill'. On the fourth and final day the participants were provided with the opportunity to develop their own partnership plans, based on the experiences and ideas raised during the consultation and upon their own analysis of the opportunities within their own organisations' environment.

In all there are three sections in this manual. Section one gives an introduction, section two presents the proceedings of each day session-wise and section three has the annexes which include opening remarks by UNDP and WHO, list of participants, summary report: participant evaluations and the condom party.

This manual has been very well prepared and will be of very good use to NGOs and business sector who would be interested or already involved in AIDS prevention activities.

AIDS Education for Student Youth

AIDS education for student youth: A training manual[19] edited by Dr. Bhagbanprakash has been prepared by a core resource team comprising academics, health specialists, youth coordinators and counsellors from reputed national and international bodies like WHO, UNICEF, NACO, University and Government departments.

This manual is designed as a resource guide to help in the training of NSS and other youth programme functionaries. Since training for UTA is likely to be organised by more than one agency, it is claimed by the editor that the training component has been standardised. The categories of functionaries to be trained include, personnel working at the Regional Centres, State Liaison Cells, the NSS Programme Coordinators at the University level and the NSS programme officers and student peer leaders at the college and +2 school level, besides the faculty of the NSS training centres in the country. In addition it has been suggested that the teachers/ functionaries incharge of student welfare can also be covered by the manual.

The claim by the editor who was also one of the members of the Core Resource Team, that the six modules in the manual are presented in detail to facilitate its use by NSS personnel and students responsible for project planning and implementation needs to be thoroughly examined. In fact one can find large number of facts, concepts and terminologies having incomplete and inadequate explanation.

To quote few: question No. 20 in page 23 (module I) on how can you test for the presence of HIV virus? does not provide an answer to the question. Instead it explains details about antibodies. In fact another core team has copied the same question and answer while preparing a training package for school children titled "AIDS education in schools: A training package".

In module II on Human sexuality: concept clarification, hardly any detail is provided on key terminologies and concepts. The portion (page 55) dealing with 'sex organs of boys and related functions/ process' does not provide adequate and complete information. For instance the function of penis has been shown only as the male organ for sexual intercourse. It has not said anything about its use for passing urine. Similarly about the testicles it has been mentioned as "two round glands". Similar misinformation and inadequate explanations can be seen throughout the manual.

An Orientation to HIV/AIDS Counselling

An orientation to HIV/AIDS counselling: A guide for Trainers[20] by WHO provides seven modules apart from providing a glossary of training terms. The seven modules are: (*i*) basic information on STD/HIV. (*ii*) HIV counselling: its nature and purpose (*iii*) Values and attitudes of a good counsellor (*iv*) Effective counselling teachniques (*v*) Sexuality and sensitive issues (*vi*) Pre-and post-test counselling, and (*vii*) Problem - solving counselling.

The modules are designed to train HIV/AIDS care providers for example, nurses and social workers in hospitals, health centres and other health and welfare sectors, both in the governmental and non-governmental departments, and to be used by a team of resource persons who have counselling experience as well as experience in inservice training of health and social workers.

Although these modules have presented lot of literature on various aspects of counselling, lot of improvement can be brought about if appropriate editing and vetting is done. Categorical statement like "This guide has been designed to help almost anybody become a counsellor" can invite unwanted criticism and may weaken the very purpose of the manual.

Sexuality, Young People and Care

Sexuality, young people and care[21] by Jeni Bremner and Anthony Hillin provides basic information on the questions for consideration in HIV prevention with young people, and draws out implications for local policy developments. It provides a means for identifying areas for priority action in organisational systems, and gives pointers for action for devising training plans, all of which will help ensure that practice complies with anti-discriminatory principles and children act guidance.

The authors say that this paper is derived from their general experience of working in the area of HIV and sexuality since 1985 and in particular in running sex and sexuality courses for residential care workers working with young people and their families since 1987. These courses have varied in length from a half a day to eight days.

They have highlighted issues which they felt were central to staff being able to do the work effectively and which were repeatedly identified by workers during training programmes.

In all there are nine chapters, an introduction and a glossary. The chapters are on safer sex; oppressions and internalised oppression; young people, sex, sexuality and HIV prevention; cross cultural work on sexuality and HIV; gender; working with young lesbians and gay men; common themes arising from work on sexuality; legal considerations in working with young people on issues of sex and sexuality; and issues for managers.

These chapters have been written in polite fashion with adequate statistical information and references. This book will be of immense use to trainers, NGOs, school teachers and those involved in family education and youth guidance in relation to HIV.

A Trainer's Guide

A trainer's guide[22] by Cathie Wright and Jo Burns is a guide to workshops on sexuality in the context of HIV/AIDS. This guide is designed to support trainers in running a course of four workshops for workers working with young people about sexuality in the context of HIV/AIDS. The overall aim is to enable workers to feel more confident, informed and skilled in discussing sexual issues with young people and in encouraging young people to value themselves enough to make responsible choices about relationships and sexual behaviour.

The four workshops are on (*i*) sexuality and identity. (*ii*) sexuality and safer sex (*iii*) sexuality and counselling and (*iv*) follow-up day. This manual contains a sample evaluation form and as many as six handouts on topics like teenage sexual behaviour and the impact of AIDS, notes on counselling skills, human sexual response etc.

This guide is very useful for training workshops and can be used with necessary changes keeping in view the social, cultural and religious background of various groups and societies.

AIDS Education in Schools: A Training Package

The attempt made by NACO and NCERT to develop an educational package "AIDS Education in Schools: A training Package"[23] is timely and most needed in India. In fact it is "an indication of the realisation that education has an important role to play in stemming the spread of HIV/AIDS" as stated by P.R. Dasgupta, the then Project Director, NACO in the preface to this educational package. The consultation provided by UN organisations like UNESCO, UNICEF, WHO and UNFPA for the preparation of contents of this package is most welcome in the Indian situation.

The training package has touched upon numerous issues on HIV/AIDS and has developed a module for students activities. The design and structure of the package has the perceived scope and potential to meet the needs of the teachers and master trainers.

It is assumed in the educational package that module I (i.e. content/enrichment material) is a prelude to module II (i.e. suggested students' activities). However, the package does not seem to have adhered to this assumption. A critical assessment of some of the chapters in module I and some of the suggested students' activities from module II has revealed that the package contains inaccuracies, inconsistencies, misdirection and misinformation.

In module I, Chapter I is on 'Why Aids Education': The envisaged aim of the package is to impart AIDS education to students in schools. The main consideration should have been to visualise the consequences of such a package on the behavioural pattern of school going children. Rather the package is giving undue emphasis on the impact of AIDS on issues such as national development, women etc. No doubt these are important issues but the real purpose gets defeated because of diffusion. There are documented cases and studies to show the involvement of school going adolescents in sexual activities and injecting drugs. These aspects need to be highlighted. The focus should be to provide accurate and complete information about AIDS and to ensure responsible behaviour instead of mixing it with extraneous issues.

Care should have been taken in the use of terminologies. For example, "sexual activities" would be more appropriate than "sexual intercourse". There is documented evidence that lot of homosexual and lesbian activities take place among young people. These are high risk activities as far as the spread of HIV is concerned. The content of this chapter do not provide adequate teaching material for one hour talk-cum-discussion on major points which are listed in page 61 (Appendix II).

In short this chapter in its present form will not be useful for the target group. It needs revision.

Chapter II on HIV/AIDS/STD: Basic Information, has several flows. Categorical statements like "AIDS is a new phenomenon" may be avoided. It is around us since last 17 years and even more. This would mean that many students were born after the detection of the first HIV/AIDS case.

While explaining transmission of HIV, the text is almost silent on injecting drugs. If the objective is to curb the high risk behaviour among students then the text should have contained adequate information about the dangers inherent in injecting drugs.

Para 3 on page 12 states that "it should be noted that the possibility of transmission of HIV through normal injections in clinics and hospitals is extremely low". In fact this is not true as far as India is concerned. The disposable needles and syringes are recycled and again used. Proper sterilisation is not done even in the best of hospitals in the capital. Even the medical and paramedical staff do not adhere to the prescribed guidelines and standards. The text has completely ignored the ground reality.

Instead (*i*) it would have been appropriate to educate the children so that they are able to demand and make sure that **properly** sterilised needles are used; (*ii*) carry a fresh disposable needle and syringe while visiting health clinics; (*iii*) they ensure that the disposable needle used for injecting them is destroyed on the spot by a needle destroyer. The author(s) of this chapter should have kept in mind the target group. This chapter projects a medical approach with medical terminologies without adequate explanation of the subject matter.

Chapter III is on HIV/AIDS: Its Prevention and Control. This chapter lacks clarity, straightforward messages and proper elaboration. Rather it opens up with a negative notion: "How to prevent and control HIV/AIDS is a very difficult question". There is paucity of information and materials are sketchy. The contents of this chapter are mostly picked up from the previous chapter. Mentioning of risky behaviour like injecting drugs is almost absent.

The discussion on "sexual intercourse" could have been incorporated in a more graceful manner. Hardly any effort is made to explain about the transmission of HIV through sexual activities. The whole approach of this chapter is based on assumed notions rather than rooting it in the empirical reality of target group. This chapter requires revision so as to incorporate adequate messages related to the prevention and control of this killer disease. A large area of subject matter is left out which needs to be included in the package.

Chapter IV is on Importance of Counselling, Care and teachers' role. The author(s) of this chapter have not made evident of any knowledge of counselling. An authentic academic exercise on counselling requires some exposure to practical experience. Statements like "Counselling is a new concept in India" are nothing but misinformation. Author(s) would have avoided devoting half a page of sketchy information on counselling. Further, the discussion on the concept of Family Planning is unwaranted. This sketchy discussion hangs in isolation without its content related on family life education.

It will be very useful if a full chapter on counselling is included in the package. The chapter may provide information about the concept, principles, techniques, methods, functions, requirements and aims of counselling before and after HIV testing etc. is provided.

First para (P.22) makes demands on teachers to function as a resource for "accurate information" in matters related to sex and sexuality. Since teachers are not provided with the "accurate information" on sex and sexuality in module I, one cannot expect them to impart the same to students. Being a teacher or a parent or an adult or a married person is no guarantee that a person has accurate information on such topics. In academic matters things need not be taken for granted. The package has been designed for adult teachers. Let us not presume that parents or anyone else will object imparting accurate information about sex and sexuality to teachers. A beginning has to be made. The tendency to overlook real life situations will only do more harm.

There is again repetition of messages which have already been mentioned. Repetition in itself is good in a training package, but it losses its importance and purpose when things are repeated only to fill pages.

Chapter VI on Question that young students may ask has several drawbacks. A few instances are cited below for clarification.

Answer to question No. 2: "where did HIV come from? states that there are a few scientific opinions about the origin of AIDS. The text has failed to mention at least the four commonly talked of theories about its origin. Simply mentioning about the existence of scientific opinions leaves a vacuume in the minds of students.

Answer to question No. 9 on advantages and disadvantages of testing for HIV states that "he/she will know to practice responsible sexual behaviour". The veracity of the statement remains unclear.

Module II is on Students activities like question box, group discussion, value clarification, role play etc.

The idea of question box is excellent. However, if the cited objectives in the text are to be met, then the package should have components on practical implications of sex and sexual activities.

Students are expected to discuss in groups for about 15 minutes on topics like "sexual intercourse". Sexual intercourse is just one of the sexual activities. There are several other sexual activities that can transmit HIV. Further the text, i.e., Module I is silent on facts of life and family life education.

As mentioned in the text, the statements for teacher training and for students' activity have no clarification in Module I. How can we expect the teacher to clalrify queries and doubts of students?

It is, therefore, suggested that: (*i*) The present training package should be immediately revised; (*ii*) an independent academic body or a committee may be constituted to examine this package; (*iii*) The course preparation team should keep in mind the target group i.e., students and teachers while developing the course contents; (*iv*) topics related to facts of life and family life education should be incorporated and elaborated in the text; (*v*) social scientist, psychologists, social workers, and NGOs having work experience with HIV/AIDS infected persons should be involved in the preparation of fresh package.

SUMMARY

In this chapter an attempt has been made to present the role of teachers in HIV/AIDS and life skill education. In brief the chapter has touched upon areas and issues which included: why to introduce HIV and life skill education in educational curriculum, some of the objectives of HIV and life skill education, some of the strategies and methods for life skill education, promotion of value education, moral education, culture of life and planning for HIV/AIDS and life skill education. It has also provided details of two programmes of study on HIV/AISD namely, CAFÉ and DAFE being offered by IGNOU through distance learning mode. The chapter ends with a review of literature based on some of the books on HIV/AIDS and related topics in circulation.

REFERENCES

1. Priya, Ritu: "HIV/AIDS Education and Behaviour Modification" in HIV/AIDS Education and care, IGNOU, New Delhi, 2001.
2. AIDS livelihood and social change in Africa (summary of a conference organized by Wageningen Agriculrual University, Wageningen, the Netherlands) in MEMISA MEDISCH, Rotterdam, December, 1999.
3. *Ibid.*
4. Gracious Thomas, "HIV/AIDS": A handbook for young people, Sky Group Publishers, Changanassery, 2005.
5. David E. Bloom and Joyce V. Lyons (editors): Economic Implications of AIDS in Asia. UNDP Regional programme Division, Regional Bureau for Asia and the Pacific, HIV/AIDS Regional project, New Delhi 1993;
6. Rober A. Glick(ed) Law, Ethics and HIV. UNDP Regional Programme Division, New Delhi, 1993.
7. John Hubley, Shankar Chowdhury, V. Chandramouli: The AIDS handbook —A guide to the understanding of AIDS and HIV. Popular Prakashan, Bombay, 1995.
8. Gracious Thomas: AIDS in India: Myth and Reality. Rawat Publications, Jaipur and New Delhi, 1994.
9. Gracious Thomas, N.P. Sinha and Johnson Thomas K.: AIDS, Social Work and Law. Rawat Publications, Jaipur and New Delhi, 1997
10. Gracious Thomas: AIDS and Family Education. Rawat Publications, Jaipur and New Delhi, 1995.
11. NACO, National AIDS Control programme India. Country Scenario update. Ministry of Health and Family Welfare, Govt. of India, Dec. 1995.
12. Multimedia Self-study kit for professionals who counsel people living with HIV/AIDS, (1994 National HIV Frontline Forum). NCM Publishers, Inc. New York, 1994.
13. Larry Siegel (editor): AIDS and substance abuse. Harrington Park Press, New York, 1998.
14. Lyn Frumkin and John Leonard: Questions and Answers on AIDS. PMIC Los Angeles, 1994.
15. Jenny Huddart and Joyce V. Lyons: NGO Responses to HIV/AIDS in Asia—Case studies. Regional Bureau for Asia and the Pacific, UNDP, New Delhi, 1992.
16. Donald Abrams, Deborah Cotton and Kenneth Mayer: AIDS/HIV treatment directory. American Foundations for AIDS Research (AMFAR), Volume 7, Number 2, 1994.

17. Sasha Alyson (editor): You can do something about AIDS. The stop AIDS project, Boston 1990.
18. Joyce V. Lyons and Karen Y. Morita: Promoting NGO/Business sector partnerships for AIDS Prevention: Consultation proceedings and manual. UNDP, New Delhi, 1993.
19. Dr. Bhagbanprakash (editor): AIDS education for student youth. UTA/ NSS, Department of youth Affairs and sports, Ministry of Human Resource Development, Government of India, New Delhi, 1994 (3rd edition).
20. WHO, An Orientation to HIV/AIDS Counselling: A guide for trainers. World Health Organization, Regional office for South - East Asia, New Delhi, 1994.
21. Jeni Bremner and Anthony Hillin: Sexuality, young people and care. Central Council for Education & Training in Social Work (London & South East Region), London, 1993.
22. Jo Burns and Cathie Wright: A Trainer's Guide. HMSO Publications, Edinburgh, 1993.
23. AIDS education in schools: A training package. NACO Ministry of Health & Family Welfare, Govt. of India, New Delhi, 1994.

3

Global and National Scenario

Introduction

AIDS which has become a pandemic is thought to be the most recent global health problem facing people from all walks of life. The HIV infection is now found on every inhabited continent. It has crossed all boarders. Sex outside marriage activities and sharing drug injecting equipment are the two major means of HIV transmission among adults. From an evolutionary perspective, sex outside marriage must be one of the oldest methods for transmitting diseases among adults, and sharing equipment for injecting illicit drugs must be one of the most recent methods. Alcohol consumption has been identified as an important behavioral factor that can contribute to HIV infection; it has been consistently associated with HIV risk behaviors over time. Significantly higher rates of HIV infection are found among samples of alcoholics and individuals who meet criteria for alcohol dependence than in the general public. In this chapter an attempt has been made to describe the Global and National Scenario of HIV/AIDS.

GLOBAL SCENARIO

By the end of 2004, according to UNAIDS/World Health Organisation (WHO) estimate about 40 million men, women and children worldwide have been infected with the HIV[1]. More than 90 percent of those infected are in developing countries. Although not yet highly visible throughout Asia, experts consider the HIV to be well established in India, Myanmar and Thailand, and present in almost all other countries in Asia and pacific region.[2]

In 1987 WHO[3] changed its method of reporting AIDS cases from a rate measured in cases per million to the total number of cases occurring per country. In 1992 the greatest totals of European cases were in France, Italy, Spain, Germany and the United Kingdom.

Countries with the highest rates of AIDS cases were Switzerland (65), France (66) and Spain (67). In the Americas, Canada, Brazil and Mexico had the largest number of cases outside the United States. Bermuda and Barbados had reported rates of AIDS cases among the highest. Australia, Thailand, Singapore, India and Indonesia had reported substantial number of new infections among in Southeast Asian and Pacific countries.

The first medical reports of the syndrome were published in the United States in June 1981[4]. For two years preceding these reports, a small but growing number of homosexual men and their physicians in New York city, Los Angeles and San Francisco were noticing rare or unusual disease symptoms—pneumocystis pneumonia, Kaposi's Sarcoma in young men - and a host of infections not found in otherwise healthy people. The ailments seemed to be related to inexplicable deterioration in the men's systems.[5] Physicians were initially helpless in finding answers to several of their questions regarding what had gone wrong with the body's defence system of their patients. Some of them believed that probably they were identifying a new sexually transmitted disease. There were also suspicions that the new disease might have developed as a result of blood transfusion and in some cases among intravenous drug users.

By the end of 1981 doctors in the Zairean's capital, Kinshasa had also began to document dozens of cases where their patients' multiple infections seemed to relate to a collapse of the body's immune function.[6] In Zambia there was the appearance of a new and more aggressive form of Kaposi's Sarcoma linked with immune deficiencies, prompted a physician working there to observe the similarity between the symptoms of her Zambian patients and those which had broken out among American homosexuals.[7]

As the medical profession started to track backwards through the 1970s it become clear that some of the earliest known cases of AIDS had been seen by Belgian doctors among Africans. The first seems to have been a thirty-four year old Zairean airline secretary, who flew to Belgium with her child in 1977, to find out the reasons for their persistent respiratory and intestinal infections.[8]

Late 1980 and early 1981 saw doctors at a Parisian clinic baffled by a case of pneumocystis pneumonia in a Portuguese man having recently arrived from Angola, in a Zairean woman, and in a French woman who had recently come from Zaire.[9] Of the two hundred patients affected by the new disease in Europe, fifty-two were Africans.[10]

In Haiti, the tell-tale combination of Kaposi's Sarcoma and uncontrollable opportunistic infections seems, in retrospect, first to have appeared in 1978-79.[11] Coinciding with the earliest cases of Kaposi's Sarcoma in homosexual men in the United States, and with the arrival of the first African patient with the new disease in Europe, Haitian refugees with immunodeficiency diseases were seen in increasing numbers in New York city and Miami during 1980-81. By mid 1982, the CDC had documented thirty-four such cases. By October 1982, researchers in Haiti had diagnosed sixty-one cases.[12]

The roughly simultaneous appearance of AIDS in the United States, Europe, Africa and Haiti promoted the question: Had AIDS been around for sometime, unnoticed because the characteristic collection of opportunistic infections so indicative of underlying immune impairment had not been recognised.[13] After combing through medical histories of past patients, investigators found a small number of probable cases of AIDS, going back nearly thirty years in three continents.[14]

The number of AIDS cases reported to the Global Programme on AIDS (GPA) in adults and children rose to 1,69,811 by mid - 1995 from 985,119 a year earlier. This represents almost a 20 per cent increase over the past year. But GPA believes that the true number of cases may be four times this, in the region of 4.5 million. The estimate takes into account under diagnosis, under-reporting and delays in reporting.[15]

Only about half of the reported AIDS cases were from the developing countries, but GPA estimates that these countries account for well over three-quarters of actual cases. The number of AIDS cases is only a fraction of the number of people estimated to have been infected with HIV, and who are therefore likely to go on to develop AIDS. According to GPA estimates, about 18.5 million adults and more than 1.5 million children have been infected with HIV since the beginning of the pandemic in the late 1970s and early 1980s.[16]

Incidence of AIDS in Representative Countries

The accuracy of reporting AIDS cases varies greatly from country to country for many different reasons. Despite the incompleteness of reporting, the UNAIDS/World Health Organisation maintains a tally of all cases reported to it. The global summary of the HIV/ AIDS epidemic upto December 2004 is presented in Table 3.1.

Table 3.1
Global Summary of the HIV and AIDS Epidemic, December 2004

Number of people living with HIV in 2004	**Total**	39.4 million (30.9-44.3 million)
	Adults	37.2 million (33.8-41.7 million)
	Women	17.6 million (16.3-19.5 million)
	Children under 15 years	2.2 million (2.0-2.6 million)
People newly infected with HIV in 2004	**Total**	4.9 million (4.3 -6.4 million)
	Adults	4.3 million (3.7-5.7 million)
	Children under 15 years	640 000 (570 000 – 750 000)
AIDS deaths in 2004	**Total**	3.1 million (2.8-3.5 million)
	Adults	2.6 million (2.3-2.9 million)
	Children under 15 years	510 000 (460 000 – 600 000)

Source: UN AIDS/WHO: AIDS Epidemic update December, 2004.

On the basis of available data on the current global status of the pandemic and recent trends in its spread, WHO has generated a plausible range of projected new HIV infections during the 1990s. In making projection of the future magnitude of the pandemic, WHO used the lower limits of its estimated regional ranges of HIV prevalence; so the results of the forecasting should be considered conservative. During this decade, around 10-15 million new HIV infections may be expected in adults, mostly in developing countries. During the same period, as many as 5-10 million children will be HIV infected at birth or through breast-feeding, the majority of them in Subaharan Africa. According to UNAIDS estimates, by the end of 2004 the total number of people living with HIV was 39.4 million, the number of newly infected with HIV was 4.9 million and the number of deaths was estimated to be 3.1 million.[17]

AIDS Status in Africa

Dr. Frumkin and Dr. Leonard reports that cases of AIDS were first noted in Africans seeking treatment in Europe only shortly after AIDS was recognized in the United States. Subsequent epidemiological studies found that AIDS was widespread throughout Central Africa with most cases linked by heterosexual contact. Testing of stored blood documented HIV in Africa as early as 1965 and reviews of medical records found cases consistent with AIDS in Africans as early as 1975. A sample of stored blood collected in Africa in 1959 contained HIV, making it the oldest known isolate of the virus. In addition, an English sailor who had been in Central Africa in 1958 was found retrospectively to have AIDS by analysing preserved tissues for the presence of HIV. All of these findings indicate that HIV was probably spreading through parts of Africa before it arrived in the United States and in Europe.[18]

Sub-Saharan Africa has just over 10 percent of the world's population, but is home to more than 60 percent of all people living with HIV—some 25.4 million. In 2004, an estimated 3.1 million people in the region became newly infected, while 2.3 million died of AIDS. Among young people aged 15-24 years, an estimated 6.9 percent of women and 2.2 percent of men were living with HIV at the end of 2004. Adult HIV prevalence has been roughly stable in recent years. But stabilization does not necessarily mean the epidemic is slowing. On the contrary, it can disguise the worst phases of an epidemic—when roughly equally large numbers of people are being newly infected with HIV and are dying of AIDS.[19]

Southern Africa remains the worst affected subregion in the world, with the data from selected antenatal clinics in urban areas showing HIV prevalence surpassing 25 percent having risen sharply from around 5 percent in 1999.

South Africa continues to have the highest number of people living with HIV in the world. An estimated 5.3 million people were living with HIV end—2003 in South Africa—2.9 million of them women. Unfortunately, there is no sign yet of a decline in the epidemic. Overall HIV prevalence among pregnant women was 27.9 percent in 2003, compared with 26.5 percent in 2002 and 25 percent the year before that. Latest data suggest prevalence levels are still increasing in all age groups, except for pregnant women older than 40 years of age.

At the start of the 21st century, some 23.3 million Africans south of the Sahara were estimated by UNAIDS/WHO to have HIV infection or AIDS. That is almost 70 percent of the World's total in a region that is home to just 10 percent of the world's population. As prevention efforts elsewhere reduce the number of infants acquiring HIV, the continent's lead in terms of child infections is more compelling than ever: UNAIDS/WHO estimate that nearly 90 percent of the half a million children born with the virus or infected through breast feeding in 1999 were living in sub-Saharan Africa[21]

Why in Africa more women than men are infected is not fully understood. A combination of factors are clearly involved, including the fact that HIV passes more easily from men to women through sex than from women to men. However, a prime factor is surely the difference in age patterns of HIV infection in men and women. Women tend to become infected far younger than men for both biological and cultural reasons. According to recent studies in several African populations, girls aged 15-19 are around five or six times more likely to be HIV-positive than boys of their own age. The infection rate in men eventually catches up, but not until after they reach their late 20s or early 30s. Clearly, older men who often coerce girls into sex or buy their favours with sugar daddy gifts—are the main source of HIV for the teenage girls.[22]

AIDS IN ASIAN COUNTRIES

(i) Thailand

Thailand has also shown that a well-funded, politically-supported and pragmatic response can change the course of the epidemic. National adult HIV prevalence continues to edge lower, with the latest estimates, putting it at 1.5 percent at the end of 2003.[23] Recharged commitment and revised strategies are now needed, however, to confront an epidemic that has entered a new phase. As many as half of annual, new HIV infections have been occurring among cohabiting couples, as more women are infected by husbands who are (or were) clients of sex workers. While still an important factor in HIV spread, brothel-based sex work has been overtaken by other patterns of risky behaviour. An estimated one-fifth of all new HIV infections are occurring through unsafe injecting drug use compared with about one-twentieth a decade ago.[24] Exceptionally high levels of HIV infection are being detected in parts of the country. In northern Thailand, 30 percent of drug injectors are infected with HIV, while median HIV prevalence as high as 51 percent has been found in other parts of the country. Yet, scant prevention resources are deployed on this front. The fact that injecting drug use is illegal should not block the path of effective action. A pragmatic approach—such as that adopted toward sex work in the 1990s—is much more likely to bring success. The same holds for men who have sex with men, among whom HIV prevalence as high as 17 percent has been detected.[25]

Table 3.2
Regional HIV and AIDS Statistics and features, end 2002 and 2004

	Adults and Children living with HIV	Adults and Children newly infected with HIV	Adult Prevalence (%)*	Adult and Child Death Due to AIDS
Sub-Saharan Africa				
2004	25.4 million	3.1 million	7.4	2.3 million
	[23.4–28.4 million]	[2.7-3.8 million]	[6.9-8.3]	[2.1-2.6 million]
2002	24.4 million	2.9 million	7.5	2.1 million
	[22.5–27.3 million]	[2.6-3.6 million]	[7.0-8.4]	[1.9-2.3 million]
North Africa and Middle East				
2004	540 000	92 000	0.3	28 000
	[230 000-1.5 million]	[34 000-350 000]	[0.1-0.7]	[12 000-72 000]
2002	430 000	73 000	0.2	20 000
	[180 000-1.2 million]	[21 000-300 000]	[0.1-0.6]	[8300-53 000]
South and South-East Asia				
2004	7.1 million	890 000	0.6	490 000
	[4.4-10.6 million]	[480 000-2.0 million]	[0.4-0.9]	[300 00-750 000]
2002	6.4 million	820 000	0.6	430 000
	[3.9-9.7 million]	[430 000-2.0 million]	[0.4-0.9]	[260 000-650 000]
East Asia				
2004	1.1 million	290 000	0.1	51 000
	[560 000-1.8 million]	[84 000-830 000]	[0.1-0.2]	[25 000-86 000]
2002	760 000	120 000	0.1	37 000
	[380 000-1.2 million]	[36 000-360 000]	[0.1-0.2]	[18 000-63 000]

(Contd.)

(*Contd.*)

	Adults and Children living with HIV	Adults and Children newly infected with HIV	Adult Prevalence (%)*	Adult and Child Death Due to AIDS
Oceania				
2004	35 000	5000	0.2	700
	[25 000-48 000]	[2100-13000]	[0.1-0.3]	[<1700]
2002	28 000	3200	0.2	500
	[22 000-38 000]	[1000-9600]	[0.1-0.3]	[<1000]
Latin America				
2004	1.7 million	240 000	0.6	95 000
	[1.3-2.2 million]	[170 000-430 00]	[0.5-0.8]	[73 000-120 000]
2002	1.5 million	190 000	0.6	74 000
	[1.1-2.0 million]	[140 000-320 000]	[0.4-0.7]	[58 000-96 000]
Caribbean				
2004	440 000	53 000	2.3	36 000
	[270 000-78 000]	[27 000-140 000]	[1.5-4.1]	[24 000-61 000]
2002	420 000	52 000	2.3	33 000
	[260 000-740 000]	[26 000-140 000]	[1.4-4.0]	[22 000-57 000]
Eastern Europe and Central Asia				
2004	1.4 million	210 00	0.8	60 000
	[920 000-2.1 million]	[110 000-480 000]	[0.5-1.2]	[39 000-87 000]
2002	1.0 million	190 000	0.6	40 000
	[670 000-1.5 million]	[94 000-440 000]	[0.4-0.8]	[27 000-58 000]

(*Contd.*)

(*Contd.*)

	Adults and Children living with HIV	Adults and Children newly infected with HIV	Adult Prevalence (%)*	Adult and Child Death Due to AIDS
Western and Central Europe				
2004	610 000	21 000	0.3	6500
	[480 000-760 000]	[14 000-38 000]	[0.2-0.3]	[<8500]
2002	600 000	18 000[	0.3	6000
	[470 000-750 000]	13 000-35 000]	[0.2-0.3]	[<8000]
North America				
2004	1.0 million	44 000	0.6	16 000
	[540 000-1.6 million]	[16 000-120 000]	[0.3-1.0]	[8400-25 000]
2002	970 000	44 000	0.6	16 000
	[500 000-1.6 million]	[16 000-120 000]	[0.3-1.0]	[8400-25 000]
Total				
2004	39.4 million	4.9 million	1.1	3.1 million
	[35.9-44.3 million]	[4.3-6.4 million]	[1.0-1.3]	[2.8-3.5 million]
2002	36.6 million	4.5 million	1.1	2.7 million
	[33.3-41.1 million]	[3.9-6.2 million]	[1.0-1.2]	[2.5-3.1 million]

*The proportion of adults (15 to 49 years of age) living with HIV/AIDS in 2004, using 2004 population numbers.

The ranges around the estimates in this table define the boundaries within which the actual numbers lie, based on the best available information.

Source: UNAIDS/WHOU: AIDS Epidemic update–December, 2004.

(ii) Vietnam

Widespread injecting drug use by sex workers makes Viet Nam's epidemic particularly explosive. In Ho Chi Minh City, 38 percent of almost 1000 sex workers included in one survey injected drugs- and fully 49 percent of those injecting sex workers were infected with HIV (compared with 8 percent of those who didn't use any drugs). In the northern port city of Haiphong, nearly 40 percent of all sex workers said they injected drugs, compared to one in six sex workers who did likewise in the capital, Hanoi. Drug-using sex workers are about half as likely to use condoms as those who do not use drugs, according to another study in Ho Chi Minh City. These trends probably explain a good deal of the steep rises in HIV prevalence detected in some of the Viet Nam's cities, where the virus now appears to be spreading freely among groups that are at high risk of exposure to HIV. HIV prevalence of 8 per cent was detected in a 2003 Ho Chi Minh city survey among men who have sex with men.[26]

Warning signs that HIV transmission could increase dramatically through sexual risk behaviour are not lacking:[27]

- In female sex workers, HIV prevalence increased five-fold in the four years to 1998, reaching 2.6 percent.
- National surveillance suggest that the HIV infection rate in male STI patients doubled to 1 percent in the same period.
- A study in two STD clinics in southern Vietnam found somewhat lower HIV rates but exceptionally worrying patterns of sexual behaviour. Every one of the over 800 men in the study had had sex with a prostitute at some point in his life, and three-quarters of them had done so in the past three years. Fully 70 percent of these men had never used a condom.
- In the same study, 45 percent of the men picked up sex workers on the street while just 38 percent visited brothels. The distribution of sex workers frequented sound another alarm bell. Generally, HIV prevention activities are easier to conduct in brothels than among street-based prostitutes, even in countries such as Thailand and Vietnam where brothels (and indeed prostitution) are illegal.

(iii) East Timor and Pakistan

East Timor and Pakistan, could be poised for HIV outbreaks. Until very recently the majority of HIV infections and AIDS cases reported in Pakistan were among migrant Pakistani workers who had been deported from the Gulf States. However, there has been a recent report of an HIV outbreak among injecting drug users in a small town in Pakistan's Sindh province. Just under 10 percent of the drug injectors in the town of Larkana reportedly tested HIV-positive.[28] Studies among Pakistani truck drivers have found that one in three has never heard of condoms, and 19 out of 20 who bought sex from women did not use condoms. Meanwhile, nearly six out of 10 sex workers in East Timor have never heard of AIDS, four out of 10 do not recognise a condom when shown one, and zero out of 10 consistently use condoms with their clients.[29]

(iv) Malaysia

The AIDS picture in Malaysia is far from clear, mainly because it is derived largely from HIV and AIDS case reports that focus on injecting drug users. Such reports indicate that 55 percent of people detected with HIV between 1998 and 2001 were drug injectors. A study carried out in Penang has found that 17 percent of drug injectors who agreed to testing were HIV-positive.[30] It is possible, though, that other significant factors in the epidemic are being missed. For example, when surveillance was last conducted among sex workers, in 1996, HIV prevalence was 6.3 percent Kaual Lumpur and 10.2 percent in Selangor.[31]

Ministry of Health official data show that by the end of February 1992 the country had only 46 cases of AIDS, of whom 33 had died, and 2,900 HIV-infected persons. Reliable sources within the ministry point out that the number of AIDS cases reported constitute about 80 percent of the actual number of cases, which would put the actual number at around 58, and that the actual number of HIV-positive cases would be around 5,800, double the number officially reported.[32]

Data from the Ministry of Health show that the major group (17 percent) comes from the ranks of the unemployed. Many experts believe that the number of injecting drug users among the Indonesian migrant population in Peninsular Malaysia is much smaller than that of the local population, and that the HIV infection and AIDS are not a problem among them.[33]

(iv) Lao PDR

Lao PDR is considered as one of the twenty least developed countries in the world. The Government figures show that about 84 percent of the people in Lao are literate although most people in this poor country had very little opportunity for formal education. With a high birth rate, low life expectancy, and low per capita income, any outbreak of an epidemic can throw the country into unimaginable disaster. With an estimated population of 4 million, the country is land-locked by HIV-infected giants like Thailand, China, Myanmar, Viet Nam and Cambodia.

With inadequate health facilities, it is almost impossible to estimate the actual prevalence rate of HIV in this country. As of April 1992, the Lao Government had officially reported only one case of AIDS to WHO office in Bangkok. However, Lao authorities have identified an additional eleven HIV-infected persons in two major cities, Vietiane and Savannakhet. The WHO has not yet confirmed or projected the number of HIV-positive and AIDS cases in Lao. Available data indicate that AIDS is concentrated in Urban areas, but no monitoring is being undertaken in smaller towns or rural areas to provide a comparison.[34] The potential target groups include the construction workers, truck drivers, salesmen, migratory labourers and poor village women who are forced to work as sex workers to support their families.

(v) Philippines

As other countries have discovered, where risky behaviors are occurring, HIV will follow—unless prevention efforts are effective. Philippines has taken such lessons to heart and are trying to reduce risky behaviours before the virus acquires a firm presence. The efforts have had partial success to date, particularly among the clients of sex workers. In 2003, for example, over one-half of registered sex workers in the Philipphine's Angeles City said they used condoms with all clients last week; however just 6 percent of hostesses in karaoke bars and night clubs consistently used condoms. But if sustained and expanded, prevention efforts could enable these countries to avoid the sorts of epidemics recorded elsewhere.[35]

The first case of HIV in the Philippines was detected in 1984, and by June 1992, 335 cases had been reported. However, later reports by the Philippine Department of Health suggest that as many as 4,000 to 7,000 Philippines may be infected. Concern is growing that the country may now be in the same position as Thailand was right before the Government initiated active surveillance programmes.[36]

Based on reported HIV and AIDS cases, sexual relations were the main mode of transmission in the Philippines (50 percent heterosexual, 13 percent homosexual, and 5 percent bisexual). Unlike in Thailand, fewer than 1 percent of reported cases in the Philippines contracted the virus through intravenous drug use. While 33 percent of patients believed they had contracted the virus abroad, 46 percent indicated that they were infected in the Philippines.[37]

According to UNAIDS/WHO, in the Philippines, HIV infection appears to remain contained at low levels, with no significant growth even in groups at traditionally high risk of infection. This is probably partly because registered sex workers are screened every two weeks for other sexually transmitted infections, which facilitate the spread of HIV, and are treated for any STIs found. In addition, sex workers report relatively high levels of condom use. According to national behavioural surveillance conducted in 1997, nearly three-quarters of registered prostitutes said they had used a condom with their most recent clients.[38]

(vi) Indonesia

The Republic of Indonesia[39] is an archipelago consisting of 13,000 Islands lying between the Asian and Australian continents. The estimated 187 million population as of 1993 is unevenly distributed in about 6,000 Islands. Indonesia has about 300 ethnic groups residing in its 27 provinces covering 302 Regency/Districts and about 6,000 sub-districts.

The first case of AIDS found in Indonesia was recorded as a foreign tourist who died in Bali, in 1987. On a vast archipelago such as Indonesia, where research has revealed ample opportunities for wider HIV transmission, the epidemic will assume diverse patterns. Risk behaviuor among injecting drug users in Indonesia is very common. A recent survey in three cities found 88 percent of the injectors had used non-sterile needles or syringes in the preceding week, yet fewer than one-third said they felt at high risk of HIV infection.[40] When injecting drug users are tested for HIV, very high infection levels are found. One in two injecting drug users in Indonesia's capital Jakarta, now test positive for HIV, while in far flung cities such as Pontiank (in west Kalimantan province on the island of Borneo) more than 70 percent of drug injectors who request HIV tests are discovering that they are HIV-positive[41]

Conditions also favour HIV spread through sex work. In seven Indonesian cities, an average 42 percent of sex workers had either or both gonorrhoea or Chlamydia in 2003. Condom use ranges from irregular to rare. In 2002, fewer than one in five sex workers operating out of massage parlours and discotheques in Jakarta said they used condoms consistently. Among sex workers in brothel areas (a group that ought to be easier to reach with interventions), rates of condom use with all clients in the previous week stood at a meager 4 percent.[42] The situation is even more troubling in parts of Indonesia's easternmost province of Papua, where HIV prevalence among sex workers in Sorong, for example, had reached 17 percent by 2003, over five times the national average for sex worker.[43]

(vii) China

Since the detection of the first AIDS case from among a foreign tourist group in China in 1985 surveillance centres on AIDS have been set up by health authorities in most of the provinces/ municipalities/autonomous regions and the prefectures under its jurisdiction. In order to strengthen its activities, the State Council approved and promulgated, in 1987, "Certain Regulations Relating to the Surveillance and Management of AIDS" as jointly submitted by nine departments concerned, including the Ministry of Public Health, the Ministry of Foreign Affairs, and the National Tourism Administration. Upto November 1992, a total of 261 AIDS cases and 969 HIV- positive cases have been reported from 18 provinces and autonomous regions (out of the 30 provinces/municipalities/ autonomous regions of the country).[44]

Although moving at a varied pace, HIV has spread to all of China's 31 provinces, autonomous regions and municipalities. In some, such as Henan, Anhui, and Shandong, HIV was already spreading a decade ago among rural people who sold blood plasma to supplement their incomes. Elsewhere, the virus has established a more recent but firm presence among injecting drug users and, to a lesser extent, sex workers and their clients.[45] Much of the current spread of HIV in China is also attributable to injecting drug use and paid sex.[46]

(viii) Japan

Data from Japan show that HIV prevalence has risen steadily among male blood donors in that country, while staying relatively stable among women. This suggests that HIV transmission is occurring mainly among men who have sex with men, some of whom might also be transmitting the virus to female sex partners. In 2003, there were some 340 newly reported HIV cases among Japanese men who had contracted their infection through sex with other men, just over three times the number of reported infections among men who report acquiring the virus heterosexually. Indeed, since 1999 there has been a rapid increase in the annual number of HIV infections attributed to male-to-male sex.[47]

(ix) Cambodia

According to UNADIS/WHO update 1999, Asia's highest levels of infection continue to be recorded in Cambodia, where an ever-improving surveillance system suggest that HIV is well established in the general population in all provinces. HIV prevalence among pregnant women in 1998 exceeded 2 percent in 12 out of the country's 19 provinces. Nationalwide, on average some 3.7 percent of married women of reproductive age were living with HIV in 1998. Prevalence in men may be somewhat higher— 4.3 percent of male blood donors were infected with HIV compared with 2.5 percent female donors.

In Cambodia, fewer men are now visiting sex workers and there has been a significant rise in condom use in commercial sex. The combined effect has been a steep drop in sexually transmitted infections and a steady decline in HIV prevalence. New testing technologies that allow researchers to estimate what proportion of infections were recently acquired show a significant drop in new HIV infections (or incidence). A 2003 survey of men aged 15 to 24 years in a low-income area of the capital, Phnom Penh, found that only 8 percent of them had ever bought sex from a sex worker.[48]

(x) Nepal

Unsafe injecting drug use is the wellspring of Nepal's epidemic, too. Use of non-sterilize injecting equipment is widespread and accounts for the high HIV prevalence—22 percent to 68 percent across the country in 2002—among male injectors, many of them younger than 25. Younger injectors appear more likely to report risky practices in parts of Nepal; in the east, for example, injectors under 25 were three times as likely to report using non-sterilize equipment at last injection compared with older injectors.[49] Nepal's epidemic also highlights the potential links between HIV infection and mobility. Injecting drug users from cities with low prevalence, but who had injected drugs elsewhere, have been found to be two to four times more likely to have acquired HIV than those who had remained in their home cities.[50]

(xi) Myanmar

Myanmar, which has one of the most serious epidemic in Asia, is an example. The situation varies across the country, but HIV has already become entrenched in lower-risk population in several parts of Myanmar. By 2003, 12 out of 29 sentinel sites for pregnant women were recording HIV prevalence above 2 percent. At Pyay and Hpa-an, respectively, 5 percent and 7.5 percent of pregnant women tested HIV-positive. About 2 percent of new military recruits tested HIV-positive at two sites in 2003. Exceptionally large proportions of injecting drug users have acquired HIV: in some places, 78 percent of drug injectors tested positive in 2003. Between 45 percent and 80 percent of drug injectors have tested positive for HIV injections in sentinel surveillance each year between 1992 and 2003.[51]

Status of HIV/AIDS in United States

The first cases of AIDS were reported in 1981. By the end of 1992, more than 250,000 Americans had developed AIDS and more than 170,000 had died nearly three times more Americans than those who died in the Vietnam war. It was estimated that in 1993 alone about 40,000 to 80,000 will get infected in the U.S.A.[52]

In the second decade of the AIDS epidemic, gay men still accounted for the majority of AIDS cases reported each year and continue to suffer an enormous burden. However, AIDS is becoming more prominent in the young and in heterosexual men and women. AIDS is now one of the three main causes of death for women and men 25 to 44 years old in this country. It is among the top 10 causes of death for children 1 to 4 years old. AIDS is now becoming a disease of families.[53]

Studies[54] reviewing the number of reported cases during the course of epidemic find that the cumulative, number of cases doubled rapidly from 1978 to 1982. During 1982, AIDS cases doubled every 12.7 months; in years before that, the rate of doubling was higher. These analyses estimate that 1984 may have been the year with greatest number of new infections, a total estimated to be about 160,000.

Rates of infection in homosexual and bisexual men peaked in 1984 and then fell substantially; by 1991 infections accumulated in this group were estimated to total 590,000. The profile of new infections in drug users is slightly different. The growth rates plateaued until 1983, and then decreased after 1986 for an estimated cumulative 265,000 by 1991. The decline in the growth rates in these populations may reflect infection of the majority of the individuals at risk; that is most that were at risk were already infected by the mid 1980s, excluding small numbers of people newly entering the group. The heterosexual epidemic lagged several years behind homo-sexuals and drug users. The rate of doubling of new cases was very fast into the mid 1980s which is representative of early stages of an epidemic. By 1986, about 15,000 new HIV infections occurred annually in heterosexuals with a total of about 100,000 thought to be infected by 1991.[55]

In the United States of America the epidemic has altered demonstrably during the past decade. An estimated 40,000 people have been infected with HIV each year in the United States in the last ten years, but the epidemic is now disproportionately lodged among African Americans and is affecting much greater number of women. The majority of people living with HIV in the United States of America are men who have sex with men. Evidence in recent years of increasing cases of syphilis and other sexually transmitted infections among men who have sex with men triggered concerns that risk behaviour was on the rise and that a new wave of HIV infections could follow.[56]

(xii) Canada

In Canada, most recent estimates indicate that some 56,000 people were living with HIV at the end of 2002[57] as many as one-third of them unaware of their HIV status. Indigenous persons appear twice as likely to be HIV- infected compared with non-indigenous persons. Most new HIV infections in Canada in 2002 were attributable to unsafe sex between men (40 percent) and injecting drug use (30 percent and declining slightly in recent years). There has been an increase in infections linked to unsafe heterosexual intercourse, a small percentage (less than 10 percent) of them among refugees or immigrants from high-prevalence countries in sub-Saharan Africa and the Caribbean.[58]

(xiii) Europe

In the 12 Western European countries with data for newly diagnosed HIV infections, HIV diagnoses in people who were infected through heterosexual contact increased by 122 percent between 1997 and

2002. HIV diagnoses among men who have sex with men increased by 22 percent in 2001-2002 in Western Europe, reversing the slow decline seen in the previous years. Data on new diagnoses should not be mistaken for HIV incidence, however, since data may reflect an increased uptake of testing services. The recent rise in new HIV diagnoses in the United Kingdom appears partly attributable to increase in HIV testing. In Germany, where greater treatment access had already boosted uptake of testing in the late 1990s, a recent increase in diagnoses (from 642 HIV diagnoses in 200 to 742 in 2002) likely reflects an actual increase in new infections.[59]

In Spain, as in several other European countries, HIV prevalence among drug injectors can vary considerably in different parts of the country. A survey of drug injectors at Spanish drug-treatment centres in Catalonia still found HIV prevalence of 38 percent in 2001. In Portugal (where the rates of new HIV diagnoses are higher than elsewhere in Europe), injecting drug use still accounted for almost 50 percent of HIV diagnoses in 2002. In France, some two-thirds of new HIV diagnoses in 2003 were in people infected during heterosexual intercourse, while in the United Kingdom the proportion was about 49 percent and in Germany 41 percent. A significant number of female sex workers are still being infected in some countries, such as the Netherlands, where a 2002-2003 study found 7 percent of sex workers in Rotterdam were HIV- positive. In the countries of central Europe (including Czech Republic and Hungry), numbers of new HIV infections have stayed stable since the late 1990s, with most of the new infections being recorded in Poland. In the Czech Republic, Hungary, Slovenia, and the Slovak Republic, sex between men is known to be the predominant mode of HIV transmission. Overall in these countries, thousands of new infections are occurring every year and large number of HIV-infected persons are unaware of their HIV status. The main challenges are to provide early and effective treatment and care to all HIV-infected people, to rejuvenate prevention efforts and adapt them to the changing pattern of the epidemic, and to reduce the psychosocial, economic and physical repercussions of HIV infections.[60]

(xiv) Russian Federation

The UNAIDS/WHO update of 1999 on AIDS epidemic say that the world's steepest HIV curve in 1999 was recorded in the newly independent states of the former Soviet Union, where the proportion of the population living with HIV doubled between end 1997 and end-1999. In the larger region comprising the former USSR as well as the remainder of Central and Eastern Europe, UNAIDS/WHO estimate that the number of infected people rose by a third over the course of 1999, reaching a total of 360,000.

The bulk of new HIV infections were caused by unsafe injection of drugs and occurred in two countries, the Russian Federation and Ukraine.

In the Russian Federation, nearly half of all cases of HIV infection reported since the start of the epidemic were reported in the first nine months of 1999 alone. While reported infections admittedly represent only a fraction of real HIV infection, little has changed in the reporting system and public health officials therefore believes this massive rise in reported cases accurately reflects trends in the overall epidemic.

The virus has been recently introduced into networks of drug injectors in Russian cities where HIV was previously virtually unknown. This is true of smaller provincial cities as well as of large metropolitan areas.

- HIV prevalence rose rapidly among drug injectors in Moscow. Over 2700 cases of HIV were reported in the Russian capital in the first nine months of 1999 along – three times as many as in all previous years combined.
- An even more stratospheric rise was recorded in the towns and cities around Moscow, with over five times as many infections reported in the first nine months of 1999 as in all other years combined.
- The virus has spread far and wide. In the Siberian city of Irkutsk, nearly 1300 infections have been reported, most of them in 1999.

The HIV epidemic among drug injectors in Ukraine started earlier than in the Russian Federation, and the consequences are now being seen in the number of people progressing to AIDS. Some 90 percent of all AIDS cases reported in 1998 and 1999 in the entire Eastern European region were in Ukraine, according to the European Centre for the Epidemiological Monitoring of AIDS.

The Russian Federation has the largest number of people living with HIV in the region, and accounts for some 70 percent of all HIV infections officially registered in Eastern Europe and Central Asia.[61] An estimated 860,000 people were living with HIV in Russia at the end of 2003, fully 80 percent of them aged 15-29 years and more than one-third of them women.[62] HIV prevalence is increasing steadily. Infection levels measured among pregnant women have risen from less than 0.01 percent in 1998 to 0.11 percent in 2003. In St. Petersburg, prevalence increased from 0.013 percent in 1998 to 1.3 percent in 2002- a hundred-fold increase.

Official estimates put HIV prevalence in the Russian prison system at 2 percent to 4 percent at least four times higher than in the wider population. As injecting drug use has increased, so has the proportion of prisoners who have histories of injecting drug use, as well as the number of them who are HIV-positive. Russia is now developing a programme that will include prevention education for prisoners, access to condoms and to bleach (for cleaning injecting equipment).[63]

Erupting with astounding speed over the past decade, Ukraine's firmly-rooted epidemic continues to expand. Newly registered HIV infections have been increasing annually since the turn of the century by 7 percent in 2000, 13 percent in 2001 and 25 percent in 2002. Just 10 years ago, there were only 183 officially registered HIV cases in Ukraine, but by mid 2004 more than 68000 cases of HIV infection had been officially registered.[64]

In the Baltic states, HIV transmission is occurring at a brisk rate, even if the overall number of infections remain low. At 2300 in 2002, the total number of HIV diagnoses in Latvia has risen five-fold since 1999. Just four years ago, Estonia reported 12 new HIV cases; in 2003, 840 people were newly diagnosed with the virus. In Lithuania, the 72 new HIV cases detected in 2001 increased more than five-fold the following year. Injecting drug use still accounts for the largest proportion of newly reported infections in these countries but sexual transmission is slowly gaining ground. In Belarus (where more than 5000 people had been officially diagnosed with HIV by mid 2003) and Moldova (where the figure stood at just under 1800), most infections are occurring among young drug injectors and their sexual partners.[65]

Uzbekistan's epidemic is now developing swiftly. Already, commercial sex appears to be playing a large role. The proportion of women among people living with the virus has grown annually from just over 12 percent in 2001 to almost 18 percent in 2003. In Kazakhastan, where a total of just over 3600 HIV cases had been reported by mid-2003, sentinel surveillance conducted in 2003 had shown prevalence level of 3.8 percent in injecting drug users and 4.6 percent in sex workers but there are no data concerning men who have sex with men.[66] In Azerbaijan, where one in four street drug injectors in the capital, Baku, have been found to be HIV-positive. Among street-based sex workers, HIV prevalence of 11 percent has been detected and among their counterparts working out of cafes and saunas, prevalence of 6 percent has been found.[67]

(xv) Latin America

More than 1.7 million people are living with HIV in Latin America. In 2004, around 95000 people died of AIDS, and 240 000 were newly infected. Among young people 15-24 years of age, an estimated 0.5 percent of women and 0.8 percent of men were living with HIV at the end of 2004.[68] Two countries in this region—Guatemala and Honduras—have national adult HIV prevalence of over 1 percent. But lower prevalence in other countries disguises the fact that serious, localized epidemics are also underway in several other countries—not least **Brazil,** which accounts for more than one-third of the people living with HIV in Latin America.[69]

HIV in Argentina remains concentrated largely in the urban areas of Buenos Aires, Cordoba and Santa Fe provinces, with an estimated 65 percent of HIV infection occurring in the capital Buenos Aires and its surrounding areas. However, the epidemic is changing. Throughout the 1980s and much of the 1990s, HIV transmission occurred mainly through injecting drug use, predominantly involving men. But sexual transmission of HIV mainly from infected drug users to their female partners, as well as between men who have sex with men—has become more prominent, accounting for an estimated 80 percent of all reported AIDS cases.[70] One recent study in Lima, Peru, for example, found that almost 90 percent of HIV-positive pregnant women had had just on or two sex partners in their lifetimes 2003.[71] With an estimated 110,000 people living with HIV at the end of 2003, Venezuela has one of the largest epidemics in the region. There, HIV is spreading mainly through unsafe sex, of it between men, a significant proportion of whom also have sex with women.[72] Bolivia's epidemic is concentrated largely among sex workers and their clients, and men who have sex with men.

In Central America, where the epidemic to a large extent is still concentrated in large urban areas, the number of HIV infection have been rising in several countries (including El Salvador, Nicargua and Panama) since the late 1990s, but HIV prevalence remains highest in Gautemala and Honduras. Among people living with HIV, men outnumber women by roughly 3:1 in most countries.[73]

To the north in Mexico, national prevalence in the adult population has remained well under 1 percent, but shows marked regional variance. On the treatment front, Brazil remains a beacon among developing countries. It continues to offer all people living with HIV access to antiretroviral drugs via its national health system when they need it. As a result, the survival time of AIDS patients has increasingly dramatically.[74]

Australia

The annual number of new HIV diagnoses in Australia has gradually increased from 650 in 1998 to about 800 in 2002. A growing share of those diagnoses was in people who had become infected in the previous year—which suggests that the increase in new diagnoses could be linked to a revival of unsafe sex. The annual number of HIV diagnoses in women has stayed relatively stable, but more of those diagnosed infections occurred through heterosexual intercourse—either in a high-prevalence country or with a partner from a high-prevalence country.[75] The per capita rates of HIV diagnoses among Indigenous people in Australia since 1993 have been similar to those in non-Indigenous people.[76]

Middle East

HIV infections in Algeria, Bahrain, Kuwait and Oman have also been attributed to injecting drug use, but its role is most evident in **Iran's** growing epidemic. About 15 percent of all HIV infections since the start of the epidemic in Iran were reported in 2003 alone.

Iran's epidemic is growing in the wake of a dramatic rise in the overall number of people who inject drugs. In recent years, Iran has improved its methods for estimating the number of people with behaviours that heighten the risk of HIV exposure. According to an epidemiological survey of drug use published by the Ministry of Health in 2002, the population of injectors could be growing at 5 percent to 10 percent a year.[77] In 2003, it was estimated that there could be as many as 200,000 injecting drug users in the country.[78]

Although overall AIDS cases remain relatively few in number, drug injecting is already the most common cause of AIDS in some countries, accounting for two-thirds of reported cases in Baharain in 1998 and half in Islamic Republic of Iran. In Tunisia, injecting drug use is responsible for more than one-third of AIDS cases. In Egypt, one AIDS case in 10 is among drug injectors. Recent studies by the United Nations International Drug Control Programme

(NUDCP) in a few countries of the Middle East—Egypt, Iran and Lebanon—indicate that the magnitude of the drug abuse problem should not be underestimated. By most conservative estimates, the number of addicts are counted in the millions in this part of the world. A relatively high proportion of these addicts inject drugs, and needle-sharing is very common.[79]

The UNAIDS/WHO report of 1999 also states that sexually transmitted infections are not uncommon in the Eastern Mediterranean region. It is estimated that around 10 million cases occur in the region every year, although reporting rates are low—fewer than 6 percent of that number were reported in 1998. STI rates are particularly high among young adults and in urban areas. Sexually transmitted infections are an important indicator that high-risk sexual practices do exist in the region, as national behavioural surveys confirm.

SITUATION OF AIDS IN INDIA

The HIV positive population is not uniformly distributed nor is it rising at a uniform rate. The determining factors are: the time and place when the infection appeared, the effectiveness of prevention campaigns, the means of transmission and the presence or absence of other sexually transmitted disease (STDs). Other factors, such as an underfunded and understaffed health surveillance system, suggest that it is not always possible to estimate the extent of infection in a country accurately.[80]

The National AIDS Control Organization (NACO) has been issuing regular reports on the state-wise cumulative occurrence of AIDS cases. The latest available data upto March 2005 is given in Table 3.3.

According to the estimates provided by the NACO/UNAIDS/WHO, India at present has approximately 5.1 million HIV-positive cases. If this trend continues, India will become the country with the largest number of HIV infected persons shortly. As on March, 2005, 103857 AIDS cases have been reported to NACO from different states and union territories.[81] Of these over 85 percent were thought to have acquired the infection from sexual activities. Maharashtra, Tamil Nadu, Andhra Pradesh, Gujarat and some of the North-eastern states have higher infection rate. Let us briefly discuss the existing situation of the spread of HIV/AIDS across the country region-wise.

Table 3.3
State-wise distribution of the Reported Cases of AIDS as on March 31, 2005

Sl. No.	State/UT	AIDS Cases
1.	Andhra Pradesh	11280
2.	Assam	225
3.	Arunachal Pradesh	0
4.	A & N Islands	33
5.	Bihar	155
6.	Chattisgarh	0
7.	Chandigarh (UT)	1119
8.	Delhi	950
9.	Daman & Diu	1
10.	Dadra & Nagar Haveli	0
11.	Goa	508
12.	Gujarat	5406
13.	Haryana	440
14.	Himachal Pradesh	223
15.	Jharkhand	0
16.	Jammu & Kashmir	2
17.	Karnataka	2343
18.	Kerala	1769
19.	Lakshadweep	0
20.	Madhya Pradesh	1314
21.	Maharashtra	12963
22.	Orissa	128
23.	Nagaland	736
24.	Manipur	2866
25.	Mizoram	106
26.	Meghalaya	8
27.	Pondicherry	302
28.	Punjab	292
29.	Rajasthan	1153
30.	Sikkim	8
31.	Tamilnadu	48180
32.	Tripura	5
33.	Uttranchal	0
34.	Uttar Pradesh	1383
35.	West Bengal	2397
36.	A,bad Mun. Corp.	520
37.	Channai M.C.	0
38.	Mumbai M.C.	7042
	Total:	**103857**

Source: NACO, Ministry of Health and Family Welfare, Govt. of India

Southern Region

The first few sero-positives reported in the country were from Chennai in 1986. Table 3.3 presented in this chapter indicate that as on March, 2005, Tamil Nadu reported to NACO about 48,180 cases of AIDS becoming the second to top the list of states having highest number of AIDS cases in the country, Andhra Pradesh being the first among the states in South India.

The sero-surveillance began in Kerala in 1985. But, people here seem to refuse to face the reality of AIDS and hide from it when they come face to face with it. A large number of its work force is employed in the Gulf or in metropolises like Mumbai, Delhi, Kolkatta, Chennai, Hyderabad, etc. The disease is contracted abroad or in the red-light districts of the metropolises. Gulf countries are now testing for AIDS and those who are found to display symptoms are immediately send back. Thus, Kerala is susceptible to the invasion by the virus and the state is unaware of the seriousness of the threat. As on March 31, 2005 Kerala has reported that it has 1769 cases of AIDS (Table 3.3.).

It may be noted that large number of HIV infected from the country as well as from abroad turn to treatment at Ayurveda hospitals in Kerala. Some of the famous Ayurveda treatment centres in the state include the Amala Cancer Hospital at Thrissur, Nupal in Kochi, Kotackal in Malapuram and PNVM at the Madhave Pharmacy in Kochi.

Children are regularly refused admission to schools if they or their parents are found to be HIV infected. Similarly in Trissur, residents of the area have threatened to demolish an institution taking care of the AIDS patients who are refused treatment in hospitals. There are also several similar incidents reported from this highly literate state. These incidents should be an eye-opener to the Government, the media and the anti-AIDS campaigners who in their over-enthusiasm or ignorance create an exaggerated scare about the disease. The scaring reports in the media and the wrong methods followed by Government agencies engaged in anti-AIDS-awareness campaign often cause negative awareness, leading to social ostracism of HIV/AIDS victims and barbaric acts. Fear campaign is not the answer to HIV/AIDS prevention.

Northern Region

Reports available (Table 3.3) indicate that Uttar Pradesh (1383), Madhya Pradesh (1340) Chandigarh/Punjab (1411) and Delhi (950) top the list among the North Indian states. There has been less testing in northern region, but Delhi reports increasing levels of infection among professional blood donors and venereal disease patients. Other states in the region like Rajasthan, Himachal Pradesh, Jammu & Kashmir, Bihar and Haryana have also reported several cases of full blown AIDS. The trend only indicate that practically every state in the region is infected with the AIDS virus.

As many as 21 Thalassemia patients undergoing treatment at the NDMC- Charak Palika Hospital in Moti Bagh, New Delhi have been detected to be suffering from the killer disease AIDS.[82] These patients were reported to have contracted the dreaded disease from infected blood transfusion. Thalassemia patients are required to undergo blood transfusions once in a month.

The Charak Palika Hospital is the largest blood transfusion centre in Delhi and caters to the need of over 200 child patients of Thalassemia. The hospital acquires about 450 units of blood every month from the Indian Red Cross Society Blood Bank. The blood supplied by the Red Cross Blood Bank is duly tested to check the presence of HIV which causes AIDS. It is certified HIV free. The detection of so many HIV-positive cases among the Thalassemic in Charak Palika Hospital indicates a strong possibility that it has been supplied with infected blood units. The number of HIV-positive patients in the hospital may be more as not all the Thalassemic patients undergo the test.

Employees at LNJP Hospital were demanding an insurance cover of Rs. 25 lakh to assist in the surgery and care of AIDS infected patients. Consequently, a 14 year old Thalassemiac boy, has been awaiting urgent spleen-removal surgery, for over three months. The employees refused to assist in the surgery when they learnt that the boy was carrying HIV. As a result the patient continues to suffer. In a number of Thalassemics, the spleen needs to be removed when it gets enlarged and there is risk of rupture. Delhi alone has about 1,100 Thalassemic patients and many of them require spleen removal.[83]

There is also superstition that one could get cured of STDs/ AIDS by having sex with a virgin. On 4 August 1994 a constable named P. Jayapaul of the Railway Police Special Force (RPSF) allegedly raped a nine year in the belief that sexual intercourse with a virgin would rid him of the killer disease AIDS. The girl died and her battered body was recovered from a tent behind the temple in the RPSF Campus at Daya Basti, near Sarai Rohilla, New Delhi.[84] Several such cases go unreported across the country.

It is reported that none of the six blood banks in the Amritsar city of Punjab including two run by the government, has been conducting HIV tests on blood donors. According to official sources, besides the non-availability of ELISA test kits, the high cost of performing the tests has been a major deterrent. In the government hospitals situated in Amritsar more than 12,000 units of blood is utilised annually which is collected mostly by the local Red Cross Society. The doctors say that HIV test on each donor costs between Rs. 300 and Rs. 400 which the private blood banks avoid to keep the supply cost low. In the government run blood banks also, the blood safety norms are not being followed either due to apathy of the officials or due to lack of proper facilities, say doctors.[85]

It is well known, that Bihar has the highest number of TB, leprosy and kala-azar cases. The Department of Venereal Diseases in Patna Medical College Hospital substantiates the fact that sexually-transmitted diseases are on the rise and every possible type of social group is affected. A survey by the Psychiatry Department of the same hospital states that the knowledge of safe sexual conduct and sex education is lowest among the medicos and doctors.[86]

Bihar's borders are open to Nepal—a favourite destination for foreigners as also Sikkim. States with a high HIV-positive ratio also lie close to Bihar such as the north-eastern states like Manipur and Nagaland. A large number of Bihar-origin are settled in the north-eastern states and have married locals, but come back to their roots once in a while. With large number of migrant labourers who migrate to Mumbai, Kolkatta, New Delhi and some pockets of Maharashtra and Gujarat, the scope for faster spread of HIV infection is thus open.[87]

Reports gathered from various states in the northern region through various sources indicate that there has been less testing for HIV in this part of the country. Apart from the shortage of trained personnel, most of the so-called centres for HIV testing are very poorly equipped with testing kits and other facilities.

Western Region

Bombay in Maharashtra seems to be the most vulnerable city in India from the point of view of risk factor and susceptibility to HIV/AIDS infection, but, the infection has spread into other parts of the state, like the districts of Sangli, Kolhapur, Nagpur, Aurangabad and some rural areas.[88] The large number of confirmed HIV/AIDS cases in Maharashtra reflect two things: the extent of transmission as well as the fact that the testing system is far better developed than in other parts of the country. But, many factors suggest that the state is already severely hit.

It is estimated that there are one lakh prostitutes in Central Bombay alone and reports show that twenty to thirty percent of these prostitutes are infected with HIV.[89] According to a study conducted by the Tata Institute of Social Sciences, Bombay,[90] there are approximately two million prostitutes in India, residing in 817 red light districts, with more than 5 million children labelled as illegitimate. The number of call-girls or high society prostitutes have not been included in this survey. A large number of their numerous clients are also infected and will pass on the virus to their sexual partners. No effort has been made to test the children of prostitutes for HIV as about 30 percent of the HIV-positive women are estimated to be passing on the virus to their children.

"The steep curve you see in Bombay of HIV positive case is even steeper than in Africa", says N.K. Shah,[91] Director of Disease Prevention at WHO in New Delhi. Shah stresses that with a million people moving through Bombay every day, the AIDS virus has a strong possibility of being transmitted outside the city. And though Maharashtra tests blood supplies much more strictly than elsewhere in India, health officials admit that about thirty to forty percent of the blood supplied comes from small clinics that are not within the purview of Health Department or the State Food and Drug Administration. Such a situation, according to health officials, means that widespread transmission has already occurred within the general population and into the rural areas of the state.

A survey[92] conducted by some social workers from the Indian Health Organization (IHO), Mumbai, on the sexual life of the truck drivers, reveals that about 90 percent of the truck drivers visit prostitutes on highways, red-light areas, hotels and dhabas. About 81 percent of the drivers and cleaners took part in homosexual acts. According to Dr. Gilade (IHO) over 60 percent of the truck drivers are suspected to be HIV carriers. The report also states that among the truck drivers, who engage prostitutes, 28 percent visit them on highways, 45 percent in red-light areas, 25 percent in dhabas and 2 percent in pick-up points. While 82 percent of the respondents admitted that they don't use condoms, 92 percent were aware of STDs. In all 64 percent of the respondents had very little knowledge about HIV/AIDS, while, 24 percent were totally ignorant.

About 45 jawans of the Army's 1st battalion of the Assam Regiment have tested HIV positive after their return from Cambodia, reports Ramesh Sharma.[93] After confirmation of the test, the infected jawans were shifted to the Pune-based Armed Forces Medical College (AFMC) where they have been kept in the new AIDS ward. A battalion normally consists of 600-650 jawans and 20-22 officers. Given the high percentage of HIV infection in a single battalion, several questions arise: Could it be that the jawans had contracted the AIDS virus before they left for Cambodia? Were they screened before leaving for their overseas assignment?

A study[94] on AIDS Awareness in Rural Community was conducted by the Department of Preventive and Social Medicine, Rural Medical College of Pravara Medical Trust, Loni, Ahmednagar with the help of USAID in 1992-93. The survey was conducted in 20 villages and covered 50 houses, each using random sample thus covering 1000 respondents. A total of 712 males (71.2 percent) and 288 females (28.8 percent) above 15 years of age were interviewed for AIDS awareness. Among the 34.5 percent illiterate respondents as many as 17.4 percent were found to be aware of AIDS while among the literate 52.2 percent were found to be aware of AIDS. In all 29.4 percent respondents reported that they acquired knowledge about AIDS through television and radio, while 6.5 percent came to know about it from doctors and 4.1 percent from nurses. While 94.4 percent respondents did not know anything about the signs and symptoms of AIDS, 77.1 percent showed ignorance about any preventive measures.

Table 3.3 shows that as on March 31, 2005 Maharashtra had as many as 12,963 AIDS cases. Some of the other states in the western part of the country, that reported full blown AIDS cases include: Gujarat 5406, Goa 508, Rajasthan 1,153 and Daman and Diu 1.

Dr. J.K. Kosamiya[95] of the Preventive and Social Medicine Department at Surat Medical College has conducted study of social environment and HIV sero-prevalence in male at risk population of Surat city. This study comprised 313 patients of STDs, 178 prisoners, 236 diamond workers and 126 jawans of the state reserve police. The overall sero-prevalence in the study group was 2.4 percent. It was high among the prisoners (5 percent) followed by STD patients (3.5 percent) and diamond workers (0.8 percent). The only mode of transmission observed in this study was sex. Several social and environmental factors were recorded in this study. HIV sero-prevalence was higher in two extreme groups in relation to individual income, educational status and living conditions. It was high among individuals residing without families, single (unmarried, divorcee or widower), those with touring jobs and recent migrants to the city. HIV sero-prevalence was higher in men with extra and pre-marital relationships, multiple partners, having relation with commercial sex workers and homosexuals. The incidence was also found more in persons, who were suffering from or had a history of STD or genital ulcer disease.

Bhawani Shankar who heads a social organisation in Rajasthan conducted a two-year study of village prostitution. According to him, the Rajnat and four other tribes are spread over 144 sex centres in Rajasthan which include villages and small towns. In the eastern part of the state where the study was conducted at least 20,000 women are known to be involved in sex trade. Most of them have never heard of AIDS or seen a condom. About 2000 of them are estimated to be carrying the AIDS virus.[96] Nandlalpura is a village in western Rajasthan where every woman is or was a prostitute and every girl child probably will become one. It is a Rajnat tribal village and it is how the people of this village survive these days.

Generations of Rajnat were travelling minstrels and dancers, dressed in brilliant turbans and swirling skirts of rainbow colours, welcomed in the sandstone fotresses of the maharajahs and queens who ruled the western desert. Today most men in Nandlalpura are unemployed, except for ferrying customers in jeeps from the highway. Highways in the state serve the sexual appetites of truck drivers and men from towns close by, particularly Jaipur and Ajmer.

According to NACO[97]report Baina in Vasco-de-Gama, the largest town in Goa has some 2000 female sex workers, most of them coming from neighbouring states. There is a STD clinic in Baina. Though situated in a relatively spacious building, it is not popular. Most STD patients prefer the services of private practitioners. Every year the clinic staff arranges for HIV testing of sex workers. The results have showed a progressive growth of HIV prevalence from 1 percent in 1987 to 27 percent in 1993. Following this finding the state government assisted by NACO and WHO has set up an intervention project in Baina.

Eastern Region

Among the North-Eastern states a significant increase of infection among injecting drug users, noticed initially in 1990 in Manipur, has now been found to extend to Nagaland and Mizoram as well. The HIV prevalence among injecting drug users in Manipur is floating between 60 percent to 70 percent and it reached 50 percent in Nagaland and 6 percent to 10 percent in Mizoram.[98]

It is seen from Table 3.3 that as March 31, 2005 Assam had 225 full blown AIDS cases while Manipur had as many as 2866. West Bengal reported of 2397 full blown AIDS cases while, Nagaland had 736 cases on record. Official report supplied to NACO by Orissa show that the state had 128 full blown AIDS cases.

Calcutta the major eastern port and Paradeep port on the coastal area of Orissa, are faced with an AIDS epidemic though state officials fudge their figures to disguise this. Manipur and parts of Mizoram and Nagaland are in crisis as AIDS spreads along the drug smuggling routes from Burma. Equally worrying is the likelihood that the virus is spreading along the highways that run through these states into Assam and beyond. Most health officials in Imphal, the capital of Manipur tend to believe that the AIDS virus will not move much beyond the intravenous drug-users, who as a group have developed high rate of infection with the virus over the past years. Dr. S.C. Pal, the Director of Calcutta's National Institute of Cholera and Enteric Diseases, which has been charged with monitoring the AIDS problem in the north-east says that there has always been a tendency to underestimate the seriousness of the north-east AIDS situation. For instance, both Nagaland and Mizoram denied that drug users in their states could be infected.[99] As Manipur shows a common international boundary of 352 kms with Myanmar, heroin is easily available in the state from the notorious Golden Triangle of Myanmar, Thailand and Laos, though Myanmar's free boarders.

The HIV sero-surveillance programme in Manipur was started at the Regional College, Imphal in July 1986 but none of the 2322 sero samples screened by ELISA upto September 1989 was found to be positive. However, between February 1990 and May 1991, 1,263 HIV positive cases had been detected of which 1,186 cases were among the intravenous drug users.[100]

Assam is the gateway to Nagaland and Manipur, two states located close to the Golden Triangle area in Myanmar from where drugs are smuggled into the north-eastern states. A report that appeared in Times of India[101] claim that there were 11 full blown AIDS cases in the state in addition to the eight deaths of AIDS patients. Since 1990 at least 166 HIV-positive cases have been reported in the state.

One reason of its vulnerability was its proximity to Manipur which has the highest incidence of AIDS says Dr. J.C. Deuri, state

AIDS Programme Officer.[102] A large floating population particularly in Guwahati comprising truck drivers and security force personnel was another important factor. Both these groups were considered to be high risk since many of them utilised the services of commercial sex workers active in some areas here and along the truck route in lower Assam. A study[103] of 255 truck drivers selected at random showed that at least two-thirds of them suffered from STDs. Over 82 percent of them said that they never used condoms.

A two-day regional conference[104] on AIDS in Guwahati voiced serious concern on the "unsatisfactory" utilisation of funds provided by NACO for the north-east. Manipur which reported of 2,700 cases of full blown AIDS and 15,000 drug addicts had failed to fully utilise the Rs. 23.5 lakh provided during 1992-93. Similarly other states like Mizoram, Nagaland and Tripura too could not utilise the amount provided by the centre. NACO and a host of other funding agencies are busy training medical and para-medical staff to deal with all aspects of AIDS control in this part of the country.

A brief report of one of the studies published by NACO in its "Country Scenario: An Update" in April 1993 is on the STD/HIV and sexual behaviour base-line survey conducted in Sonagachi red-light area in Calcutta. This was the first community based random sample STD survey in India in which 450 commercial sex workers were selected. The survey, co-ordinated by the Department of Public Health of the All India Institute of Hygiene and Public Health, Calcutta (AIIHPH) was a joint undertaking by various national and state public institutions and an NGO assisted by WHO consultants in the survey design, monitoring and reporting. The overall rate of STD in this group was over 50 percent although HIV prevalence rate was still low offering a real window of opportunity for prevention of HIV epidemic in this city. A majority (69 percent) of sex workers had some knowledge of STD, most commonly about syphilis (67 percent), but only 31 percent knew about AIDS. Most sex workers (70 percent) reported to have suffered an STD in the previous year and during the previous month 34 percent received treatment for some ailment. About less than half (45 percent) took precautions against pregnancy but condom use by their client was reported at only 4 percent. At the time of the survey 42 percent of the sex workers interviewed complained of veginal discharge.

Payal Singh[105] reports about one of the most successful AIDS intervention project being initiated by the AIIHPH in Sonagachi, Calcutta. This project probably have the highest number of 'peer educators' in the world. The 65 peer educators are all sex workers. They are the backbone of this programme. The sex workers become 'peer educators' after undergoing a six week training course. The training curriculum comprises knowledge about STDs and the use of condoms as well as negotiation skills. The latter are essential for sex workers to convince clients to use condoms, particularly since they receive no support whatsoever from pimps and brothel owners on this score.

The sex workers of Sonagachi wear 'uniform' sponsored by the AIIHPH and the government—green coats over their saris and badges with a red cross which proudly state 'peer educator'. The coat and the badge do a great deal for their morale. For them they are symbols of acceptance and self-respect and clad in these they go about their new duties of visiting each brothel, speaking to each occupant, distributing condoms and reiterating the urgency of combating AIDS.

The statistics[106] on the AIDS intervention programme prove its efficacy. The number of condoms distributed per month by sex workers in Sonagachi have gone up from 1,500 in September 1992 to approximately 65,000 in April 1994. Another survey which was conducted in early 1994 indicated that condom usage which had been less than 2 percent in September 1992 had gone up to 47 percent. As a result, the abortion rate had fallen from 46 percent to 38 percent. Similarly sexually transmitted diseases had come down from 81 percent to 61 percent and the HIV level is still below 1.5 percent. The entire Sonagachi area has ten teams working to bring about AIDS awareness by the 'peer educators'.

Several intervention programmes are being initiated by NACO in the North-east.[107] In collaboration with Swedish SIDA, NACO is supporting five NGOs in Assam, Manipur and Nagaland in conducting outreach interventions with injecting drug users. The Indian Council of Medical Research (ICMR) with technical and financial support from WHO is conducting operational research on outreach programming to prevent transmission through injecting drug use. Another project is that of OXFAM and SHARAN which is linked up with NACO, WHO and the Government of Manipur to develop a model project on the home or community based care of persons with AIDS.

SUMMARY

HIV has crossed all boarders across the globe. Development of strategies for the prevention and control of this killer disease require adequate knowledge about the way in which the virus has spread among peoples all over the world. In this chapter, global scenario and notional scenario of HIV prevalence has been presented. While discussing global scenario, attempt has been made to present the global picture of the spread of HIV by providing details about HIV/AIDS scenario in Africa, United States of America, Europe, Latin America, Russian Federation, Middle-east, Australia, and a number of countries in Asia. The national scenario has been presented region-wise, namely, South, North, East and West giving available information on HIV/AIDS prevalence in various states as on March 31, 2005.

REFERENCES

1. UNAIDS/WHO: AIDS epidemic update-December, 2004, UNAIDS Genewa, 2004
2. Joyce V. Lyons: In Economic Implications of AIDS in Asia, edited by David E. Bloom and Joyce V. Lyons, UNDP, New Delhi 1993, p. I.
3. Lyn Frumkin and John Leonard: Questions and Answers on AIDS, PMIC, Los Angeles, USA, 1994.
4. "US Centres for Disease Control: Pneumocystic Pneumonia—Los Angeles", Morbidity and Mortality Weekly Report, 5 June 1981, Volume 30, number 21, pp. 250-2 and M.S. Gottlieb *et al.*: "Pneumocystics Carinii Pneumonia and Mucosal Candidacies in previously Healthy Homosexual men", New England Journal of Medicine, 10 December 1981, Volume 305, Number 24, pp. 1425-1431.
5. For a narrative account of the dawning awareness of a new immunodeficiency disease in the US, see Randy Shilts, *And the Band Played on*, New York, St. Martins press, 1987, p. 630.
6. B. Lamey and N. Malemeka: "*Aspects Cliniques et Epidemiologiques de la Cryptococose a Kinshasa*", Medicine Tropical, September - October 1982, Volume 42, Number 5, pp. 507-11.
7. A.C. Bayley: "*Aggressive Kaposi's Sarcome in Zambia*, 1983, Lancet, 16 June 1984, pp. 1318-20.
8. Morbidity and Mortality Weekly Report, J. Vandepitte *et al.*: "AIDS and Cryptococcosis (Ziare, 1987)", Lancet, 23 April 1983, pp. 925-6.
9. G. Offenstadt *et al.*: "*Multiple opportunistic Infection Due to AIDS in Previously Healthy Black Woman from Zaire*, "New England Journal of Medicine, 31 March 1983, Volume 308, p. 775.
10. R.J. Biggar *et al.* (Ed.): "*Epidemiology of AIDS in Europe*" and following articles, European Journal of Cancer and Clinical Oncology, 1984, Volume 20, number 2, pp. 157-73; N. Clumek *et al.*: "*Acquired Immuno Deficiency Snydrome in Black Africa*", Lancet, 19 March 1983, p. 642; J.B. Bruet and R.A. Ancelle, Annals of Internal Medicine: "*The*

International Occurrence of the Acquired Immune Deficiency Syndrome", November 1985, Volume 103, Number 5, pp. 670-4.

11. J.W. Pape *et al.*: *"Characteristics of the Acquired Immuno Deficiency Syndrome (AIDS) in Haiti"*, New England Journal of Medicine, 20 October 1983, Volume 309, Number 16, pp. 945-50.
12. *"Opportunistic Infection and Kaposi's Sarcoma among Haitians in the United States"*, Morbidity and Mortality Weekly Report, 9 July 1982, Volume 31, Number 26, pp. 353-361.
13. Panos Dossier, the 3rd Epidemic - Repercussions of the fear of AIDS, The Panos Institute, London, 1990, pp.5-6.
14. For details see chapter 3 of AIDS in India: Myth and Reality by Gracious Thomas, Rawat Publications, Jaipur 1994.
15. NACO, *National AIDS Control programme India: Country Scenario Update*, NACO, New Delhi, December 1995.
16. *Ibid.*
17. UNAIDS/WHO, 2004. *op. cit.*
18. Lyn Frumkin and John Leonard, *op. cit.* pp.102-3.
19. UNAIDS/WHO, 2004. *op. cit*
20. *Ibid.*
21. UNAIDS/WHO: *"AIDS epidemic update: December* 1999", UNAIDS, Geneva, 1999.
22. *Ibid.*
23. UNAIDS, *2004 Report on the global AIDS epidemic,* Geneva, UNAIDS, 2004.
24. Thai Working Group on HIV/AIDS Projections: *"HIV/AIDS projections for Thailand*: 2000-2020", Bangkok, 2001.
25. UNDP, *Thailands' Response to HIV/AIDS: "Progress and Challenges"*, UNDP, Bangkok, 2004
26. UNAIDS/WHO, 2004, *op. cit.*
27. UNAIDS/WHO, 1999, *op. cit.*
28. Shah S.A., Altaf A., Mujeeb S.A. and Menon A.: *"An outbreak of HIV infection among injection drug users in a small town in Pakistan: Potential for national implications"*. International Journal of STD & AIDS, 15 (3): 209-210, 2004
29. Pisani E., Dili STI Survey Team: *"HIV, STIs and risk behaviour in East Timor: An histric opportunity for effective action"*. Dili, East Timor, Family Health International, 2004.
30. Navarathanam. V. and Vicknasingham. B.: *"Survey of drug users in Penang and Northern Province Wellesley district"*, Penang University Sains Malaysia, 2003.

31. UNAIDS/WHO, 2004, *op. cit.*
32. David Lim: *"The Economic Impact of AIDS on Malaysia"*. David E. Bloom and Joyce V. Lyons (eds.) *op. cit*, pp. 58-59.
33. *Ibid.*
34. Anthony M. Zola: *"The Implications of AIDS for the Agricultural Sector in Lao PDR"*. David E. Bloom and Joyce V. Lyons (eds.) *op. cit*, pp. 99-104.
35. UNAIDS/WHO, 2004: *op. cit.*
36. Orville Solon and Angelica O. Barioza: *"Overseas Contract Workers and the Economic Consequences of the HIV/AIDS, in the Philippines"*. David E. Bloom and Joyce V. Lyons (eds.), *op. cit*, pp. 115-117.
37. *Ibid.*
38. UNAIDS/WHO, 1999, *op. cit.*
39. Djumhana Sumantri: *"The Ethical and Legal HIV/AIDS Related Issues in Indonesia"*. In Law, Ethics and HIV, edited by Robert A. Glick, UNDP, New Delhi, 1993, p. 167.
40. Pisani, E. *et al.*: *"Sexual behaviour among injecting drug users in Indonesia carries a high potential for HIV Spread to non-injectors"*. Journal of Acquired Immune Deficiency Syndrome, 34 (4): 403-6, 2003.
41. Monitoring the AIDS Pandemic Network, AIDS in Asia: *"Face the facts – A comprehensive analysis of the AIDS epidemics in Asia"*. Bangkok (MAP), 2004.
42. *Ibid.*
43. UNAIDS/WHO, 2004, *op. cit.*
44. Wang Yan and Zhao Ning: *"A brief introduction to the legislation of China governing the prevention and control of HIV/AIDS"*. A. Glick(ed.), *op. cit*, pp. 183-84.
45. Zangk-L, Ma S-j, Xia D-y: *"Epidemiology of HIV and sexually transmitted infection in China"*. Sexual Health, 16:39-46, 2004.
46. UNAIDS/WHO, 2004, *op. cit.*
47. C. *Monitoring the AIDS pandemic Network* (MAP) 2004, *op. cit.*
48. UNAIDS/WHO, 2004, *op. cit.*
49. MAP, 2004, *op. cit.*
50. UNAIDS/WHO, 2004, *op. cit*
51. *Ibid.*
52. Surgeon General's Report to the American Public on HIV Infection and AIDS, State Department.
53. *Ibid.*
54. Lyn Frumkin & John Leonard, *op. cit.*
55. *Ibid.*

56. UNAIDS/WHO, 2004, *op. cit.*
57. *Ibid.*
58. *Ibid.*
59. *Ibid.*
60. *Ibid.*
61. C. Rhodes, T., *et al.*: *"Behavioural factors in HIV transmission in Europe and Central Asia"*, unpublished paper, UNAIDS, Geneva, 2002.
62. UNAIDS, 2004, *op. cit.*
63. *Ibid.*
64. Euro HIV/AIDS Surveillance in Europe: *"Mid-year Report 69"*. Saint-Maurice, Institute de Veille Sanitaire, 2003.
65. *Ibid.*
66. *Ibid.*
67. WHO Regional Office for Europe: *"HIV infections epidemiology: Sentinel Surveillance and Risk Factors: A comparative study in the Russion Federation", Azerbaijan and Republic of Moldova, Copenhegane*, WHO-Euro, 2004.
68. UNAIDS/WHO, 2004, *op. cit.*
69. *Ibid.*
70. *Ibid.*
71. Alarcon J.O. *et al.*: *"Determinants and prevalence of HIV infection in pregnant Peruvian Women"*, AIDS, 17:613-618, 2003.
72. Ministerio de Salud Y Desarrollo Social de Venezuela: *"Registro de infections de transmission sexual en los services del pais, 1998-2002"*, Caracas, Ministerio de Salud Y. Desarrollo Social, 2003.
73. UNAIDS/WHO, 2004, *op. cit.*
74. *Ibid.*
75. National Centre in HIV Epidemiology and clinical Research, Australia: *"HIV/AID, viral hepatitis and sexually transmitted infections in Australia:* Annual surveillance Report 2003, Syndney, National Centre in HIV Epidemiology and Clinical Research, 2003.
76. UNAIDS/WHO, 2004, *op. cit.*
77. MAP, 2004, *op. cit.*
78. Jenkins, C., Robalino D.A.: *"HIV/AIDS in the middle East and North Africa: The costs of inaction"*, World Bank, Washington, 2003.
79. UNAIDS/WHO, 1999, *op. cit.*
80. Panos Dossier, The 3rd Epidemic, *op. cit.*
81. NACO: *"Report on Surveillance for HIV infection in India"*, NACO, New Delhi, March 2005.
82. H.T. Correspondent, 21 Thalassemics have AIDS, Hindustan Times, Sept. 8, 1994.

83. Kalpana Jain: *"LNJP staff seek insurance for AIDS surgery"*, TOI, New Delhi, 20 August 1994.
84. TOI: *"Constable rapes minor for cure"*, TOI, New Delhi, 14 August 1994.
85. Ajay Bhardwaj: *"Amritsar blood bank conduct no HIV test"*, TOI, New Delhi, 26 November 1994.
86. Mammen Mathew: *"AIDS cases shooting up in Bihar"*, Hindustan Times, New Delhi, 15 March 1993.
87. *Ibid.*
88. Government of Maharashtra: *"Status paper on Prevention and Control of AIDS programme"*, Department of Health, Bombay, August 1990.
89. Sunday, Calcutta, August 1991.
90. Social Welfare, Volume xxxvii, Number 3, New Delhi, June 1990.
91. Sunday, *op. cit.*
92. Seema Sinha: *"IHO Move to Educate Truck Drivers on AIDS"*, TOI, New Delhi, December 1993.
93. Ramesh Sharma: "45 *Combodia - returned jawans test HIV-positive"*, TOI, New Delhi, 5 September 1994.
94. Goyal, R.C., Kulkarni, A.T. and Somasundaram K.V.: *"AIDS awareness in Rural Community"(Report)* Department of Preventive and Social Medicine, Rural Medical College of Pravara Medical Trust, Loni, Ahmednagar, 1993.
95. *TOI: "AIDS waiting to erupt in Surat"*, TOI, New Delhi, 27 Jan. 1994.
96. Ranjan Roy: *"AIDS bomb ticks in Rajasthan village"*, TOI, New Delhi, 26 March 1994.
97. NACO: *"National AIDS control programme"*, India *op. cit.*
98. *Ibid.*
99. Sunday, *op. cit.*
100. VHAI: *"Health for the Millions"*, Volume xvii, Number 4, New Delhi, August, 1991.
101. TOI: *"Assam needs to take steps to check AIDS"*, TOI, New Delhi, 3 December 1996.
102. *Ibid.*
103. *Ibid.*
104. *Ibid.*
105. Payal Singh: *"Sonagachi's Sex Workers Spread AIDS Awareness"*, TOI, New Delhi, 3 April 1994.
106. *Ibid.*
107. NACO, *op. cit.*

4
Vulnerable Population

No individual or country is beyond the reach of HIV and its impact, says an UNAIDS press release. Whichever the continent, whatever the culture, whatever the standard of living, people are affected and at risk. UNAIDS estimates that there are over 20 million people living with HIV/AIDS and over five new infections take place every minute. In the most affected countries, hospitals are overwhelmed with AIDS patients; schools, farms and factories are losing skilled employees; children are being born infected or are orphaned as their parents die of AIDS. Gains made in development are being reversed.[1]

All the estimates show that the infection is increasing more rapidly in India than anywhere else in the world and one cannot predict the actual socio-economic impact of this disease. We know that most infectious deceases strike the very young and the very old. However, we are now witnessing an epidemic that strikes people in their productive years, namely, in the age group of 15 to 45. Figures available show that over 70 per cent of the currently HIV infected in India are in their productive age[2]. All calculations by world bodies show that the infection is increasing more rapidly in India than anywhere else in the world.

As the 1990s unfolded, the horror of HIV pandemic infecting the young people in India has come to light. Over 20 per cent of the infection in the country is found to be among people in the 10-24 age group.[3] Although no country-wide study is available to quote on the sexual practices of our people, particularly that of the teenagers, the results of some micro studies provide enough evidence about the active involvement of young people in sexual activities and abuse of substance which are detrimental to the spread of HIV.[4]

Some of the HIV infected people can pass the virus to the uninfected faster while the transmission efficiency will depend according to the stage of illness. However, because most people with HIV are currently not sick, most transmission occurs from those without symptoms. The reported cases of HIV infected persons in India clearly show that HIV has not spared any class, community, group, religion, profession, qualification, age, colour and sex. It is therefore appropriate that we focus our attention on target groups as well as target factors while, discussing issues pertaining to the prevention of HIV/AIDS in India although education and awareness comparing will continue to dominate any prevention activities.

Trends show that HIV transmission does not take place uniformly throughout the society. People practicing certain high-risk behaviours such as having multiple partners or injecting drugs are more vulnerable to contracting and spreading HIV. It is possible to identify groups of individuals who practice risk behaviour. Once identified special efforts must be made to create an enabling environment, which will facilitate and support behaviour change. A combination of 'Information Education and Communication (IEC)' strategies and relevant service provision such as STD care and condoms can be used to help create the right circumstances for behaviour change. Targeting those with high-risk behaviours, and thus at increased risk of contracting and transmitting HIV, is one of the important strategies for the prevention and control of AIDS.[5]

TRANSMISSION THROUGH SEX

The AIDS virus is primarily transmitted from one person to another through sexual activities. When we talk about sexual transmission, we need to examine the various categories of persons who are vulnerable to HIV infection through sexual contacts. Therefore preventive measures should be addressed to such groups so as to meet the requirement of any particular group. Let us briefly list some of these potential carriers and, or transmitters of HIV in our country.

Sex Workers

The 'sale of sex' is a universal phenomenon. This oldest profession today has acquired a very high profile. India is no exception to this. A detailed account of the extent of the prevalence of prostitution based on a study conducted by the Tata Institute of Social Sciences, Bombay,[6] states that there are approximately two million prostitutes in India, residing in about 817 red-light districts, with more than five million children labeled as illegitimate. The number of call girls, or high society prostitutes have not been included in this survey. Most of the prostitutes are reported to be engaging on an overage four clients a day, while the sex workers in brothels have to entertain about ten clients in twenty-four hours. Over 75 per cent of all HIV infections reported in India were acquired through multipartner sex.[7]

Prostitution is an integral part of the formal and informal economics of countries worldwide. It can be a big business although not usually for the sex workers. Sunday,[8] in one of its cover stories 'The Nether World', gives a detailed account of the flourishing promiscuity in India. It states that illicit sex does not always come free. A number of men are forced to look for it in the red-light districts of various cities such as G.B. Road in Delhi, Sonagachi in Calcutta and Kamathipura in Bombay. The going rate varies from Rs. 20 to Rs. 50 and most prostitutes manage to make Rs. 300 to Rs. 500 in a day - though of course - part of it goes to their pimps and other protectors.

The report further adds that at the other end of the market are expensive call girls, who charge anything from Rs. 1000 to Rs. 50,000 per night. In Bombay, young girls hailing from the southern states and from Uttar Pradesh, Bengal and Nepal live as paying guests in the suburbs, and in up-market areas like the Malabar Hill. They often get involved in these rackets. Businessmen avail the services of such networks, supplying girls to politicians and bureaucrats with whom they wish to gain favour. Some five-star hotels in metropolitan cities also posses what are called "tart charts". The ladies listed here are made available to selected clients at special rates, with the connivance of the hotel staff. Sometimes call girls are reported to be flown into Delhi for one night from Bombay to service important clients.

It is a fact that this killer disease has claimed the precious lives of hundreds of women and men involved in prostitution. Further, it has also infected the numerous clients of the prostitutes. No woman has chosen or accepted prostitution on her own. Everyone is dragged into it. That is the tale every prostitute tells the social workers, NGO functionaries and those who approach them for lending a helping hand. Usually, the reasons are many:[9]

(a) Women in India live in a society, which is very averse to the very birth of a female in the family. Parents are keen to marry them off at a tender age. Divorce, bride burning, female infanticide, child marriage, incest, and numerous form of other violence against women are rampant in our society. Many young married women become widows in their teens. Among them a large percentage are thrown out of their in-laws houses, neither are they welcomed back by their own parents. These women often land up or are forced into prostitution to look after themselves and their children. Therefore, destitution along with poverty drag many a woman into prostitution.

(b) Several women are forced into prostitution because of desertion by their husbands or lovers. Many a time, men corner young girls, by friendship or so called 'love' and promises of marriage. Once the man has drawn the women's attention and she commits her affection to him, she is brought to the city with false promises of a happy life and the like and are then sold to sex contractors and brothel owners. Faced with the crude realities of life, and unable to go back to their parents, these women are forced to look for some means of survival and agree to sell their bodies in the flesh market.

(c) Exploitation of women at work place is a common phenomenon all over the world. India is no exception to this. Whether one is in government service or in a private or unorganized sector, several women are forced to satisfy the desires of their boss or employer. Once fallen, one is deprived of her morality, and very often one is tempted to accept prostitution as a side business. Many call girls that the Indian cities shelter fall into this category. In the case of unmarried women, they find the job highly profitable and are at the services of the clients who come to them directly or in five star hotels.

(d) Sex industry is a flourishing business for many unemployed and unmarried young girls. Some of them make lot of money through this profession and live very lavish and luxurious life. In fact they also win favours from politicians and business tycoons. In fact for winning favours in any sector, sex is one of the most influential item sought and provided. One can find racketeers for this business in every state and industrial towns.

(e) Reports from various parts of the country show that many college going girls are known to be working as call girls in order to make extra money to meet the growing cost of living in cities. Various analysis show that this phenomenon is more common among girls from professional colleges who stay far away from their homes. It is a fact that most professional colleges/institutions are co-educational in nature and the rate of interaction among male-female students is high. The practice of ragging is also a contributory factor where often one is dragged into sexual acts - both heterosexual as well as same sex relationship. Dr. B.K. Singh, head of the department of Psychiatry, Patna Medical College, has some alarming statistics to provide based on some of the studies conducted. According to one study, as many as 66.7 per cent of male medicos and 25 per cent of female medicos confessed to be involving in pre or extra-marital relationship. The percentage for non-medico male and female was 54.54 per cent and 43.47 per cent respectively.[10]

(f) A report on Indian promiscuity,[11] says that every Saturday night, eight couples meet at a South Calcutta house. The men are senior corporate executives, and the women housewives, though some do baffle in business. Dressed in conservative business suits and decorous handloom saris, they epitomize the Bengali concept of bhadralok (gentlemen) until they have their first drink. After that all the men drop their car keys into a box and the women are asked to pick out one. Whichever key they pick decides which man they will spend the night with. If that turns out to be their own husband, they have to try their luck again. Calcutta is not an exception. Many cities and industrial towns in the country bear witness to this practice which has almost become a routine programme for the weekends, particularly for the well to do. One can imagine the shock and trauma that a newly wed bride of an ambitious young man has to undergo when he agrees to share his wife with senior officers. Sacrificing the dignity of one's own wife for a promotion or other petty favours is a common feature in this country in which officials and influential persons from various walks of life indulge in.

(g) For women and young girls belonging to various tribal and some of the backward communities, prostitution is a traditional occupation. This is true for many women in western Rajasthan, Uttar Pradesh, Madhya Pradesh and some of the states in the northeast. Ranjan Roy[12] reporting from Nandlalpura village in western Rajasthan alleges for generations the Rajnat women were satisfying the sexual lust of the Maharajahs(kings) and now they are available for anyone who can afford to pay Rs. 50 to Rs. 70. Young girls stepping into their adolescent period are to entertain men of all age groups. Unlike the rest of the country, in Nandlalpura a female child is preferred to a boy child. In fact the boys are found to be ill fed, neglected and poorly dressed. Girl children are given better and more food, good clothing and are kept clean.

The Kolta of Uttar Pradesh sell their wives and daughters to pimps and contractors of brothels hailing from cities. Sometimes their men (husband/father) accompany the womenfolk to cities only to avoid the suspicious eyes of police. There is no social taboo among the Kolta for prostitution has been considered as their profession. Some parts of central India still have the practice of supplying a maiden to the bridegroom along with bride.

All these only speak of a society where promiscuity is rampant while, it denies and conceals the facts. It is high time that we recognize the seriousness of the issue and take necessary steps to change the behavioural pattern across the country.

(h) There is yet another category of the so-called call girls or prostitutes comprising married women. Among them some are also employed. For one or other reason, these women are forced to take up the profession for earning to support the family and very often the husband and his business. In most cases, the husbands motivate them to involve in flesh trade when the family gets trapped in indebtedness. Therefore here too we find poverty as a leading cause for these lower middle class women to involve in flesh trade.

At the other end of the market, one can also come across couples from well to do families involving in extra marital relationship as a part of their sophisticated life. These are families where both husband and wife consciously approve each others involvement in extra marital affairs and socialization of a different nature. The end result of all these include family disharmony, neglect of children, loss of values and morality, divorce, prevalence of STDs and now getting infected with the HIV.

(i) Organized sex trade is not a new business in India. When one fails to find a job, do a business or do not posses land for cultivation, selling and purchasing females in open market becomes an alternate source of earning. This phenomenon has its history going back beyond the British period when women used to be exported by ship overseas. Today things have become more organized and women are being taken by flight for the purpose, particularly to gulf countries. Many young educated girls are into this profession without their choice and consent. Hundreds of girls coming to cities in search of jobs come in contact with people who persuade or lure them to take up the profession. Many are sold several times to different people and brothels.

There are hundreds of brokers working for this purpose. Even young ladies from well to do families land up in this profession. In fact I have come across several cases in which arranged marriages are held with the claim that the bridegroom is a green card holder or has a good job in a developed country and so on. Under this pretax passport and visa for the bride is arranged and the poor lady is sold abroad. There is no statistics available to show the extent of such exploitation. But the fact is that organized flesh trade exists in India in various forms. In fact hundreds of adolescent girls of Nepal origin are sold like hot cakes in various cities not only in northern India but also in metropolitan cities like Bombay. Apart from this organized sex business is also a part of tourism package.

(j) Devadasi system is a practice in our country since time immemorial when young girls of about ten years of age of a certain section of society were trained as skilled courtesans and were initiated into a profession through a ritual in a temple. This practice is still prevalent in India in large scale particularly among some of the economically and socially weaker sections of the society. These girls are being sexually exploited even before they enter the adolescent stage.

Dharam Singh,[13] the then social welfare minister of Karnataka informed the state assembly during question hour that more than 1400 devadasis in the state (official figure) suffer from the killer virus HIV. He said that the devadasi system had become a social menace and action was being taken to curb the practice. Among the 21,862 devadasis in the state (official figure), most of them belong to Belgaum, Bejapur and Raichar districts. It may be noted that the devadasi system is prevalent in several states particularly Andhra Pradesh, Tamil Nadu, Maharashtra, Orissa and Karnataka. Once they develop disease like STDs most of them are thrown out. They find no other option than to join the flesh market for earning their livelihood. Today these ladies and their clients are at high risks of contracting the HIV.

(k) For the girl child of a prostitute, this profession becomes her traditional occupation. While other communities dread the birth of a girl child and celebrate the birth of a son, the girl child of a prostitute is welcomed by her mother, the brothel keeper and the pimps as a potential source of income. At least half of the estimated six million children (believed to be females) of the prostitutes have no other option than to follow the profession of their mother. Given the present circumstances in the country, many of these children of prostitutes are likely to be infected either from their HIV positive mothers or through the pimps and other customers who engage them for sex at very tender ages.

It may be noted that the problem of prostitution has been discussed mainly in terms of its impact on health, particularly STDs/HIV/AIDS, commercialization and exploitation of women. However, the worst affected by the circumstances are children born to the prostitutes. They are vulnerable to the sex business, right from their birth and at every stage of their growth, particularly from childhood to the stage of adolescence. Born with the stigma of being 'illegitimate offspring', they are shunned by the rest of the community.

The situation of a prostitutes child is not better than that of stray animals. The child's mother is busy with her customers for which there is no fixed time. The infant is forced to sleep below the bed used by the mother for her business. The child is given opium or tobacco water to sleep, which prevents it from disturbing the mother and the customer. Older children loiter around, as their mothers neither have home of their own, nor do they have any time to attend to their children. Even the socialization within the family is absent because there is no family or home. The female child is exploited by the pimps, mother's customers and strangers before she is able to understand the purpose of the acts. Often these children see their mothers in sexual act, which frequently entails rough scenes. They are forced to put up with the traumatic and frightening experience from infancy, and by the time they are about six or seven, they would know all about facts of sexual life. This creates a feeling of insecurity, rejection and vulnerability in the child. And what to talk, if it is infected with the HIV virus either from their mother or the strangers who exploit them sexually.

Rakesh Bhatnagar[14] reports that the Supreme Court is divided on prevention of prostitution, but its two-judge bench expressed unanimity on setting up juvenile homes for the sex workers' offsprings and children engaged in prostitution. The division among Justice K. Ramaswamy and Justice D.P. Wadhwa came on a public interest petition filed 10 years ago by lawyer Gaurav Jain seeking setting up of separate schools for the sex workers children. In the 96-page verdict, Justice Ramaswamy elaborately dealt with the plight of sex workers in particular and women in general. He also relied on lawyer V.C. Mahajan Committee report while enlarging the scope of public interest litigation in such matters and also Articles 142 and 145 of the Constitution.

Homosexuals and Lesbians

Like the sex workers, homosexuals and lesbians can be also categorized into various groups. Apart from the scattered population where same sex relationship is prevalent, one can find the presence of this phenomenon among institutionalized persons and those employed in armed forces. In the following paragraphs some of these groups are discussed.

(a) Several cases of HIV infection through homosexual and lesbian activities have been reported by study teams conducting researches in various parts of the country. The population of gays and lesbians runs into thousands in this country. They have their own groups and associations. They also publish periodicals, which are being widely circulated. In fact 1994 saw the first national seminar of homosexuals in the country when it was held in Bombay.

NACO[15] has initiated an intervention programme among "men who have sex with men" (MSW) in Madras based on the situation assessment of the issue. The results of the assessment showed an alarming level of risky sexual contact between men, greater than had been expected.

A recent study[16] reveals the frequency of sexual contacts among school children. About 25.2 per cent of students are of the opinion that students of their age group have sex with a partner of the same sex. Another survey[17] conducted by the social workers from Indian Health Organization on the sexual life of truck drivers reveals that about 81 per cent of the drivers and cleaners took part in homosexual acts. One of the studies[18] conducted by the Department of Psychiatry, Patna Medical College Hospital shows that 26.47 per cent male medicos and doctors have had homosexual involvement, while the figure for female counterparts was 18.75 per cent.

The MCRC, JMI[19] conducted a study on AIDS awareness among adolescents in the city of Madras, in which a total of 498 respondents of both the sexes within the age group of 13-24 years of high, middle and low income group in and out of the formal educational system were interviewed. Among the 90 respondents, who attempted the question as to whether one has had sex with a person of the same sex, as many as 23.3 per cent replied in the affirmative. It may be noted that among the 2097 reported cases of AIDS as on 30 November 1995 to NACO one per cent (1.0%) comprised the homosexuals.

The truth is that the Government of India has also accepted the fact that we have homosexuals and lesbians in our society and denial is no more an escape mechanism. However, as reported earlier, there is no proposal under consideration of the government to supply condoms to prisoners in Tihar Jail. This was informed by the then Minister of State for Home Affairs, Mr. P.M. Sayeed to Lok Sabha on 5th May, 1994.[20]

(b) It is a recognized fact that we have population explosion in our country. Along with it there is also a growth in crimes. Although we may be increasing the number of para-military forces to keep the law and order situation under control, hardly any effort is made to increase the number of jails in the country or provide additional facilities to the existing ones, which are over crowded beyond any reasoning. For example the Tihar jail built to house 2,500 inmates has over 8,500 inmates now. This is almost the same situation in the jails situated in other parts of the country.

The fact is that Indian legal procedures are too lengthy and an undertrial may have to spend the rest of his/her life as an undertrial. Practice of homosexuality and forced sodomy among the jail inmates are common phenomena. In fact Dr. K.K. Aggarwal[21],

President of the New Delhi Chapter of the Indian Medical Association made a sensational announcement after heading a team of doctors to Tihar jail that about 90 per cent of male inmates practiced homosexuality.

Although there is a hue and cry about this announcement in various circles the fact is that the extent of the prevalence of same sex relationship within the prisonsers could be more than the rate in the general population who have access to every form of sexual relationships. In any case, it is high time that the authorities and activists involved in anti-AIDS works recognize the prison inmates as a potential high-risk group for HIV transmission. This has been the case in several countries fighting the AIDS pandemic. While several countries have initiated action for the free supply of condoms, Isreal has gone to the extent of considering a proposal to allow heterosexual activities among prisoners by permitting their spouses to visit them once a week in the prisons. The policy makers and influential authorities do not want to recognize the existing sexual practices among prisoners in our jails.[22]

(c) Persons employed in armed forces such as the military, airforce, navy and the para-military forces iive away from their hometown. In most cases their duty demands them to be away from their spouses for long intervals. It is a known phenomenon worldwide that these people indulge in various types of sexual activities and homosexual acts are very common. Although in developed countries provision is made to supply 'comfort women' even in the battlefield during an operation, such practices are hardly available for those serving in Indian armed forces. Therefore one is forced to satisfy one's needs through same-sex relationship. Whether it is same-sex affair or through 'comfort women' both these are high-risk activities as far as the spread of HIV is concerned There is enough and more evidence and reported cases to show that these jawans(male or female) do indulge in same-sex, heterosexual and bisexual activities in their camps.

According to Ramesh Sharma[23] nearly 45 jawans of the Army's 1st battalion of the Assam Regiment have tested HIV positive and another 100 jawans of the same battalion are reportedly suffering from sex-related diseases after their return from Cambodia. This battalion which returned in the last week of March had gone to Cambodia as part of the United Nation's force to oversee the conduct of general elections in that country.

Sources say that the HIV cases were detected during routine medical tests on the jawans after they returned from their foreign assignment. The medical officers were initially panicked as they had not anticipated so many HIV cases and there weren't enough AIDS testing kits. Extra AIDS kits had to be requisitioned to cope with the situation.

After the confirmation of the tests, the infected jawans were shifted to the Pune-based Armed Forces Medical College(AFMC) where they have been kept in the new AIDS ward. The 100 jawans suffering from other STDs have been sent to different army hospitals for treatment. It is not the first time that HIV has been detected among armed forces personnel. But this is the first time that so many jawans of a single battalion have tested HIV positive. A battalion normally consists of 600-650 jawans and 20-22 officers. What is important is that HIV has not spared any class or group and new programming to cover all these high-risk groups is of utmost importance.

(d) We have large number of hostels and boarding houses spread all over the country for school children, college students as well as for working persons particularly women. Same-sex relationship is not an unknown affair in these institutions. Besides there are also large number of institutions set up to take care of the beggars, juvenile delinquents, orphans, handicapped, women who are deserted or rescued from brothels etc. Apart from large-scale sexual exploitation in various forms, which at times involve organized sex-trade, there are also reports of same-sex relationships prevalent in such institutions. Various authorities and the legal system in the country is very well aware of these phenomena. It is high time that target-oriented intervention programmes are initiated to: protect these weaker sections of the society; free them from exploitation by their guardians; creating awareness among all parties involved about the impending disaster that HIV can bring about and to change the life-style of all those concerned.

(e) Among the groups vulnerable to HIV infection through sexual activities include the adolescents and street children. Sexual experimentation usually begins when one enters the adolescent stage. Studies among school children, school dropouts and street children across the country show that young boys and girls involve in sexual activities during the teenage period. However, the street children which include the rag pickers, runaways, children of sex workers and the neglected children are found to be involving or forced to be involved in sexual activities even before they are ten. Many are being exploited by elders for various reasons.

There is a widespread belief among certain less literate persons that sex with a virgin would cure one from STDs and HIV/AIDS. Several tiny girls are forced into sexual activities by those infected with these deadly viruses. Many of them die and those that manage to survive lead a life full of fear, shame and despise from one's own dear ones.

Among the street children same-sex relationship as well as heterosexual experiments are very common. Social workers and functionaries working among street children from various parts of the country report that these tiny kids learn all about sex and sexuality before they are ten. Marie Stopes[24] admits that 40 per cent of women who come for abortions are unwed mothers under the age of twenty. Many school and college going girls seek abortion even without the knowledge of their parents.

Target-oriented and factor-oriented intervention is essential to contain the spread of HIV among this high-risk group. There is no accurate estimate of the number of street children in the country. The Government of India estimates the number to be around 18 milllion, while the operation Research Group places the figure at 44 million. Swami Agnivesh claims that there are at least 60 million child labourers which include these street children. Therefore, one cannot simply overlook this section of the society while evolving strategies for the prevention and control of HIV/AIDS/STDs.

Eunuchs

Involvement of eunuchs in flesh trade is not a new phenomenon in our country. Eunuchs were employed by kings to take care of the harem References of eunuchs can be found in the historical and religious books of various countries and religions. Today they have assumed importance as a high-risk group who could transmit the HIV. Experiences of people working among HIV support group, homosexuals, lesbians and other sex workers in the country speak volumes about the involvement of eunuchs in flesh trade.

Apart from serving the homosexuals and lesbians, eunuchs are also found to be running brothels in various cities. They are also instrumental in persuading women to take up prostitution. Eunuchs also serve clients in selected hotels and holiday homes.

It is estimated that about 40,000 castrations take place every year in India, of which three-fourth die of infections caused by the crude practice.[25] Young boys particularly in the adolescent stage are brought to their camp under one or other pretext and their genitals are chopped off with the kitchen knife or through the help of a barber. In some cases a physician's help is also sought to surgically remove the genitals of young men. These doctors are believed to be taking huge amounts for their service. Since most castrated men die of infection, the services of physicians are sought.

Wadhwa[26] in one of his reports claims that there are about 5000 eunuchs in Delhi alone and the president of All India Hijra Kalyan Sabha - an organization that has been fighting for the rights of eunuchs for over a decade - say that there are about 1.2 million eunuchs in the country. It is believed that not even one per cent of eunuchs are 'born eunuchs'. These people are considered as a social menace although some persons attach religious importance to them. An estimated 200,000 eunuchs from various parts of the country gather in a temple at Koovagam, a small village in Tamil Nadu every year to celebrate an annual festival in which they become brides of the deity Araven.[27] It may be noted that the Election Commission of India has recognized this group and they are now able to vote like "men and women" and are allowed to opt for either sex as per their wishes for their enrolment in the voters list and for the purpose of identity cards.

It is important that any HIV prevention and control programme should also focus on eunuchs who are a potential high-risk target group for the spread of HIV. It is unfortunate that our executive wing lacks wisdom and they are being guided by influence and petty gains. As mentioned earlier, the Ministry of Health and Family Welfare (NACO) has recognized the need to initiate prevention programmes for AIDS among homosexuals while the Ministry of home failed to recognize the fact that the prison inmates involve in same-sex relationship by denying the free distribution of condoms among the prisoners. Similarly while the Election Commission of India has recognized the eunuch's right to vote, the Ministry of Health and Family Welfare (NACO) has failed to see them as a potential high-risk group for HIV transmission. By any measure, the Eunuchs are a high-risk group than the barbers for whom the Assam government has initiated sensitization programme, which is also a necessity.

Sperm Donors

Transmission of HIV from one person to another could also take place without a direct person to person sexual activities, yet involving sexual fluid, namely, the sperm. Hundreds of thousands go for donor insemination (DI). India is not an exception to this. As a result there are several instances when aged ladies such as a grandmother gave birth to their grand children. There is so much of meddling with human body that there is no limit to the extent of its misuse. On the one hand we speak of respect for the individuals, morality and value system, while closing both the eyes to the crude practices in which one is involved. As a result, the chances of getting infected with the HIV is also crossing all limits and boundaries.

There was a big newspaper report[28] about Ahmedabad going for its first voluntary sperm bank in the state set up with the help of the US medical experts. Dr. Vineet Mishra, In-charge of the high-risk pregnancy unit of the institute of Kidney Disease and Research Centre, says that over three lakh infertile couples go for artificial insemination every year with semen from either the husband or a donor. He alleges that unhealthy and poor quality genetic materials are provided by quacks and pathologists who use semen obtained from professional donors like the labourers, beggars or street vendors who are readily available for as little as Rs. 20 each time. At the other end of the market are the high profile donors like good-looking, handsome and smart medical, computer and engineering students who charge anything between Rs. 1000 and Rs. 2000 each time. There are also several news paper and other periodical reports, giving information about the involvement of students from professional institutions of learning who stay far away from their homes and involve in sperm donation which provided them additional pocket money for meeting the ever-growing cost of living in urban centres. They do not bother about the number of children they father before getting married.

Many women are forced to seek abortion when they learn about the status of the semen donors. There are documented cases at least in some countries when HIV has been transmitted through artificial insemination.

There are many issues surrounding the donation of semen particularly in a country where one boasts so much about religious, moral, philosophical, social and cultural values. What has happened to this so-called strong and sacred "husband-wife" relationship? What will be the personal, psychological and social lives of children born through artificial insemination, the identity of whose fathers is not known? What an agonizing experience it would be for the child to know its genetic heritage? And now what trauma would it cause to the mother, the child and the husband of the women if the semen donated to them contained HIV? Therefore every effort needs to be taken to focus on this target group (or target factor) seeking DI to prevent the unabated spread of HIV. Like the blood donors, semen donation has become a big business whose beneficiaries include the sterilized men, people already infected with HIV and other deadly diseases including hepatitis B. In fact, instead of reducing social and human problems, perhaps we are on the way to creating a new social disorder with new problems and human sufferings.

The fact is that the many sperm banks situated in the country hardly have the facilities for screening genetic materials for HIV and other diseases. Further there is hardly any direction from health authorities to maintain minimum standards. Above all, several of these banks provide secret services to the customers who want to maintain confidentiality. It also enables the sperm bank operators to charge huge amounts from their clients who may have to undergo DI several times before one is able to conceive. The exact success rate is not known for there are many quacks operating the so-called sperm banks across the country. It is high time the health authorities take serious note of the situation and do the needful instead of waiting for the disaster to occur.

TRANSMISSION THROUGH BLOOD

Because of the nutritive value, adequate oxygen content and temperature, blood is a good source for the growth of organisms. There are several diseases which are transmissible via blood such as HIV/AIDS, syphilis, malaria and other viral infections. Therefore transmission of blood can lead to transmission of blood transmissible diseases. In fact studies have shown that transfusion of HIV infected blood is the most efficient means of transmitting HIV infection. The transmission rate of HIV via blood is estimated to be 90 per cent.

Blood banks and blood donation began in India in 1941 during the Second World War as a war necessity. When Japan invaded Burma, it became almost certain that India will be their next target. Therefore, the British government launched massive action plan to meet the challenges. Subsequently, in early 1942 the then Governor General of India directed all the provincial governors to set up blood banks as one of the measures to provide blood to the wounded soldiers.[29] Later it became a business for many, and one can find hundreds of blood banks spread across the country of which many do not have the required license.

There are several ways in which an individual can be infected through contaminated blood. An attempt has been made to discuss details about some of the potential target groups who are at risk of HIV infection through blood. This will enable us to categorize some of the high-risk groups for whom target-oriented prevention programmes can be planned.

(i) Health Care Providers

The exact estimate of health care providers in the country is not available. In any case their number exceed over a million which alone shows the urgency of imparting accurate and complete information regarding safety measures in handling patients. A recently conducted study(1997)[30] of 260 health care workers at the All India Institute of Medical Sciences (AIIMS) by the Centre for Community Medicine at AIIMS, revealed that as many as 86 per cent of the doctors did not use appropriate precautions against HIV. In fact among the respondents, as many as 20 per cent doctors and 32 per cent nurses had more than 15 exposures in a month. While 58.3 per cent doctors and 53.7 per cent nurses had accidental exposure to patients blood and body fluid, 35 per cent doctors and 45 per cent nurses had a break of skin. It is amazing to note that about 20 per cent of the doctors did not know the routes of HIV transmission.

If this is the situation at the premier medical institution of the country which also runs HIV/AIDS awareness and education programme for people from various walks of life across the country one can imagine the plight of health care workers spread over the nook and corner of the country where they live without access to urban facilities. Therefore there is an urgent need to do all that the country can, to first provide, adequate training to the health care providers.

(ii) Professional Blood Donors

There are an estimated 1401 blood banks in the country managed by different agencies; 727 in the government sector and 674 in the private/voluntary sector.[31] The requirement of blood in the country, assessed on the basis of the number of hospital beds (as per WHO criterion) i.e. 6 to 16 units (average 11 units) of blood per hospital bed, is estimated to be 60 lakh unit per annum. At present the total collection of blood is about 30 lakh unit per annum which denotes an overall shortage of 50 per cent.[32]

Although no exact estimate of the number of professional blood donors is available, India has anything between 50,000 (official figures) to 200,000 (professional Blood Donors Association figures) who sell their blood regularly. It has become a profession in a poverty stricken society on the one hand, while marching ahead towards free market economy on the other. While the sex workers sell their body, the professional blood donors sell their blood to the hundreds of blood banks situated across the country.

According to a study conducted in 1989, out of every 1000 professional donors, 39 tested positive in ELISA tests as opposed to 14.5 per thousand voluntary donors.[33] Government and voluntary blood banks including that of the Red Cross Society, rely entirely on voluntary and replacement donations. Unfortunately, even these blood banks are unable to meet safety standards because of shortage of equipment and personnel.

An analysis of the blood banking system in the country would be alarming. A report[34] about the situation of illegal blood banks in the state of Bihar say that there are about 200 blood banks in the state capital alone providing blood to the needy without any licence or facilities for testing. If this is the case in just one city in the country, the number of blood banks and the number of professional blood donors could be a hundred times more than the figures quoted earlier.

According to Dr. Dilip Sen,[35] a leading Pathologist, every nursing home in Patna has its own illegal blood bank which augments their commercial viability. This is also admitted by the Director-in-chief, Bihar Health Services, Dr. Prabhas Chandra, who said at a workshop on AIDS in Patna, that a majority of the 76 known private and government blood banks are functioning without licence or despite the fact that their licenses have lapsed. Dr. Sen is more than sure that these banks which thrive on the greed of professional donors, are supplying blood to patients without testing them for Australian antigen or Hepatitis B etc.,

Ajay Bhardwaj[36] reports from Amritsar that none of the six blood banks in the city including two run by the government, has been conducting HIV tests on blood donors. According to official sources, besides the non-availability of ELISA test kits, the high cost of performing the tests has been a major deterrent. It is reported that in the government hospitals in the city, more than 12,000 units of blood has been utilised annually which is collected mostly by the local Red Cross Society. The doctors say that HIV test on each donor costs between Rs. 300 and Rs. 400 which the private blood banks avoid only to keep the supply cost low. In one of the raids carried out on private blood banks, the investigating team had found 10 of the 49 blood samples infected with HIV. In order to predict the way HIV is likely to spread in a particular group of people, it is important that we discuss briefly about the known sources of HIV infection. Although HIV has been isolated from a number of bodily fluids and tissues, including blood, saliva, tears, breast milk, semen, vomit etc. the virus can transmit from one person to another only through certain well known ways. People have become infected via blood transfusions, infected blood products including donated organs and via the sharing of syringes and hypodermic needles.

Apart from the professional blood donors, there is a large contingent of general population who donates blood as voluntary donors on emergency cases. The fact that only about 50 per cent of blood is collected through blood banks shows that the rest of the 50 per cent is pooled from other sources, namely, voluntary blood donation. It may be noted that the voluntary donors are of two types. One-the close relatives or friends of patients, and two-the voluntary donors who are motivated to donate blood through organised blood donation camps generally held in educational institutions, offices and blood donation camps organised by public agencies.

Therefore, one can find various categories of blood donors who need to be made aware of the impending disaster that HIV and other deadly diseases could bring about through blood and blood products. These target groups are to be informed about the precaution required for donating blood, particularly, of the need for ensuring the use of sterile needles and undergoing HIV test. Because most professional blood donors belong to the lower strata of the society whose behaviour pattern is not certain, one has to be doubly sure before collecting and transfusing blood of such donors. It could be that several of them might be involving in high risk activities including unprotected sex and substance abuse. There is also an urgent need for educating the para medical staff at the blood banks about the safety measures to be followed in blood collection, supply and transfusion. The same precautions are also required for those involving in organ donation and transplantation.

(iii) Intravenous Drug Users

It is important and necessary for everyone to understand the relationship of substance abuse to HIV/AIDS. Substance abuse and AIDS are biopsychosocial diseases. According to Jones,[37] both AIDS and Alcohol and drugs are influenced by physical, psychological behaviour and environmental conditions. There is no single or simple magic bullet to either cure or prevent the occurrence of alcoholism or drug addiction or of HIV/AIDS. There are the risk factors of being mood altered and judgement impaired, the transmission factors of sharing injecting drug equipment, paraphernalia, and their co-factors of the progression of the disease in terms of compromised immune system, high stress, pre-existing illnesses, and also the transmission factors of pregnancy in terms of father to mother to foetus. When we speak of risk behaviours of addicts of HIV infection it is important to understand: Addicts share their booze and their bottles, their drugs and paraphernalia. When we speak of paraphernalia it is not just needles, but syringes, works, cookes, spoons, dishes, cotton and filters and waters. Addicts also share their sexual partners.[38]

Injecting drug users are a potential channel in the transmission of HIV. The virus causing AIDS is passed on to an individual while sharing a needle and syringe used by an HIV infected person. Small volumes of contaminated blood remain inside the previously used needles and syringes thereby providing opportunities to transmit the HIV virus to the subsequent users.

The injecting drug abusers are one of the high-risk groups in the country particularly in the northeastern states. According to Thomas[39] the drug scene in north-east and Manipur in particular is somewhat like what happened in Edinburgh in England in the years 1984-86. It was estimated that 40 per cent of Britain's HIV infected drug users lived in Edinburgh. This percentage is similar in the Indian context to Manipur because of the easy availability of pure heroin or number four. While addicts elsewhere in India chase or smoke smack or impure adulterated street heroin, the Manipur youth prefer to inject it. Moreover, because of sharing the tribal nature, the young people in the tribal belt of Manipur tend to inject heroin in-groups, sharing contaminated needles. Such sharing of needles become even more necessary for the intravenous drug user in Manipur as the government took a tough stand and ensured that the addicts did not get needles. So the intravenous addicts bought ink droppers and fitted a needle to it and used it for injection. When the government got tougher and ink droppers were not freely available, the addicts emptied small shampoo sachet (of what is known as 'morch shampoo' in Manipur) and rigged in needles.[40]

A survey conducted by Merchant[41] among 235 brown sugar addicts in Bombay showed that 86.7 per cent (204) were in the age group of 15-26 years. Nearly 70 per cent of the addicts surveyed spend on an average Rs. 40 to Rs. 200 per day on drugs. About 3 per cent spend more than Rs. 450 a day. In all 89 per cent of the addicts had difficulty in communicating with their parents while 56 per cent of them lacked a "father figure" at home.

The above description only show the extent of the prevalence of substance abuse in the country. Although no exact figures are available to quote, deliberations in various conventions put the figure at around one million, which could be more or less. What is important is that the NACO and other agencies involved in de-addiction and anti-AIDS activities have recognized the seriousness of the prevailing situation. However, all focus are on North-east, and the rest of the country where substance abuse is rampant is all together forgotten. This anomaly in wisdom cannot be explained by any rational consideration and every effort needs to be taken to do the needful to contain the further spread of HIV among the substance abusers across the country.

(iv) Thalassemic Patients

Another group of people at high risk are the Thalassemic patients in the country who comprise mainly children. Scores of thalassemic children from various parts of the country have been reported to be HIV infected from blood transfusion. The exact number of thalassemic children in the country is not known. Figures presented at HIV/AIDS conferences, seminars and workshops in various parts of the country put the estimate of thalassemic major babies born in India annually at around 5000, half the number dying without their problem even being diagnosed. Thalassemia is a hereditary disease, in which there is abnormality in the protein content of the haemoglobin molecule. The affected, red cells cannot function normally and hence lead to anaemia. Other symptoms include enlargement of the spleen and abnormalities of the bone marrow. Patients with this disease are treated with repeated blood transfusion, almost once in a period of six weeks.

With the rapid spread of HIV in the country and the already reported large number of thalassemic patients getting infected through blood transfusion across the country because of the negligence of health care providers, undefended health delivery system and inadequate number of trained personnel, it is absolutely necessary that preventive measures are adopted on a priority basis by everyone involved in taking care of the thalassemic patients. It is a high-risk group for HIV infection and concern should be shown to their cause.

Supreme Court Judgement on Revamping Blood Banks: In a Public Interest Litigation (PIL) the Supreme Court of India, in a historic judgement on 4th January, 1996, directed the Union of India and State Government to take various steps towards coordinated management and revamping of blood banking activities in all its facets of collection, testing, quality control, storage, archiving, rational use, monitoring, training and research. Some of the directives of the judgement are: [42]

a) The Union Government and all the State Governments/ UT administrations shall establish National/State Blood Transfusion Councils by 15th July, 1996, as a 'Society' registered under the Societies Registration Act, 1860. The Object Clause of the Constitution of the Councils assigns the task of ensuring coordinated management of blood banking services in all its facets.

b) To licence all the blood banks by 31st Dec., 96(later extended to 17th May, 1997)

c) To take steps to discourage the prevalence of professional donation of blood so that the system is completely eliminated by December 31, 1997.

d) To secure a grant of 100% exemption from Income Tax to the donors in respect of donations made to the National/ State Blood Transfusion Councils.

e) To consider the advisability of enacting separate legislation for regulating the operation of blood banks.

The judgement provides a good tool for revamping the Blood Transfusion Services ensuring adequate availability of safe blood and blood products. The follow up of the judgement was the formation of the National Blood Transfusion Council in May, 1996. State Blood Transfusion Councils have also been set up in all the states and UTs. Section 80-G of the Income Tax Act has also been amended by the Government to provide for 100% deduction from total income to the donors in respect of donations to the National and State Councils. The operationalization of blood banking activities have also been covered under the Drug and Cosmetics Act/Rules, which are in the process of revision.

(v) Other Target Groups

Apart from the high-risk groups described above, there are a number of people who also require adequate information about safety measures in order to prevent the transmission of the HIV virus through blood. These include:

a) persons working in barbershops and beauty parlours;
b) persons involved in using skin piercing instruments for the purpose of piercing nose, ears etc.
c) persons involved in tattooing;
d) persons selling kidney and other organs;
e) recipients of blood and blood products; and
f) persons involved in home care of the HIV infected.

Care has to be taken while planning any programme for sensitization among all types of risk groups so that adequate provision is made to address the issues not only to the risk groups but also to their beneficiaries or clients as well as their immediate relatives.

TRANSMISSION FROM MOTHER TO CHILD

Child victims are the horrifying new faces of AIDS in India with a large number of cases being reported from various parts of the country. One of the main three known routes of HIV transmission from one person to another is the transmission from a mother to her child. There are many differing opinions, but one does not know the following:[43]

i) Since all babies inherit their mother's antibodies, it is only logical that if a mother has positive antibodies to HIV, then her baby will be born with them too.

ii) After 6-18 months the maternal antibodies in the baby disappear, and up to 75-80 percent of babies born to HIV positive mothers will not carry the virus. This means that there is a 20-25 per cent risk of the child having HIV infection.

iii) The most commonly known way of a baby becoming infected with HIV is through womb. There is very little medical information to suggest that the virus is transmitted at the time of birth or through breast-feeding.

If the mother is HIV negative, and if her sexual partner is HIV positive, then there is a risk that the woman may become infected while trying to conceive. Further, there is every likelihood that the child conceived would also become HIV infected. Similarly, if the mother is HIV positive, there are more chances for the child in the womb to be HIV infected. As mentioned earlier, donor insemination also could be a risky factor.

Many women will need more than one attempt before they become pregnant with donor insemination and will therefore be exposed repeatedly to any infections the donor has which can be passed on via his semen. Virtually all babies born to HIV positive mothers will have antibodies to the virus. This is because babies are born with 'maternal antibodies' from their mothers which provide protection until their own immune system are fully developed.[44] According to NACO about 30 per cent children born to HIV positive mothers are likely to be infected. Whatever be the claim, any HIV antibody test on a child before the age of 18 months will be inconclusive.

HIV has been transmitted through breast milk in a very small number of cases.[45] There is a higher prevalence rate of HIV in colostrum (early milk) than in later milk. Further, blood transmission may theoretically also occur via cracked and bleeding nipples, and should an HIV positive woman choose to breast feed, extra care would be necessary to avoid this complication.

An HIV infected woman can transmit the virus to her child before, during or shortly after birth. Transmission from an infected mother to her unborn child now accounts for more than 75 per cent of all paediatric AIDS cases.[46] The WHO has described how HIV infection affects mother and children through the following:[47]

HIV crosses the placental barrier and infection can also occur at the time of delivery. Transmission to the foetus occurs in 20-50 per cent of seropositive women. The risk of foetal infection is lower in a symptomatic women. The risk of intrauterine infection is higher in women who had recently acquired the infection, women with AIDS and in women who had previously delivered infected offspring. HIV infection does not have any adverse effect on the course of pregnancy, delivery or lactation. Pregnancy does not affect the course on HIV infection. Maternal HIV infection is associated with a higher rate of premature delivery and intrauterine growth retardation. At least part of this association might be attributed to consistent risk factors like smoking, drug addiction and anaemia in HIV-infected women. Progression of HIV infection is rapid in infancy.

According to WHO[48] half of the infected infants will die by two years of age and over 90 per cent will die by five years of age. Infected infants born to HIV infected mothers will become orphaned early in childhood (as their parents die of AIDS) and face all the attendant social consequences. It appears that the HIV epidemic has already nullified to some extent, the decline in maternal and under-five mortality rates (45 MR) achieved over several decades of MCH care. It is possible that in the current decade, maternal infant and under-five mortality rates may show a deep rise due to the HIV epidemic.

When we talk about mother to child transmission, the target groups that need awareness and education are the tens of thousands of sex workers spread across the country, children born (or will be born) to them, the tribal communities that indulge in prostitution, those women who provide sex to the truck drivers and their clients on the highways, the women who opt for donor insemination, travelling executives who seek sex while away on tour and their partners etc. apart from the ordinary people in the street and in the country side.

SUMMARY

HIV has not spared anyone because of one's social and economic status, colour, sex, age, profession, religion or cultural background. However, the early experiences showed that certain groups of people were more vulnerable to contracting the HIV. In this chapter, the author has made an attempt to describe the so-called high-risk groups in India who are most vulnerable to HIV/AIDS. These high-risk groups include: Sex workers, Devadasis, Certain tribal communities, Truck Drivers, Adolescents and Street Children, Homosexuals, Lesbians, Eunuchs, Thalassemic patients, Intravenous Drug Users, Sperm Donors, Milk Donors, Organ Donors, Blood Donors, Health Care Providers and Children born to HIV positive mothers.

REFERENCES

1. UNAIDS, World AIDS Day 1996: *One World, One Hope*. Geneva, 15 March 1996 (Press Release).
2. Gracious Thomas, *Prevention of AIDS: In search of answers*. Shipra Publication, New Delhi., 1997, p.36.
3. Lal Shiv, Preventing AIDS : Educating youth to protect themselves from infection. Swasth Hind, New Delhi, November-December 1993.
4. Gracious Thomas, *AIDS and Family Education*. Rawat publications, Jaipur, 1995, pp. 131-137.
5. NACO, National AIDS control programme - India, country scenario update, December 1995. New Delhi.
6. Social Welfare, Central Social Welfare Board, New Delhi, June 1990. (A brief report of the findings were published. Now the figures could be much more).
7. NACO, National AIDS control programme India, country scenario - An update, MHFW, Govt. of India, New Delhi, 1993.
8. Sunday, Calcutta, 13 June, 1992.
9. Gracious Thomas, Prevention of AIDS: In search of answers, op.cit. pp. 39-41.
10. Mammen Mathew, *AIDS cases shooting up in Bihar*. Hindustan Times, New Delhi, 15 March 1993.
11. Sunday, Calcutta, 25-31, August 1991.
12. Ranjan Roy, AIDS bomb ticks in Rajasthan Village. TOI, 26 March 1994.
13. UNI, 14,00 Devadasis have AIDS. Hindustan Times, New Delhi, 8 January, 1993.
14. Rakesh Bhatnagar, SC for homes for sex workers children. TOI, 17th July 1997.
15. NACO, op. cit. p. 61.
16. Arya, Hema and Sengupta, Sumita, *Teenage promiscuity" so much too Soon*. TOI, New Delhi, 29 April 1994.

17. Sinha, Seema, "IHO Move to Educate Truck Drivers on AIDS" TOI, New Delhi, December 1993.
18. Mammen Mathew, op. cit.
19. MCRC, JMI, 'A study of AIDS Awareness among adolescents in the city of Madras." MCRC-JMI, New Delhi, 1994.,
20. PTI, No condoms for Tihar inmates. TOI, New Delhi., 6 May 1994.
21. Anjali Deshpande, What can a short chat tell a heart specialist about AIDS in Tihar? TOI, New Delhi, May 5, 1994.
22. Gracious Thomas, op. cit.
23. Ramesh Sharma, 45 Cambodia - returned jawans test HIV positive. TOI, New Delhi, 5 Sept. 1994.
24. Arya, Hema.et.al.op.cit
25. Times of India, New Delhi, 21 April 1994.
26. Wadhwa, Soma *Man or Woman, Eunuchs can vote now*. TOI, New Delhi, 6 November 1994.
27. Impact, Gay and Lesbian News for New Orleans and the Gulf South, Volume 19, No. 11, May 27-June9, 1994.
28. TOI, Sperm bank being set up in Gujarat. TOI, New Delhi, 25 Sept. 1994.
29. Jagdish Bhardwaj, Blood of the professional - A report on the exploitation of professional blood donors by the blood banking system in India. ABVA, New Delhi, 1991.
30. Kalpana Jain, AIIMS Staff run high risk of HIV infection, says study. TOI, 27 July 1997.
31. V.N. Sardana(Joint Director, Blood Safety, NACO), Blood Banking Services in India. Health for the Millions, VHAI, December 1996.
32. *Ibid.*
33. Sakina Yusuf Khan, The kiss of death. TOI, New Delhi, 25 Sept, 1995.
34. Mammen Mathew, op. cit
35. *Ibid.*
36. Ajay Bhardwaj, Amritsar blood banks conduct no HIV test. TOI, New Delhi, 27 Nov. 1994.
37. A. Billy, S. Jones *Substance Abuse and HIV* 1994 National HIV Frontline Forum Multimedia Self-study Kit. NCM Publishers, Inc. New York, 1994, pp. 12-17.
38. *Ibid.*
39. T.K. Thomas *The drug scene in India*, In the Dream and the Dragon: The truth about substance abuse. TRAC Publication New Delhi 1994, p. 177.
40. *Ibid.*
41. Yusuf A. Merchant, Brown Sugar Addiction- the Indian perspective. The DrugAbuse Information Rehabilitation and Research Centre, Bombay 1986.

42. NACO, National AIDS Control Programme India : Country Scenario—an update, December 1996, New Delhi, 1997
43. Terrence Higgins Trust, HIV, & AIDS; Information for women. London, 1990.
44. HIV and the under 5: A guide for workers and carers. George House Trust, Manchester, 1994.
45. *Ibid.*
46. WHO, AIDS prevention: What maternal and child health (MCH/FP) Service providers need to know. WHO, NEW DELHI, 1992.
47. *Ibid.*
48. *Ibid.*

5

State Efforts in HIV Prevention

The AIDS epidemic continues to pose a threat to the very existence of the human species on earth. It is a challenge, it is a demon, it is unpredictable, it is huge, it is unstable, it is invisible, it is dangerous and it has almost become an insurmountable task for the medical researchers to counter its movement, let alone develop a vaccine. Time has come to accept and acknowledge that AIDS affects everyone. It reaches anybody, across the border, religion, culture, race, profession, age, gender and socio-economic status.

Almost every country on this planet has reported the prevalence of HIV. Every single day more than 16,000 people—7,500 adults and 1,000 children—are projected to get infected with HIV[1]. In the United States, AIDS is the leading cause of death among men in the age band of 25-44 and it is the third-leading cause among women of that age group. But the disease is already the leading killer of black women who come under the same age bracket[2]. Studies, mainly in industrialized countries, indicate that about 60 per cent of adults will progress to AIDS within 12-13 years after getting infected with HIV.[3]

Statistics regarding routes of HIV transmission show the following trends:

- heterosexual (male-female sex) accounts for more than 70 per cent;
- homosexual (male-male sex) 5-10 per cent;
- transmission of HIV infected blood or blood products accounts for 3-5 per cent, and sharing of HIV infected injection equipment by drugs 5-10 per cent[4].

Mother-to-child (vertical) transmission accounts for more than 90 per cent of all infections in infants and children. Around

25-30 per cent of all infants born to HIV-infected women themselves become infected with HIV before or during birth, or through breast feeding[5]. In 1995 approximately 500,000 children were born with HIV infection (about 1,4000 per day)[6]. In 1995, 1.3 million people—1 million adults and 0.3 million children below the age of five—died of HIV/AIDS associated illnesses. The number of cumulative HIV/AIDS deaths reached 5.8 million as of July 1, 1996.[7]

It is alarming to note what Dr. Hira[8] of AIDS Research & Control Center (ARCON) has to say about this epidemic. In Mumbai, for example, he says it has spread faster than in Africa. Between 1993 and 1997, ARCON estimates that rate of HIV infection among pregnant women grew from 0.8 per cent to 4.2 per cent, among voluntary blood donors from 0.6 per cent to 2.8 per cent. ARCON's conservative estimates indicate that 0.8 per cent or three million of the sexually active population in India are HIV infected and more than a 100 thousand (a lakh) have full-blown AIDS. By the year 2000, India will have 8 to 12 million HIV carriers and 1.1 million AIDS patients. Dr. Hira feels that unlike North America and Europe where more than 70 per cent of HIV is spread through intravenous drug use and gay sex, in India 75 per cent of HIV is spread through sexual activity of heterosexuals only and one per cent through gay sex. The socio-cultural lessons of the west haven't proved very useful to the Indian. This warrants that they must conduct their own studies and adopt a multidisciplinary approach to the disease.

Prevention of HIV is a Challenge

While statistics are important, what is more important is what, is done with those statistics? It is time to act prudently. It is time to pool all wisdom, knowledge, skills and resources to fight the pandemic. It is time to deal with the disease and the people who are infected with compassion, concern, love and care. It is time for the quacks to stop talking about a cure that does not exist. It is time to learn from the initiatives taken and success achieved by those countries which are worst affected by the pandemic during 1980s.

Speaking at the opening ceremony of the XI International Conference on AIDS in Vancouver, Eric Sawyer, one of the founders of ACTUP, New York alleged "Human Rights violations and genocide continue" to kill millions of impoverished people with AIDS. Governments are killing poor people in developing countries because they are providing only a tiny amount of AIDS funding which is limited to prevention efforts and does not pay for AIDS care. The truth is hatred of the poor and of the disenfranchised communities continue to allow discrimination, stigmatization, violence and even murder of people living with AIDS to remain unchecked. People with AIDS do not have any protection against human rights violations.[9]

Signal from all over the world evolved as a result of studies, workshops, conferences, seminars, evaluation reports and experiences of people living with HIV clearly show that 'prevention' is the most significant factor in the management of HIV/AIDS. However, prevention in many ways is more difficult than cure. It demands more time, more effort, more money, more investment in human resources, moves slowly, shows less tangible results over a long period of time because of its involvement in behaviour change and lack of reward in any form. While we wait with our fingers crossed for a vaccine to be developed or drugs for cure, prevention is the only option available left to tide over the AIDS pandemic.

In a country with much proclaimed cultural, religious and traditional values, AIDS has presented a big challenge to the policy makers, political leaders, religious leaders, parents, academics, physicians and NGOs to contain the deadly disease. Given the nature of this disease and the routes of its transmission which has stigma attached to it, everyone involved in AIDS work in the country is dumbfounded. Much water has flown under the bridge ever since the government of India launched its multisectoral programme with international collaboration. Unfortunately nothing substantial has been done to contain the unabated spread of the killer disease. It is a fact that hundreds of blood banks still operate without a license; no comprehensive education and health policy has been initiated; no modification has been made in the existing age old laws; little provision is made to sensitize the masses about

HIV and its transmission etc. These are sufficient to show the lackadaisical approach of the government machinery responsible for AIDS control and prevention in the country.

Success Stories in HIV Prevention

Most of the developed countries and some of the developing nations across the globe launched broad-based HIV prevention programmes that have started yielding results. There is a remarkable progress in prevention of HIV in several countries which have been recorded by AIDS Control and Prevention (AIDSCAP) in its final report of the status and trends of global HIV/AIDS pandemic, July 1996. According to this report there is a decline in HIV incidence and/or prevalence in gay men in the US, Australia, Canada and Western Europe; decline in prevalence in young women in Uganda; decline in HIV incidence in young men in Thailand and remaining low of HIV prevalence among injecting drug users in a number of countries including Australia. [10] UNAIDS reports that there is a reduction of mother-to-child rate by two-thirds in industrialized countries through the administration of antiretorviral drugs to HIV-infected pregnant women and their newborn babies.[11]

As far as Thailand is concerned, since 1991 the strategy of 100 per cent condom use by men has been promoted all over the country to ensure condom use in the commercial sex industry. Together with the hard-hitting public awareness campaigns, this has resulted in an 80 per cent decrease in sexually transmitted diseases in Thailand from 1989 to 1994. Further, the Thai HIV prevention efforts have made substantial progress in reducing the number of new infections each year which has dropped almost four-fold since 1990.[12]

This success in HIV prevention is attributable to the broad base response of Thai society, a response which extends all the way from the national level down to the community level. Active condom promotion, improved STD control, mass media, workplace and school-based AIDS education, and efforts to promote compassion and support to those affected have all been important components to this effort. Government, NGOs, business, schools and communities as well as self-help groups of people with HIV/AIDS, have all taken an active role in this response. [13]

The National AIDS Control Programme of India was launched in 1987. The strategic plan for prevention and control of AIDS began implementation in 1992, with support from World Bank, WHO and other international agencies. Although much publicity has been given to condom programming, it covers only about 5 per cent of the eligible couples who use it mostly for contraceptive needs. Low level of awareness, lack of political will and lack of funds, equipment's and trained manpower are all hurdles in achieving success in the prevention and control programmes of AIDS in India.

STRATEGIES OF THE NATIONAL AIDS CONTROL PROGRAMME (NACP)

The Government of India constituted a National AIDS Committee in 1986. On the basis of the recommendations of that Committee, a National AIDS Control Programme (NACP) was formulated in 1987. It has been strengthened and consolidated since 1992 and a strategic plan 1992-97 was prepared and launched with a World Bank soft loan of 84 million US dollars. This project has come to an end on 31 March 1997[14]. Up to 1996, only about one-fourth of the credit was utilised. All the states and Union Territories were urged by NACO to utilise the remaining amount within the project period.[15] The future of the programme is not clear till the present day. However, let us briefly discuss the strategies defined under this strategic plan for 1992-97 [16] before we embark upon suggesting any modification or evolving new strategies.

The Aims

The aims of the plan were to establish a comprehensive, multisectoral programme for the prevention and control of AIDS in India, which would:

- prevent HIV transmission
- decrease the morbidity and mortality associated with HIV infection
- minimise the socio-economic impact resulting from HIV infection.

These aims were to be achieved through meeting a series of medium term objectives, which include the following:

a) to establish effective surveillance in all states to monitor the epidemic
b) to provide sound technical support
c) to ensure a high level of awarenéss of HIV/AIDS and its prevention in the population
d) to promote the use of condoms
f) to target interventions at groups identified as high risk
g) to ensure the safety of the blood
h) to develop the services required to provide psychosocial support to HIV infected persons, AIDS patients and their associates.

Strategies

In all, nine strategies were defined to meet the objectives mentioned above. They are:

1. Programme management
2. Intersectoral collaboration
3. HIV/AIDS surveillance
4. Sexually transmitted diseases
5. Condom programming
6. Targeted intervention
7. Blood safety programme
8. Information, education, communication (IEC) and
9. Reduction of impact.

Let briefly examine each of these components independently to see the constraints and drawbacks in the implementation of the programme during the past five years.

An initial and maiden attempt to develop such a strategic plan may not necessarily result in a foolproof document - the strategies under discussion being no exception. Political uncertainty, financial limitations, lack of trained personnel, socio-cultural background in which we live, varied high-risk groups, size of population, geographical vastness of the country, poverty, illiteracy, inadequate health delivery system etc. play decisive roles in the implementation of any policy in a democratic country like India.

1. Programme Management

In order to accomplish the objectives of NACP, efficient programme management constitutes one of the most significant components of the overall programme. Establishing an effective mechanism for intersectoral collaboration, strengthening of technical and research capabilities, enhancing programme managerial capability, efficient flow of funds and an in-built mechanism for monitoring and evaluation are some of the highly relevant management needs of the AIDS Control Programme. Taking these needs into account, due emphasis has been accorded to the component of programme management in the strategic plan. The broad objectives of this programme component are:

a) establishment of an effective Programme Management mechanism at national and state levels;

b) provision of technical, financial and operational support to the staff and organizations implementing programme activities.

These objectives are addressed through four strategies: (1) the creation of intersectoral collaboration for AIDS control and the mobilization of opinion leaders; (2) development of an efficient mechanism for the programme coordination and management at both national and state levels; (3) strengthening the technical and research capabilities of the programme; and (4) monitoring, making reviews and an evaluation of the programme.

A large number of management and coordinating bodies have been constituted at the national and state levels, details of which can be seen from figures 5.1 and 5.2 respectively.

Implications

The relevant management needs spelt out in the programme management component of the strategic plan are most essential and a welcome step towards the management of HIV/ AIDS related activities in the country. The establishment of an effective mechanism for inter-sectional collaboration is an excellent bureaucratic idea stemming from the already existing practice prevalent in the democratic system of government in the country.

It is alleged that the result of the system is delay in action and delay in agreement which leads to compromise on issues ultimately leading to focussing on a "common minimum programme" wherein no individual department or ministry owns responsibility. The experience of those five years (1992-97) is right before us. Several ministries and departments were approached for collaboration. For implementation of a particular programme, one has to run from pillar to post to get things moving. No single department or ministry was willing to own responsibility and was passing the buck among themselves. As a result not even one-fourth of the credit made available by the World Bank was utilized during the first four years. [17]

It is alleged that there was delay in planning, organising and implementing most of the programmes by NACO. With a weak management mechanism at the top which lacked will, the responsibility of strengthening the technical and research capabilities, enhancing programme managerial capability, efficient flow of funds, proper monitoring and timely evaluation became a Herculean task. It is unfortunate that towards the end of the strategic plan period (92-97) almost all-responsible officers right from the top have been replaced. In fact the National AIDS Committee which is the forum to bring together various ministries, NGOs and private voluntary organizations has been dissolved and is being reconstituted.[18] This has helped everyone to walk away quietly owning no responsibility and accountability. In short, we may say that the programme management component was a waste of time, energy and money.

Inter-sectional Collaboration

A number of activities has been undertaken to ensure intersectoral collaboration for AIDS Control and prevention programme in association with departments and ministries within the government of India, bilateral agencies, NGOs and corporate sectors.

Collaboration within the Government of India is mainly by seeking the involvement of National Service Scheme (NSS), National Council of Educational Research and Training (NCERT), Ministry of Information & Broadcasting, other Ministries and departments having related activities of HIV/AIDS/STD prevention and control and the Indian Council of Medical Research (ICMR).

The bilateral agencies involved include UNISEX, UNDO, UNDCP, UNSEEN, UNAIDS, and bilateral donor agencies such as the Swedish International Development Authority (SIDA), the US Agency for International Development (USAID), the Norwegian Agency for Development (NORAD), the Overseas Development Administration (ODA) and the European Community (EC).

Apart from the governmental and bilateral agencies, a large number of International NGOs like Ford Foundation, Oxfam and Population Services International and national NGOs like Christian Medical Association of India, Voluntary Health Association of India, etc., are also involved in programme financing and implementation of HIV/AIDS prevention and control programmes. A couple of corporate sector organizations like Confederation of Indian Industry (CII), the Bengal Chamber of Commerce and Industry and the Tata Iron and Steel Corporation is also involved in the fight against HIV/AIDS in the country.

Implications

Inter-sectoral collaboration is an important aspect in implementing any result-oriented programmes particularly in the field of prevention and control of AIDS and for the development of vaccine/cure and rehabilitation of the AIDS patients. In fact NACO has done a wonderful job in seeking collaboration of a large number of agencies within the ministries, departments, national and international bodies.

However, many important issues were either left unnoticed or purposely avoided for reasons known only to NACO and if there is a controlling agent above it. In practice, the heads of the department/ministry or other agencies represent all the decision making meetings and conventions. Normally such persons find hardly any time to attend meetings. It is alleged that they come for meetings more often than not, unprepared. In fact most of the meetings end up by constituting committees and sub-committees and delegating powers and responsibilities. In effect, it only causes delay, wastage of time, energy and money.

Normally the bureaucrats and officers from the departments/ ministries find hardly any time even to learn about the what, why and how of the problem of AIDS. The presence of representatives from World bodies, particularly UN organizations is taken as a prestige issue with content and satisfaction. It is alleged that very often these representatives have no choice but to agree to the pressures of the government representatives.

National and international donor agencies, NGOs and private voluntary organisations take pride in associating with a government venture for various reasons, such as building up a useful rapport. It helps them get huge government funding to suit their purposes and find a protective shield against all sorts of harassment from auditors, income tax authorities, police etc. In the process it has been found that several bureaucrats, Members of Parliament and state assemblies run their own parallel NGOs to which hundreds of thousands of rupees are diverted.

As a result one can see a mushrooming of NGOs for AIDS related activities, duplication of work by bilateral agencies and lack of purposeful implementation of projects. Let us quote a couple of examples here :(i) Bilateral agencies were denied permission to finance NGOs directly; (ii) several modules produced in collaboration with international agencies are of poor quality in terms of content, accuracy and presentation: AIDS education in Schools: a training package; an orientation to HIV/AIDS counselling, AIDS education for student youth; a training manual etc. are some of them; (iii) a lot of delay is caused in granting permission to agencies in the execution of their projects, etc.

One point which is guaranteed in inter-sectoral collaboration is an attractive reporting which run into pages, about the involvement of several agencies whereas the results themselves are insignificant in comparison with the achievements made in several developing countries.

3. HIV/AIDS Surveillance.

In 1935, the Indian Council of Medical Research (ICMR) started screening blood samples from some high-risk behaviour groups to determine if HIV was present in India. In 1986, the Christian

Medical College (CMC), Velour, detected an HIV seropositive sample taken from a commercial sex worker in Madras. HIV surveillance entered its second phase in May 1986 when its objective was re-defined as identifying the geographical spread of HIV infection and determining the major mode of HIV transmission. The second phase indicated that HIV infections had reached almost all parts of the country and that heterosexual transmission was the major mode of HIV transmission in India. In November 1987 HIV surveillance entered the third phase and special groups such as blood donors were targeted. In October 1990, the overall responsibility of surveillance was taken over by the Directorate General for Health Services (DGHS) from ICMR. Until 1994, surveillance was based on data generated from 62 surveillance centres situated in different parts of the country. The main objective of the current surveillance system is to be able to monitor trends in specific high-risk groups, and also monitor trends in-groups considered to be low risk such as antenatal clinic attenders.

A sentinel surveillance system has subsequently been adopted, which follows a pre-defined scientific protocol. This includes strict sampling procedures in limited sites with specific population groups. Based on the existing information on HIV prevalence among various groups and on the existence of high-risk behaviours and socio-economic factors, STD clinic attenders, injecting drug users in Manipur, Maharashtra, Delhi and Nagaland and pregnant women from Maharashtra and Manipur are chosen. The trends of HIV infection will be monitored among these groups over a period of time. For surveillance purposes, serial testing with two (ELISA, Rapid, Simple) tests have been recommended without reference to Western Blot. In order to implement this programme, a training module on HIV sentinel surveillance was prepared and implemented for all the State Epidemiologist and State AIDS programme officers in 1993. NACO has also developed a report format for reporting the trends periodically to NACO.

A network of physicians responsible for AIDS case diagnosis and management has been set up to improve case management and reporting. The Christian Medical Association of India (CMAI) has been entrusted with the task of training physicians throughout the country. Up to the end of 1995, about 2200 doctors have been trained in the diagnosis and management of AIDS cases. Similar training programmes for private general practitioners and nurses are underway. NACO believes that the AIDS case referral and reporting system could supplement the HIV sentinel surveillance data in monitoring the epidemic and could contribute to the planning of hospital and community care for AIDS patients.

Implications

HIV/AIDS surveillance is one of the most important components of the strategic plan for the prevention and control of AIDS in the country. However, the way in which HIV surveillance started in India speak volumes about the attitude of the physicians, law makers, and people responsible for law and order situation in the country. Some groups believed to be involving in high risk activities were forced to undergo blood test and actions were taken against them if they were found to be HIV positive. The scenario has not changed much even though India too has entered the second decade of the rapid spread of AIDS in the country. AIDS patients are still turned out of the hospitals from metros, village communities eliminate the HIV infected, schools close their doors to the children of the infected, police continue to harass the HIV positive persons, employers refuse employment to the infected and so goes the story.

It is believed that those responsible for drafting the strategy had little knowledge about issues surrounding HIV/AIDS. Bilateral agencies seem to have failed in their efforts to convince the Indian bureaucrats and policy makers about the crucial issues for reasons best known to them. Those who had the privilege of going abroad for exposure visits, training etc. may have enjoyed the trip but were quite inept to carry with them healthy practices successfully followed in countries which have made substantial contribution for the prevention and control of AIDS. Unfortunately, the meaning of the very word "confidentiality" has been misinterpreted for the convenience of the people responsible for screening and reporting HIV cases.

It was to say the least, blunder for the Directorate General of Health Services to take over the responsibility of surveillance from ICMR. ICMR is an autonomous body and the government had very little control over its functions. Being an autonomous body it could have done a marvellous job sincerely and with a purpose. When the DGHS took over the responsibility and the NACO had the control over the system. It is alleged that there was no limitation to the extent of suppressing facts to suit the needs of the government. In the ultimate analysis one can find that the entire process was a calculated attempt to conceal actual facts. Rosy pictures are given about the HIV status only to divert the attention of the people. Some people argue that, if the government ventured for an appropriate intervention, it would cause a serious set back to its economic reforms. The result is that HIV is intruding into every nook and corner of the country and India now has the dubious distinction of being the AIDS capital.

It may be noted that the 62 surveillance centres situated in various parts of the country had the responsibility of only generating data regarding the prevalence of the disease. However, there is no mechanism to inform a patient (if found to be HIV positive) that he/she is HIV infected. Some of the ministers, physicians and state AIDS cell officials term it as "maintaining confidentiality". What a serious crime? The system has deliberately chosen to allow the infected to continue to spread the disease until one meets a dog's death.

There are wide variations in the estimates of HIV/AIDS cases provided by such agencies as WHO, NACO, IHO and others in the country. There is no accurate system of reporting or of calculating estimates. The strategy of counting heads obviously is no solution: one has to address the prevailing situation in the country.

The plan of action for adopting the sentinel surveillance system is yet another method to avoid extension of provisions to the masses and fixing responsibilities for the spread of HIV to selected groups. Because some initiatives are taken by certain agencies to project the actual situation existing in states like Maharashtra, Manipur and Tamil Nadu, a general understanding is given to the media and the public that these are the most vulnerable states in India. Certainly, the situation for example in Kerala where most of its population live outside the state (many in gulf countries) and that of Delhi is no better.

India still lack proper testing kits, trained personnel for the job and the much-needed counselling programme. Everyone everywhere speak of counselling while very few institutions provide training in counselling. When the country has miserably failed to appoint professionally trained social workers and counsellors in hospitals, what to talk of counselling for the HIV infected!

The most unfortunate fact of all is that training to physicians, nurses, counsellors, teachers, etc., are given by way of 2 to 5 days of attendance in a workshop or a seminar where more than half the time is wasted in inauguration, parties, valedictory function, forms to fill up for purposes not known to anyone and so on. How much of real business transactions can take place in which the participant receive adequate information and gain skill? In fact one can come across several resource persons who were not even sure of the routes of HIV transmission and many other relevant topics. Above all most of these so-called resource persons copy ideas from the West, which are usually not welcomed and accepted by the participants.

4. Sexually Transmitted Diseases

The control and prevention of sexually transmitted diseases is now recognized as one of the major strategies to control the spread of HIV infection and AIDS. There is growing evidence that the presence of a STD greatly facilitates both acquisition and transmission of HIV infection.

A centrally sponsored national STD programme has been in operation in India since 1946. Currently, STD prevention services are available at 5 regional STD reference centres; 372 STD clinics in Medical Colleges, and centres/units in district and taluka hospitals. The NACO document says that most patients seeking health care for STD are men while women with STD remain without treatment because of ignorance and stigmatization.

The Ministry of Health and Family Welfare has adopted a policy to integrate STD control into the existing health care system. A consultant (STD) has been employed by the NACO to assist the Additional Project-Director (Tech.) in all activities relating to STD control. A number of STD programme officers have been appointed in the state AIDS Cell as well. Efforts are also made for the prevention of STD and HIV through IEC activities. A generic set of educational material on STD for people with low literacy for use in health care facilities has been developed. A programme for the orientation and training of private health care providers in STD case management is being developed by the IMA in collaboration with the NACO. As on December 1995, three states namely Maharashtra, Tamil Nadu and Karnataka have already started to collect information on STD prevalence and incidence.

It may be noted that India has a high incidence of STD, with an estimated annual incidence rate of 5 per cent or 40 million new cases each year. Many people either fail to seek help or suffer from re-infection or persisting infection. This has important implications for any attempts to prevent the spread of HIV.

Implications

The decision to include sexually transmitted diseases as a component of the strategic plan for the prevention and control of HIV/AIDS is timely and most appropriate. However, it is painful to note that the Ministry of Health and Family Welfare has adopted a policy to integrate STD control into the existing health care system. When the country has an estimated annual incidence rate of 5 per cent, or 40 million new cases each year, the policy to integrate STD control into the existing health care system may not be adequate. This is below any standard of the country in comparison with its economic reforms. We should not perpetuate the already declining state of affairs of our health care system.

One cannot explain by any rational consideration why the ministry has adopted such a policy in spite of the recognition of the fact that the control of STDs is crucial for the prevention and control of AIDS. Further, there is already the centrally sponsored national STD programme, which is in operation since 1946. What is required today is to provide adequate input by way of expertise, finance and infrastructure facilities for the testing, treatment and care of the STD patients.

HIV being one of the STDs, one may wonder how the ministry could think of giving a step-motherly treatment to the programme for the prevention and control of STDs. If one has to achieve desired goals in the prevention and control of HIV/AIDS, it is essential that the prevention programme of STDs should go along with it. In fact, it is only causing duplication of services, wastage of time, energy and money.

Another aspect is that by and large, the Indian women with STDs remain without treatment because of ignorance and stigmatization. Having realised this fact, it is the duty of the state to make all out efforts to integrate the prevention strategies for STDs and HIV under one umbrella. It is high time that we recognised the seriousness of the existing situation in which STDs and HIV transmission have close association. Further, the estimates of both STDs (which is already an uncontrollable number) and HIV are only a fraction of the actual number as we do not have a well defined operational system for diagnosing and reporting.

It may be noted that the STD control programme currently reaches about 5 to 10 per cent of the STD patients in the country. In a number of states STD programme officers are still not appointed. There are no social workers or counsellors available in STD clinics. Most STD clinics are poorly equipped. Effective STD drugs are unavailable in PHCs. Funds for drugs and consumable items are not being utilized by some states because of delay in release of funds by state finance departments.[19]

5. Condom Programming

In recognition of the fact that some people have multiple sex partners, and engage in sexual behaviour which put them at risk of acquiring STDs (as evidenced by high STD rates in the country) the government of India strongly supports the promotion of good quality, low cost condoms for the prevention of STD and HIV infection. According to the NACO, condom market in India is currently relatively small, catering mostly to contraceptive needs of users, and covers only 5 per cent of eligible couples.

Two issues to be overcome in the promotion of condoms for disease prevention are (i) the negative quality and image perceptions of Nirodh (a brand of condom) and (ii) the almost exclusive association of condoms with family planning/spacing.

One of the main strategies outlined in the strategic plan for the prevention and control of AIDS in India is to provide technical assistance to companies to manufacture condoms in conformity with the international specifications laid down by the WHO and improve the quality assurance system. Schedule "R" of the Drugs and Cosmetics Act, which stipulates minimum quality standards for condoms manufactured in India has been reviewed. A revised version of Schedule "R" which will bring condom specifications within the quality parameters as described by WHO has been notified in the "Gazette of India - Extraordinary" dated June 9, 1995. The manufacturers have agreed to meet the new specifications for all future orders by the Department of Family Welfare. The dry, unlubricated Nirodh condom is being phased out.

Social marketing of condoms will be an important strategy to increase the acceptability of and access to condoms. The free distribution of condoms, although important as a means of introducing first time users to the product is not recommended on a large scale. Preference should therefore be given to social marketing of condoms, where the user pays a subsidised price for the product.

Implications

Although condom programming is just one of the nine components of the strategic plans, much publicity has been given in India for condom use. In fact it has gone to the extent of giving an idea to the general masses that HIV is transmitted only via **sexual intercourse**. This emphasis can be seen practically in all AIDS campaign leaflets, spots, manuals, etc., being brought out by the NACO and other agencies within the country. The effort to create awareness about HIV transmission through other routes is almost insignificant in comparison with the attention paid to condom programming. In spite of all this publicity, condom programming has not yielded the required results.

The strategic plan has recognised the fact that the condom freely distributed (Nirodh) through the health delivery system is of poor quality. It is alleged that five years of effort by the NACO has not brought about any change. It only shows lack of political will and there is no accountability sought for from responsible authorities. In fact there was a lot of media report about the massive condom free distribution programme and the beneficiaries were the "balloon industries" who used to collect the condoms in large quantities through quacks, beggars, vendors, etc., in return for small monetary gains. Whereas NGOs working among sex workers even from Delhi complain of short supply of condoms for free distribution.

Another issue sought to be overcome through the condom programme strategy is the exclusive association of condoms with family planning. A close look at most of the publications (if not all) brought out for AIDS awareness programme by the ministry and various other agencies in the country, one cannot come across any reference to this issue in the literature nor in any of the multimedia packages. This lackadaisical approach only shows the limited extent of knowledge on the subject, lack of interest on the part of functionaries, and the lack of seriousness of purpose and guidance. It only gives an impression that certain programme activities are listed and given publicity to satisfy the authorities without looking into the results. More often than not, these ideas are just copied from some other countries while no effort was made to look into the strategies adopted by them.

One of the major drawbacks in the intervention with school children and adolescents is the resistance from parents and teachers who are yet to be given appropriate messages. The on-going publicity campaign with the caption "use condoms to have sex" borrowed from abroad only aims at spreading a new culture of "sexual freedom" in this otherwise taboo-ridden and traditional society, still upholding and nurturing religious values. In short, no proper planning was done while adopting and implementing a strategy like the one aforementioned.

Government cannot escape with excuses that they lack money and technology. Huge amounts earmarked for the purpose are not sanctioned and disbursed to the agencies/state governments concerned on time. Reports show that amounts for a particular year is sanctioned towards the end of a financial year and by the time one receives the amount, the financial year comes to an end. How can any programme be successful with so many bureaucratic hurdles on the way? The ultimate result is complete failure of the system. It is alleged that in order to avoid responsibility and accountability, every now and then officials are transferred. This means a new team with little knowledge of the field to score the next innings is pressed into action. Ironically, it brings to India 'victory' in terms of providing the highest number of HIV/AIDS cases in the world.

6. Targeted Interventions

The objective of the targeted interventions is to reduce HIV transmission among population groups at increased risk of HIV infection through health promotion and education and the provision of appropriate facilities and services. In order to identify the distribution and location of high-risk groups, surveys have been undertaken in many parts of the country.

Based on an initial assessment by a WHO consultant in early 1992, the Municipal Corporation of Greater Bombay set up a targeted intervention for sex workers in Kamathipura and Khetwadi, the major brothel areas of Bombay. The intervention includes outreach activities, condom promotion and provision of STD control services. Initially funded by WHO, the project is now supported by, The Swedish International Development Agency (SIDA).

In May-June 1992 an STD/HIV community based random sample STD survey was conducted in the Sonagachi area of Calcutta; the first such study in India. Building on this survey, an intervention project was designed with three components; clinical services provision for the diagnosis and treatment of STDs; IEC for behavioural change and promotion of condoms. Initially, the project was technically and financially supported by the WHO followed by the support from the NORAD. Currently the Overseas Development Administration (ODA) United Kingdom, is providing support as part of a broader Sexual Health Project in the state of West Bengal.

An assessment of sex workers outside brothels in Chennai (Madras) was initiated in 1992. The assessment revealed that out of the total of about 3000 sex workers, about 400 were based in 70 to 100 small brothels distributed over the whole city. WHO provided financial and technical support to the research and intervention.

Following a situation assessment, an intervention programme among men who have sex with men (MSM) was initiated in Madras on 15th March 1994 by the Community Action Network with financial assistance from the NACO. The inaugural meeting was attended by over 600 members of MSM circuits and over 100 'Ali' (eunuchs) community members.

Agencies such as NACO, SIDA, OXFAM, SHARAN, ICMR and WHO are involved in conducting outreach interventions with injecting drug users in the northeast.

The Indian Institute of Health Management Research (IIHMR) Jaipur, in collaboration with the NACO has been planning an intervention programme among the truck drivers aimed at prevention of STD/HIV transmission.

Implications

As far as programme implementation is concerned, targeted interventions assume greater importance. The strategic plan has definite objectives to be fulfilled. Surveys have been undertaken to identify distribution and location of high-risk groups. However, the results are not encouraging. The report speaks of only a couple of surveys conducted which were limited to a couple of metros and parts of northeast. The target group comprised sex workers, and injecting drug users, and one meeting with men who have sex with men was held in Madras.

It is alleged that there was no proper planning. Based on the trends seen in some of the countries abroad, certain high-risk groups were purposely selected for surveys and intervention. There was no question of identifying a group as "high-risk group" when the planners themselves decided the status of certain groups. There is no evidence of having applied any parameter for identifying high-risk groups. Things were done on the mere basis of certain assumptions. Individuals or groups who had access to the financing agencies had the privilege of conducting the surveys.

In the process, many high-risk groups and locations were left out. Even the various routes of HIV transmission was not given importance. Further, it is unfortunate that the system could hardly come out with anything substantial during the period 1992-97. There is no accountability and no machinery to fix responsibilities.

There is sufficient information about various target groups. The Assam government has shown the lead by identifying barbers as a target group for creating awareness about HIV/AIDS, although the likelihood of a barber's razor transmitting HIV is about 0.01 per cent.[20] The state government has already covered 800 barbers in their first intervention programme.

Enough information about other target groups are available in some of the books published from within India by academics interested on the subject. These groups comprise sex workers including call girls, clients of sex workers, devadasis, eunuchs, street children, clients at STD clinics, truck drivers, certain tribal communities, professional blood donors, organ donors, sperm donors, milk donors, institutionalised persons including prisoners, beggars, women in nari-niketan (destitute homes) special school for girls, homosexuals, lesbians, persons in armed forces, substance abusers, thalassemic patients, people using skin piercing instruments etc. The list could be much longer. How could a system sleep over for five years while it is fully aware of the impending disaster HIV is likely to bring about in the country?

7. Components of Blood Safety Programme

Based on the National Policy framework on Blood Transfusion Services, a strategic plan for prevention and control of HIV and AIDS through transfusion of blood and blood products in India has been developed. In 1989 the Ministry of Health and Family Welfare engaged the services of Ms. A.F. Ferguson & Co. to study the status of blood bank programme in the country.

According to their report there are a total of 1018 blood banks in the country handling 19.5 lakh units of blood annually. It has found that in the blood transfusion services, infrastructure was highly de-centralised, and lacked many critical resources namely, personnel, facilities, equipment, supplies and financial resources. There was an overall shortage of blood particularly blood from voluntary donors. Further, the testing facilities were limited and erratic.

In all, 154 zonal blood testing centres (ZBTCs) have been established all over the country to provide HIV testing facilities. These ZBTCs have established linkages with blood banks operating in the voluntary and private sectors. The ZBTCs receive samples of blood from several blood banks linked with them and after testing the samples for HIV, the results are communicated on the same day for further action. The NACO has launched a central scheme of assistance to states to upgrade blood bank services by providing minimum facilities to all blood banks in the public sector. The NACO has set up a sub-committee on quality control of blood and blood products. A computerised format has been designed for sending monthly blood screening reports from ZBTCs and district level blood banks.

The Government has formulated a short term and long term strategy for training and workforce development under the blood safety programme. Under the short term strategy, 10 training institutions in different regions of the country which are imparting short term courses have been augmented. Training modules are being prepared.

As a long-term strategy, the Medical Council of India has proposed to start post-graduate degree courses in blood transfusion services, which would pave the way for better career prospects in this field.

The specification for blood banks are given under schedule "F" (part XII-B) of the Drug and Cosmetic Rules. The rules have been amended to provide mandatory testing of every unit of blood for Hepatitis, AIDS and other blood transmissible diseases. The licensing of blood banks has been brought under the dual authority of state and central government. According to the Drug Controller's office, three quarters of the blood banks in the country have been inspected and licensed.

The total quantity of blood generated in the country is less than 50 per cent of our estimated requirement. Of this total approximately 29 per cent comes from professional donors. The ICE component of the NACO provides inputs for motivating voluntary donors by involving mass media, government institutions and NGOs.

Implications

The study conducted by Ms. A.F. Ferguson & Co. has provided lot of information about the blood banking system in the country. The scene was pathetic: the blood banks to be modernized have not received their equipment's so far; the staff provided for, under the blood safety component have not been appointed by most of the states/UTs; and the supply of test kits is erratic and inadequate. The utilization of the grant released to the states under blood safety programme has been only to the tune of 15 to 20 per cent.[21]

A number of blood banks are not licensed. According to the Ferguson report there are 1018 blood banks while Dr. Sardana, Joint Director (Blood /Safety) NACO puts the figure at 1401.[22] The 1996 NACO update put the figure at 1475. Some other reports show that blood banking has become an industry and there is mushrooming of blood banks in various states particularly in private sector. All the efforts so far have been to concentrate on the 1018 blood banks. There is no explanation as to why the system could not inspect and provide license to them. There are several reported cases in which even the blood supplied by the Red Cross Society with the label 'HIV FREE' were found to be contaminated. If this is so, what to speak of local blood banks operating all over the country, which follow no safety measures!

However, the establishment of 154 zonal blood-testing centres across the country is a welcome initiative. The purpose will be served only if trained personnel, good quality testing kits, and necessary equipment's are supplied in time.

While motivating people for voluntary blood donation is very important and necessary, deviation from the primary objective of providing safety measures for blood transfusion is not encouraging. The system should gear up to address issues, which are crucial to HIV transmission through blood and blood products. Not a word has been spoken about the use of disposables, needle destroyers, sterilization, etc.

It should be an eye opener to the system to learn lessons from some of the efforts made by certain political parties in the country. For example, the youth wing of the Kerala Congress (Mani group) has been holding seminars across the state to sensitise people on blood safety measures and they are also supplying free needle destroyers to various hospitals situated in each district. The media also has come forward to publicise the efforts.

8. Information, Education and Communication (IEC)

Efforts have been underway in many parts of the country to educate populations on AIDS, its transmission and prevention. The overall strategies and activities of the IEC component are aimed at redressing the existing situation in order to make the general population, especially men and women of various ages, youth, children and specific vulnerable groups become aware of this issue.

The objectives spelt out in the strategy are: (i) to raise awareness, knowledge and understanding among general population about AIDS, HIV infection and STDs, routes of transmission and methods of prevention; (ii) to promote desirable practices such as condom use, the sterilization of needles and syringes, and voluntary donation of blood; (iii) to mobilize all sectors of society to integrate AIDS messages and programming into existing activities; and (iv) to ensure that all relevant health workers are trained in AIDS communications and coping with strategies and thereby strengthen technical and managerial capabilities.

The strategic plan for AIDS prevention and control in India gives prime importance to IEC and social mobilization strategies to combat the spread of HIV. These include advocacy, intersectional collaboration, mass media, involvement of NGOs, training and research.

It is necessary to convince numerous policy makers and opinion leaders about the seriousness of the AIDS epidemic and of the need for securing the human rights of those afflicted. As part of advocacy, NACO has been seeking cooperation from various groups such as industrial sectors and chambers of commerce, opinion leaders at the grassroots level, railway board, prominent medical and sports persons, communication institutions, media institutions and personnel.

Inter-sectoral collaboration seeks to tap the networks available within the government sector by involving related ministries/ departments such as Department of Family Welfare, Ministry of human resources development, Ministry of labour, Ministry of welfare, Ministry of railways, Ministry of tourism, and Ministry of information and broadcasting.

Some of the specific initiatives involving intersectoral collaboration include: Universities talk AIDS by the department of youth Affairs and sports through the NSS, out reach projects like multimedia workshops, reaching out to rural youth through the Nehru Yuvak Kendras spread across the country, Vishwa Yuvak Kendras training programme for NGOs in urban centres and AIDS education in schools.

Under the mass media campaigns, the Directorate of audiovisual Publicity produced about 20 audio/video spots and juggles. A 30-episode radio programme in a creative listener-participatory mode titled "Haseen Lamhe" in Hindi and 10 other languages were broadcast in collaboration with the Department of Family Welfare. Some IEC print materials were prepared for injecting drug users in the North-East, and health education package for commercial sex industry. More materials on blood donation, package for truck drivers, etc., are under preparation.

Involvement of NGOs is an important component of the programme. Funds allocation to 16 states for direct NGO support are in the process. A pilot project to develop a model for the care of HIV infected individuals and people with AIDS has been developed in collaboration with NGOs and WHO in Manipur.

As far as training component is concerned training modules are being produced for IEC and AIDS. A youth training module and a module for nurses have been finalised.

In the area of research, efforts are made to know more about the attitudes and perceptions of Indians towards sexuality, condom uses, and basic knowledge of STDs and AIDS. In all 65 cities with a population of 5 lakhs and above situated in 30 states and UTs were selected to conduct the study. The target groups identified are commercial sex workers, male homosexuals, injecting drug users, transsexuals, frequently travelling men (truck drivers) and slum population. The study is yet to be completed.

Implications

Much has been written and spoken about the IEC component of the strategic plan for HIV prevention and control. In fact IEC has been the torchbearer for creating awareness among all populations across the globe. The Indian bureaucracy has also accorded great importance to IEC component in the AIDS programme, The objectives spelt out in the strategic plan for IEC component are appropriate.

However, the experience of the past five years (1992-97) have shown that IEC has failed to meet the objectives spelt out. It is alleged that no substantial effort was made to raise awareness, knowledge and understanding among general population. When many of the medical and para-medical personnel in the country are ignorant about the basic facts regarding HIV/AIDS, what to talk of the general population! Regarding the promotion of desirable practices, the NACO reports that hardly 5 per cent of the eligible couples use condoms for contraceptive needs. Further it also confirms the quality of the stuff. If the system is not concerned about the issues, mere formulation of strategies has no meaning. As regards sterilization of needles and syringes even the government owned hospitals in the country's capital do not adhere to the guidelines and norms issued by the DGHS. Voluntary blood donation is a good practice, which needs to be encouraged. However, being an act of charity, and of status and prestige, some efforts are being made particularly through educational institutions and by involving elected representatives, sports personalities, etc.

AIDS education is yet to be integrated into the on-going activities of varying nature like teaching, research extension, work place, etc. The technical and managerial capabilities are still left unattended. Much needs to be done to train the health workers. Confining only to seminars and workshops of 5 to 10 hours cannot provide adequate training. It can in fact cause adverse results. For example everyone cannot become an HIV counsellor. Only certain individuals who have a bend of mind for the job with adequate information, training, skill and aptitude can plunge into such areas. Whom to blame if the WHO's Regional Office for South-East Asia brings out a guide for trainers entitled "An Orientation to HIV/AIDS Counselling" in which the note for the user reads: "This guide has been designed to help almost anybody become a counsellor"! [23]

The above mentioned text is only an example. It is alleged

that people who have no expertise in the area are called upon to prepare such documents which instead of serving the purpose become harmful to the society which has numerous quacks in various fields, and counselling is not an exception to this rule.

NGOs have been encouraged to involve in the IEC projects. But they are not provided adequate exposure, training and the much-needed finance. It is alleged that when the system ignores the middlemen who consume 20 to 40 per cent of the sanctioned amount what can one expect in terms of quality. Inter-sectoral collaboration has become a catchword and it certainly causes delay in processing any proposal.

The multi-media infrastructure in the country is not adequately made use of for the purpose. Some people believe that for one or the other reason, the system is afraid of involving committed, sincere and efficient persons. In fact they are considered a threat to the whole system. Their involvement would mean transparency, accountability and a host of other requirements.

There is also allegation that hardly any result oriented research has been undertaken in any field. Many projects are being discarded half way through. There are reports about the preparation of modules. Some have been completed. Hardly any difference can be seen if one compares the same with a couple of other existing literature especially those already in circulation from international bodies. In short, the whole exercise ends up in cutting and pasting and literally copying from available sources.

9. Reduction of Impact

As the epidemic spreads, it is essential to be prepared to reduce its overwhelming impact on individuals, families and communities. This is sought to be accomplished by planning, training counsellors, setting up community based care structures and improved access to health care facilities for those afflicted.

The objectives of reduction of impact component of the strategic plan are:

1. To provide appropriate counselling services where needed to reduce social and psychological impact of the AIDS epidemic and for prevention of the spread of HIV infection.

2. To ensure that the health care workers are adequately trained to provide good quality care to patients with HIV and AIDS, and that such care is not jeopardized by misconceptions and undue fear.
3. To ensure support for community based care programmes and ensure easy access to good quality services for those in need of services.
4. To ensure that all affected by AIDS receive proper care and treatment inside and outside the clinical setting with respect for each individual's rights and dignity.

In order to achieve the above-mentioned objectives, the NACO has prepared an Indian counselling training module. An apex centre has been identified and will train three core trainers from all the identified institutions. In order to cover all states, five regional training centres have been identified. Each centre will conduct four programmes with 20 participants and would train 480 trainers at the intermediate level from different states. These trainers would then train those at grassroots level.

As part of health care services, NACO has trained 600 professors, assistant professors/lecturers on the clinical management and diagnosis of HIV/AIDS and basic counselling from different medical colleges in the country. The IMA has undertaken the training of core 'trainers of trainers' and private general practitioners. Some nurses have been trained in four orientation training programmes organised by the NACO in Delhi, Calcutta, Bombay and Chennai.

For the community based care, a pilot programme on care and support has been completed in collaboration with NACO, OXFAM, WHO and the Government of Manipur. This has led to the development of generic guidelines for community care. Further pilot programmes are being developed in Maharashtra and Tamil Nadu.

Implications

The four main objectives mentioned above sounds excellent. However, to date nothing has been done in order to achieve any of those objectives. In order to provide appropriate counselling services, the system has neither expertise nor infrastructure. It is an enormous task requiring inputs in terms of money and personnel. The family welfare programme is a crowning example in which provision for counselling was present.[24] However, it remained only in paper and no one ever thought of its necessity. Because HIV/AIDS prevention and control programme has its origin in the developed countries like USA and Europe where counselling services are a full-fledged profession, the concept also was copied by the Indian planners knowingly or unknowingly. It is alleged that having caught the tiger by the tail, the system is struggling to manage the show without adequate knowledge and expertise in the field.

Similarly, the second objective, namely, "to ensure that the health care workers are adequately trained to provide good quality care to patients with AIDS and that such care is not jeopardized by misconceptions and undue fear." Inspite of the efforts of five years (1992-97) most of the health care providers including physicians from the best of hospitals from the metros refuse to handle HIV cases. In fact there are instances when a doctor with post-graduate degree refused to accept sponsorship to undergo diploma programme on HIV/AIDS/STDs being offered by a foreign university.

There is a fear that given the present state of affairs in the system, it may take years and probably decades before the country can afford to have adequately trained health care workers. Similarly removing misconceptions and undue fear from the masses and health care providers will require a lot of effort on the part of the Government.

The concept of community based support and proper care of HIV/AIDS patients is yet another item brought in from the Western world. The Indian medical system has yet to recognize the need of involving medical social workers in the health care system before talking about community based care and support. Unfortunately there is no political will and the physicians too are not taught about the role of medical social workers.

The NACO has prepared an "Indian counselling training module" It has made an interesting reading. As mentioned earlier, the quality of the text needs to be examined by an independent team of experts. Similarly the plan for training core trainers through regional training centres and subsequently to train those at grassroots level in counselling services are mere imaginations. It is alleged that the system has once again failed to understand the society, the seriousness and extent of the problem and the religious, traditional and cultural backgrounds of our people. Some activists have alleged that it is easy to sit in an air-conditioned room and plan for a people toiling in heat, rain and snow clad mountains across the country.

What the country requires today is a strategy prepared for planning, organising, implementing and evaluating HIV/AIDS prevention and control programme. Keeping in mind the variety of people we have in the country, the kind of health delivery system available as well as the administrative hurdles, we shall discuss more about a viable plan of action in the following chapter.

SUMMARY

The government of India had formulated the National Strategic Plan 1992-1997 for the prevention and control of HIV in the country. The life of this plan has come to an end on 31 March 1997. An attempt was made to critically analyse this National Strategic Plan in this chapter. There are about nine components in this plan. They are: programme management; inter-sectoral collaboration; HIV surveillance; STD's; condom programming; targeted interventions; blood safety; IEC and reduction of impact. Each of these components have been described along with its implications which has paved way for evolving a set of action plan which are being dealt with in the following chapter.

REFERENCES

1. UNAIDS, The HIV/AIDS situation in Mid 1996 - Global and Regional Highlights, 'UNAIDS Fact Sheet, July 1, 1996.
2. Andre Picard "Women Unseen Victims of AIDS - poverty, illiteracy and discrimination combine to spread disease among females" The Globe and mail, July 11, 1996.
3. UNAIDS, op. cit.
4. *Ibid.*
5. *Ibid.*

6. The AIDS control and prevention (AIDS CAP) project of Family Health International. The Francois - Xavier Bagnound Center for Health and Human Rights of the Harvard School of Public Health and the Joint United Nations programme on HIV/AIDS, 1996. Final Report of the Status and Trends of the Global HIV/AIDS Pandemic July 5-6, 1996.
7. UNAIDS,op. cit
8. Sameera Khan, interview with Dr. Subhash Hira of Mumbai - based AIDS Research & Control Center (ARCON), "Three epidemics and a doctor" TOI 13, July 1997.
9. Eric Sawyer, Global Access to Health Care, Integration, Japanese Organisation for International Cooperation in Family Planning, Tokyo, winter 1996.
10. The AIDS Control and Prevention (AIDSCAP) project, op. cit
11. UNAIDS op.cit.
12. Thailand: Success in HIV prevention, Integration winter 1996, p.11
13. *Ibid.*
14. National AIDS control programme, India: Country Scenario update, NACO, New Delhi 1995.
15. NACO, AIDS newsletter, December 1995.
16. National AIDS control programme India, op.cit. The details of the strategic plan 1992-97 presented in this chapter is based on this NACO publication. NACO is the apex body of the Ministry of Health & Family Welfare, Govt. of India for planning, organising and implementing AIDS control & prevention programmes in the country.
17. NACO, AIDS newsletter op.cit.
18. NACP, 1995 op. cit. p. 23.
19. P.N. Sehgal, Towards effective policies and strategies for control of HIV/AIDS. Health for the Millions, VHAI, New Delhi, Nov-Dec. 1996.
20. Bulbul pal, Close Shave, TOI, New Delhi, 3 August 1997.
21. P.N. Sehgal, op. cit.
22. V.N. Sardana, Blood Banking in India, Health for the Millions, VHAI, New Delhi. Nov-Dec 1996.
23. WHO, An orientation to HIV/AIDS counselling: A Guide for trainers, World Health Organisation, Regional Office for South East Asia, New Delhi, 1994.
24. NACO, AIDS education in schools: A training package, NACO-NCERT, New Delhi, 1994, p. 19.

6

Strategies for Prevention and Control of HIV

As a result of the clinical researches based on the understanding of the dynamics of HIV, physicians especially from the West are beginning to voice some optimism on the research for an effective treatment for the AIDS disease. In the meantime, some of the Ayurvedic physicians particularly from South India claim similar breakthrough in their effort to fight the virus. However, the fight to control HIV/AIDS is an ever-widening battle while the challenge of living with HIV has become a harsh reality for the infected individual his/her family, friends, community and the state.

Medical breakthroughs were reported in the Eleventh International Conference on AIDS in Vancouver that often-reduced virus levels in the blood stream to the below detectable levels by the assay used to measure it. One of the most significant developments of course, has been the advent of the protease inhibitor era which has brought with it the demonstration of the ability to suppress viral replication to levels not previously seen said Dr. Scott M. Hammer in the plenary lecture of the conference. Presentations of data on cocktails of drugs that are producing improved survival times and rising levels of immune cells began to offer the first big hope that HIV/AIDS, which was considered a fatal, incurable disease, might become one of the chronic manageable diseases.[1]

For most people now living with HIV in India there is no hope of receiving any treatment let alone dream of a cure even if effective therapies against HIV/AIDS are developed. The fight against HIV/AIDS is going to be long drawn especially for people living with HIV in developing countries. The much advertised combination therapy involving two to four drugs are said to cost around $ 13,000 per year per person. This is simply beyond the reach of most people living with HIV. As reported in the previous chapter, at ARCON, Mumbai, the treatment per person costs Rs. 20,000 a month, which not even one per cent of the infected in India can afford.

Past experience show that scores of people in India die of diseases which are preventable and which have treatments available. But the health delivery system in the country is such that timely prevention and treatment are not given priority. The policy of the government is to wait for a disaster to occur before initiating any action. Dr. Michael Rekart was right when he said that three million people still die of tuberculosis a year though we have had a cure for tuberculosis for 45 years.[2] The estimates discussed in the previous chapter such as: that India already has over 1.5 million HIV infected; by the turn of the century about 5 to 8 million will be infected; as we step into the 21st century we will have over 1 million AIDS cases; over 8500 new cases are being added every day; about half of the infected would be women; about 1400 children are born with HIV infection daily and that India already has more infected people than any other country in the world; have not made any impact on the policy makers. As usual, our government will wait and watch for a situation when hundreds will die of AIDS on the roads before we initiate a plan and implement HIV care and support services.

ISSUES AND PROBLEMS

Millions of rupees have gone into the AIDS control and prevention programmes in the country provided by bilateral agencies during the last one decade. How much of it was put to productive use is not certain. What has been the success rate? Certainly some issues are still very clear which need to be addressed on a priority basis. Hardly any change has been brought about regarding the myths and misconceptions associated with HIV/AIDS/STDs. The health care system for the poor remains where it was a decade ago. Social stigma on those infected with HIV continue to dominate not only in the rural areas but also among the urban dwellers. HIV has crossed all borders of religion, sex, age, economic levels etc. Community care and support services are almost nil. Not one counsellor for HIV has been appointed till today. Hospitals have no room for the AIDS patients. Trained personnel, proper equipments and reliable testing kits are not available. The strategic plan 1992-97 mostly remained only on paper. A new regime for programme management has been constituted. It is alleged that during the ninth plan period (next five years) perhaps those new recruits will spend time trying to understand the disease, its magnitude and fish in the troubled waters.

An attempt has been made in this chapter to re-define the strategies already discussed in the previous chapter and evolve a viable plan of action based on the past experiences not only of India but also of developed and developing countries across the globe. Certain things are clear:

1. NACO needs to be made an autonomous body free from bureaucratic nexus.
2. Financial viability and a system to monitor smooth and timely financial advancement to all projects at all levels needs to be evolved.
3. Inter-sectoral collaboration and its strategies have to be re-defined.
4. Improvements are needed in the collection and analysis of surveillance data.
5. Massive training for HIV counsellors needs to be given top priority by involving non-medical institution spread across the country.
6. Strategies for the prevention and control of STDs need to be redefined to link it with HIV/AIDS prevention and control programme.
7. Relevance of condom programme requires close examination.
8. Targeted interventions require re-thinking and should now focus on women, young adults, adolescents and marginalised communities instead of victimising certain sections of the society.
9. Blood safety programme requires immediate attention and revamping.
10. Role of IEC to be clearly spelt out.
11. Strategy for the reduction of impact to be given top priority in the coming years.

12. Adequate position and guidance for community care and support initiatives through local bodies needs to be given utmost importance.
13. Research and evaluation should be made an on-going process attaching accountability and responsibility.

In the following pages, let us try to redefine each of these strategies with the aim of evolving a plan of action which may go a long way in the prevention and control of HIV/AIDS/STDs in the country.

1. Programme Management

Establishment of an effective programme management mechanism at national and state levels is the need of the hour. The establishment of NACO as an extended wing of the Ministry of Health & Family Welfare, Government of India was a welcome initiative. However, past experience especially the outcome of the strategic plan 1992-97 show that perhaps NACO was helpless to deliver the goods. There seems to be time only for creation of various bodies, committees and subcommittees which instead of providing functional viability, created more hurdles as far as programme planning, organisation, implementation and evaluation were concerned.

NACO was supposed to be providing technical, financial and operational support to the staff and organizations implementing programme activities. However, NACO seems to have miserably failed to fulfill this objective although it had access to technical knowledge and finance. As mentioned in the previous chapter, the World Bank had given a soft loan of US dollars 84 million of which NACO could disburse not even half of it to the state AIDS cells. Therefore money was not a constraint. During the period 1992-97 there were at least two occasions, when NACO had to relieve the services of the so-called National Consultants who were supposed to be providing technical support. It is alleged that the recruitment system seems to have been highly influenced by political interference rather than quality and excellence. By the end of the strategic plan, the Additional Secretary and Project Director of NACO was shifted to another ministry, the Additional Project Director (IEC) was shifted to another department, the National AIDS committee which was the highest level advisory body to oversee the performance of the programme was dissolved, several national consultants were removed and so on, goes the story. It may be noted that even several officials involved as representatives of bilateral agencies to NACO including WHO, UNAIDS, UNICEF etc. were either shifted from their departments or have left the country. The culmination of the episode was shifting the NACO office from the 1 Red Cross Road (Red Cross Society Building) back to Nirman Bhawan, where the Health Ministry of the Union Government is housed.

Suggestions

i The impending disaster that HIV/AIDS is likely to bring about in India - loss of human lives; draining the national economy, paralysing the existing health care system, drastic reduction of work force from among professional; etc - require setting up of a separate HIV/AIDS Ministerial portfolio both at the centre and in the states.

ii The National AIDS control organisation should be freed from the bureaucratic and political control by making it an AUTONOMOUS BODY through an act of Parliament.

iii The NACO should be headed (Chairman/Director) by an eminent physician who has adequate knowledge on the subject as well as one who has contributed substantially to HIV/AIDS prevention and control programme in the country. No upper age-bar may be prescribed. This position may be categorized as a tenure post of five years which can be reviewed with the approval of Health Ministry/ Cabinet/President of India.

iv There should be at least two Joint Directors - one from among the physicians and another from among the professional social workers or psychologists drawn from universities/institutions of higher learning/medical colleges in the country who have made substantial contribution towards the prevention and control of HIV/AIDS.

v NACO may set up few divisions headed by experts from respective fields such as: Treatment & Prevention; Blood safety; Surveillance; Research & Evaluation; STDs / Hepatitis B/C/ Tuberculosis; IEC; and an Administrative & Finance

Division to carry out all the planning, organisation, implementation, and evaluation programmes.

vi Similar steps as mentioned above should also be taken by the state for the effective management of HIV/AIDS prevention programme.

2. Programme Financing

AIDS prevention and control activities have been supported by the National Budget of the Government of India since 1987, with additional assistance coming from and through WHO since 1989-90. The signing of the credit agreement with the World Bank in April 1992 has substantially expanded the resources available at national and state levels.[3]

From the past experience (1992-97) it is found that there was non-utilization of allocated funds and delay in submission of timely accounts by several state governments. There are also reports alleging that some of the state governments diverted the funds allocated for HIV/AIDS prevention programme for some other purpose.

It may also be noted that there was undue delay in sending applications for various projects through proper channels. Further delay also was caused for screening applications at state level as well as at NACO office. This has resulted in NACO releasing finance to state governments towards the end of the financial year-in many cases by December or January. The state governments in turn took their own time to disburse the amount to various applicants. Naturally under such circumstances, many agencies and NGOs received finance at the eleventh hour. How can one expect result-oriented implementation of any programme effectively? This was followed by reports in the media that many state governments failed to utilize funds allocated to them for HIV/AIDS related work.

Suggestions

i. The Ministry of Health & Family Welfare of the Government of India should earmark substantial amount annually towards funding the NACO activities. The Ministry should follow a policy of "spend and claim". Whatever soft loans and other credits received from world bodies like UNAIDS etc. may be diverted to NACO annually on project basis without any delay.

ii. NACO should be given full freedom, responsibility and accountability for utilization of funds according to its priorities. The state AIDS cells to be established by the State Ministry of Health in line with "NACO set up" should be given at least 80 per cent of their annual budget estimates. This arrangement is feasible and a viable option similar to what is being practiced by the apex body of higher education in the country, namely, the University Grants Commission (UGC).

iii. With the above-mentioned suggestion, the prevention and control of AIDS will become the primary responsibility of the state governments. By doing so, we are eliminating scores of hurdles found in the existing system.

iv. The state governments should be given a free hand to mobilize funds from within and outside the country for the purpose of HIV/AIDS related activities. The bilateral agencies also should be allowed to directly fund the state AIDS cells on project basis.

3. Inter-sectoral and Bilateral Collaboration

A developing country like India certainly has to depend on loans, subsidy, and all sorts of grants from governmental and bilateral agencies, international NGOs and corporate sector for the prevention and control of HIV/AIDS programme. With limited resources, infrastructures, and technical expertise, the country must also seek external assistance.

The past experience shows that NACO has succeeded in attracting huge amount of resources from world bodies for the AIDS work. A large number of bilateral agencies are pouring in money for the prevention and control of AIDS. However, there are duplication of projects which is a common phenomenon in India particularly, with NGOs and private voluntary organizations. Above all, it is alleged that NACO seems to have failed in providing adequate guidance and direction for proper, timely and effective utilization of available resources and services. As a result certain states like Maharashtra, Tamil Nadu and some of the states in the northeast received lot of attention and support in terms of finance and technical expertise, whereas several states with high-risk groups remained without similar assistance for one or the other reason.

Suggestions

i. NACO as an autonomous body may like to seek cooperation from various departments and ministries within the government of India on a broad basis without attaching programme implementation responsibilities. At the state level, the state AIDS Cells also may seek cooperation of various departments and ministries for the HIV/AIDS prevention and control programme. However, all responsibilities will rest with NACO at the centre and state AIDS cells at the state level for planning, organizing, implementing and evaluating various programmes. This responsibility if shared will only create hurdles, delay in decision making and finally bowing down to "common minimum programme' which is the talk of the day.

ii. State AIDS cells should be given a free hand to independently seek cooperation and collaboration from bilateral agencies, NGOs, private voluntary agencies and corporate sector for HIV/AIDS related activities.

iii. A close look at the extent of involvement of bilateral agencies and NGOs etc. show that some selected states have the privilege of getting lot of benefits while most states are neglected. NACO may like to look at the issue and negotiate with various organizations to see that each organization is given a couple of states to work with so that there is a fair deal. This will help to ensure that HIV infected and those at risk from various parts of the country are adequately taken care.

iv. As far as major skill oriented training programmes are concerned, IMA, CMAI, VHAI and similar other agencies may be entrusted with the responsibility of training personnel on project basis.

v. In order to avoid duplication of the production of training manuals and much more so as to ensure the development of multimedia packages with accurate and complete information, agencies like IMA, CMAI, VHAI medical colleges etc. should be approached by NACO on project basis. The past experience show that many modules developed by co-opting a few so called experts who have little knowledge on the subject have produced materials which cannot be taken to the market.

vi. The sponsoring of individuals for training programmes; exposure, visit abroad; participation in seminars, conferences and international conventions through bilateral agencies or government departments should be done in such, way that there is adequate representation from every state AIDS Cells, NGOs and other agencies involved in HIV/AIDS related work. Effort should also be made to see that programme implementers at various levels right down to those at grassroots levels are given opportunities. The present practice in which only the top brass at the national level enjoy such benefits and privileges should be done away with.

4. HIV/AIDS Surveillance

In a democratic set up it is very difficult for a government to recognize and accept factual data and information on various topics, issues and problems. This was true for India regarding the reporting of railway accidents; deliberations in the state assemblies and both houses of Parliament, actual number of casualties in an accident or a natural calamity etc.

As far as HIV/AIDS is concerned, there are wide variations and discrepancies in reporting actual data. NACO as well as various other agencies operating in the country publicize statistics which are not accurate and their estimates vary. Similarly, the actual number of HIV and AIDS cases reported from various parts of the country to NACO are also not reliable.

Surveillance and reporting is periodically done for taking the nation for a ride. HIV/AIDS surveillance should have provided data based on which planning, organizing, implementing and evaluating programmes for the prevention and control of the killer disease can be initiated. Unfortunately, the data available are inaccurate and many states do not report the factual data on time. Further, the testing system and the procedure for sample selection are also faulty. Certain groups are assumed to be high-risk groups and are made targets for HIV surveillance. Above all, testing system in a couple of states like Maharashtra and Tamil Nadu are far better than most of the states in India. Therefore, to reach conclusions based on available data from a particular state is false. The present system needs modification and the following suggestions may help us to have better surveillance for HIV/AIDS in the country.

Suggestions

i. NACO as an autonomous body should initiate necessary action to see that HIV testing is taken up at all levels from primary health centres to district level hospitals in every state and districts in the country. The state AIDS cells should be given the responsibility of reporting HIV/AIDS surveillance data.

ii. Timely measures should be taken to ensure that testing kits, other facilities including infrastructure are provided to all public health centres in every district. Adequate number of persons must be recruited for the purpose. Sufficient orientation and training must be given to the staff.

iii. Target oriented approach for testing should be done away with in a phased manner. Every section of the society must be taken into consideration. Focus must be made on women, young adults, adolescents and marginalised communities.

iv. Confidentiality does not mean "not disclosing test results" to the individuals undergoing HIV test. The on-going practice is a criminal act. The existing process does not have provision to inform the individual about his/her status after an HIV test. It should be made mandatory that HIV/AIDS test results are communicated to the clients. It may be noted that pre-test counselling for all, and post-test counselling to those infected are essential.

v. Testing one for HIV/AIDS without one's consent is illegal. Therefore, prior permission in writing must be taken from a person before his/her blood or body fluid is taken for HIV testing. NACO may develop a small proforma which can be printed by state AIDS Cells in local languages for local use. People who cannot sign will need to give their thumb impressions.

vi. For an effective surveillance programme, cooperation from block level and panchayat level must be sought. This will help in ensuring that the surveillance system covers every village community in the country.

vii. HIV testing without consent of a person can be done in exceptional cases like those who want to donate either blood semen or any organ for transplantation. This will be under the sentinel surveillance system.

5. HIV Counselling

The role of counselling in health care system in India has become all the more important with the unabated spread of HIV/AIDS among people from all walks of life. As clinicians, the counsellors of HIV/AIDS have to walk right into the heart of the pains of an infected person. The counsellors have to address myriad issues that challenges the very existence of an HIV/AIDS patient his/her family, friends and community. Although much has been spoken about counselling, hardly anything has been done in practical terms. The very policy of the anonymity of testing procedure do not require any counselling. Therefore, there is a contradiction in the very strategy itself. In fact counselling is more important than condom programming as far as the prevention and control of HIV is concerned.

Pre-test counselling and post-test counselling are essential aspects in the prevention and control programme of HIV. An individual who comes for an HIV testing is faced with several problems, which may have direct or indirect impact upon the very existence of the individual. In fact one volunteers oneself for a judgement on one's life. It can be a death sentence. It can also be a clean chit for a tension free life.

All those who come for HIV test require social and emotional support, which the existing medical system is unable to provide. Very few Universities in the country offer programmes of study in psychology, social work and counselling. The medical colleges within the country have very limited seats for medical graduates to pursue studies in psychiatry. In fact some of the best institutes are not able to train more than 5 to 10 physicians in a batch. This is a discouraging proportion to the ever-growing population of the country and the enormous health related problems faced by the people.

Suggestions

i. NACO should make every effort to appoint qualified personnel as counsellors at every health care centre where HIV/AIDS testing facilities will be provided. To begin with at least one counsellor should be appointed in health care centres situated in rural areas. In urban centres, based on the number of population to be covered, more counsellors should be appointed.

ii. It is true that there is dearth of adequately trained counsellors. The state AIDS Cells should be directed to collaborate with departments and schools where programmes of study in social work or psychology are offered. Apart from recruiting the trained graduates and post-graduates from these institutes, efforts must also be made to offer short-term intensive training programme leading to a certificate in HIV/AIDS counselling for which the minimum qualification may be a bachelor's degree. This task can be assigned to CMAI, VHAI, IMA, Schools of Social work, Department of Psychology and Departments of psychiatry in medical colleges.

iii. Because of the professional nature of counselling and the changes taking place in the strategies of HIV/AIDS prevention and control programme, refresher courses also should be made available for all those who are involved in counselling HIV/AIDS related cases.

iv. Keeping in view the cultural background, social and traditional values of our people, counselling strategies must be developed to suit the existing circumstances in the country. While effort will be made to follow the basic criteria for counselling, the counsellors should be oriented to adapt approaches, which are acceptable to local community. For this reason, as far as possible counsellors should be recruited from within the states and if possible within the districts or at least within the various regions of a given state. This will enable the counsellor and the client in understanding each other and in conveying meaningful messages

6. Sexually Transmitted Diseases

The centrally sponsored national STD programme has been integrated into the existing health care system. At the same time NACO decided to include STDs as a component of the strategic plan for the prevention and control of HIV/AIDS. This is like riding in two boats at the same time.

Although the national STD programme has been in operation since 1946, even today several states have not appointed STD programme officers.[4] The existing system has hardly any provision for healthy and timely communication between AIDS and STD programmes. There is delay in release of funds for drugs and consumable items for STD while NACO has also failed in disbursing funds to the states for AIDS programme well in advance. The end result is total failure of the programme.

There is no clear-cut plan for training in STD control as well as AIDS prevention programmes. Counsellors are not appointed at STD clinics and HIV testing centres. The government has recognised the fact that in most cases women do not avail STD treatment facilities due to stigmatization. Further the existing facilities reaches only an estimated 5 to 10 per cent of all STD patients in the country while we have 40 million new STD cases every year. Control of STDs is crucial for the prevention and control of AIDS. The above figures are frightening and give a serious warning to the health care system about the impending disaster that STDs and HIV is set to bring about in the country.

When we plan measures for the prevention and control of STDs and HIV/AIDS, it is appropriate and important to consider the relationship between STD and HIV infection.

HIV has emerged as the latest type of STD which has no cure as on date. Both STD and HIV are associated with same risk behaviours, that is unprotected sexual activities involving multiple partners. Transmission of STD and HIV through other routes are not ruled out. For a person infected with STD, the acquisition and transmission of HIV infection is easier and faster. An early diagnosis and effective treatment of STD can significantly reduce the chances of HIV transmission. Most of the preventive measures for the control of STD and HIV are same. STDs are very common in urban and rural areas. HIV also has been found to be spreading both in urban and rural areas. Therefor,e one can find lot of similarities between STDs and HIV infection and the factors contributing to its spread.

Suggestions

i. Prevention and control programme for STDs and HIV/ AIDS should be brought under the sole responsibility of NACO and state AIDS Cells. Every effort must be made to integrate AIDS and STD prevention, control, care and treatment at all levels for achieving desired goals.

ii. Programme planning, organising, implementing and evaluating for STD and HIV should go hand in hand. Training of personnel for case management in STD and HIV should be integrated. There is no need to appoint separate personnel for managing HIV and STDs. In fact the existing personnel in the STD clinics should be trained in HIV case management without further loss of time.

iii. Counsellors and social workers should be given integrated training for dealing with HIV and STD clients.

iv. Every effort should be made by the State AIDS Cell to screen people from every walk of life for STD and HIV. This should be taken up following a well-planned awareness programme and by seeking consent of the clients. Free check up and testing facilities should be given to all for STD and HIV diagnosis.

v. Financial allocation to the tune of 80 per cent as suggested earlier should be made by the Central Ministry of Health and Family Welfare through NACO to the State AIDS Cells.

Adequate testing kits, other equipments and drugs for treatment should be made available to all health care centres activated for STD and HIV tests.

7. Condom Programming

NACO has accepted the fact that condom market in India is relatively small, catering mostly to contraceptive needs of users and covers only 5 per cent of eligible couples. At the same time it also reiterates the governments support for the promotion of "good quality, low cost condoms" for the prevention and control of STD and HIV infection. What should one infer from the terms "good quality, low cost condoms". For any material to be of good quality, one has to make good payments. It is certain that we cannot have good quality condoms at low cost unless the government subsidises the cost. Further, the much-publicised 'Nirodh' (one brand of condom) is of poor quality and is almost freely available in public health centres. However, not even the poorest of the poor are interested in it as one has no confidence in using the stuff. As mentioned in the previous chapter there is much demand for this government recommended condom in the balloon industries.

Dr. S.K. Harikumar, Behaviour Physician and Coordinator of VHAI-EC programme on HIV/AIDS in Kerala points out that the policy of AIDS control agencies to recommend condom as the most important preventive method needs to be modified for Kerala situation. It has been widely reported by housewives and commercial sex workers that their counterparts are very reluctant to use condoms. Government has not yet been able to ensure the quality of the "free supply" condoms and the low-income groups are not confident with them. In Kerala the chances of people accepting any practice only because it has been recommended by the authorities is limited. People like to have choices before adopting a method, which is most suitable for them. So an ideal and intelligent alternative would be to suggest many safe sexual practices, out of which one could be condom. Non-penetrative sex, sex therapy to over come sexual dysfunction's and maintenance of sexual health are some of the other issues to be addressed properly. This improved approach can help prevent the spread of HIV infection among different target groups.[5]

Some countries and international agencies continue to promote condom as the most effective method to prevent and control HIV/AIDS. As we discussed in the beginning, what is required for India is a culture specific approach in evolving preventive measures. Past experience clearly indicate that prevention education and awareness programmes have not yielded desired results. Captions and hoardings such as "use condoms to have sex' are neither acceptable to nor appreciated by most parents and teachers in India. While dealing with adolescents in a classroom setting, we need to impart messages that are in tune with the much cherished value system of the country. We have a significant population of about (80 per cent) in the classrooms who look towards preventive messages and measures which are in tune with their value system.

Suggestions

- Promotion of "abstinence until marriage" could be one of the best options. Young people are encouraged to take pledge to remain virgin until marriage. NACO and other agencies must take courage to promote abstinence programmes particularly among the school population.
- Young people should not be under-estimated. HIV is a lifestyle disease. People can change their lifestyles. For this they need to be given appropriate education and encouragements. Youth today are prepared to accept challenges. Teaching them to discipline themselves and practice behaviours that are decent and moral will go a long way in helping youth to adopt methods that would help in HIV/AIDS prevention.
- Teachers and ToTs must be provided refresher courses to gain correct knowledge and acquire appropriate skills in sensitizing students about delicate topics associated with life skill education.
- Values such as respect for the body of the other person, building good character, honesty, morality, self-discipline etc. must be incorporated into the curriculum. It will be convenient to teachers and ToTs to deal with such topics. However, efforts must be made to provide sufficient teaching materials on such topics.

8. Targeted Interventions and High Risk Factor

It is high time that the "targeted intervention alone" approach is given less priority while, "high risk factor" is adopted for future intervention programmes for HIV/AIDS prevention and control in country. In the initial stages, when the number of cases detected in various parts of the world was few the "high risk group" approach had some relevance. For example, in the early 80s, HIV high-risk groups were identified as homosexuals, followed by sex workers and blood donors. Therefore, programme initiatives were taken to contain the spread of the virus among such identified groups.

Now that we have much knowledge and understanding about the way HIV keeps spreading without any distinction of border, culture, gender, race, religion, age and socio-economic status, we have to evolve a strategy for intervention based on high risk factor than high risk group approach. Time has come to discard the high risk and low risk categorization. Because the estimates show that hundreds of thousands are already infected and millions are at risk cutting across all borders. HIV has been detected among children, men and women, sex workers, homosexuals, lesbians, professionals including physicians, working class and ordinary people all over the country. Therefore, no social group can be labeled as "low risk group".[6]

Much changes have occurred in the family set up and social and moral values, of the people not only in the urban areas but also in the rural sector during the recent past, particularly, with the advent of the concept of market economy. Travel and migration has increased many folds within the country and outside. Tourism sector has made drastic changes in the movement of people. Inter-sectoral and international collaboration in various fields has increased. More and more people seek institutionalised services which has increased the chances of HIV transmission from patients to health care providers within hospitals. There is also change in the concept of moral values. More and more people consider pre-marital sex as part and parcel of life - a phenomena endorsed by many experts, parents, physicians and other professionals. These are 'high risk factors' in terms of HIV transmission from surgical and skin piercing instruments, blood and blood products, and infection through bodily fluids while nursing and caring the HIV infected at home or in institutional setting. All these are potential routes for the spread of HIV into general population. Therefore, time right for focussing attention is on all people - men and women; children; adolescents and young adults; and the marginalised communities while initiating HIV prevention and control programme in India.

Suggestions

i. NACO should change its present strategy of targeted intervention to cover all sections of the society. Target oriented approach may be used in a limited way while sanctioning projects to NGOs and other agencies operating in a small geographical area catering to particular groups like sex workers, substance abusers, men who have sex with men etc.

ii. Every effort must be made for safe practices by the physicians and para medical personnel taking care of the HIV infected in hospital set up.

iii. The IEC component now has to emphasize attention to cover all social groups within a given state. Just as we have the WHO sponsored polio vaccination drive in the country, efforts should be made at national and state levels to cover all population for programmes involving awareness campaign, testing, counselling, and extending community care support initiatives.

iv. The intervention strategies should focus on 'risk-factor' than risk groups. Therefore, efforts should be made by NACO through the State AIDS Cells and Public Health System in the country to reach out to all people with programmes for awareness, family visits to motivate people for HIV tests (wherever doubts exist) and informing people about safe practices for home care of those infected with HIV and STDs.

v. The very fact that 40 million new STD cases are added every year in our country alone is a sufficient ground for shifting focus from high-risk groups to high risk factor. Therefore, separate programmes must be developed on risk factor suiting to the needs of people from various walks of life.

vi. The target-oriented studies initiated so far has not yielded desired results. It is time now to shift focus on to the general masses for studies to determine behavioural practices and risk factors. Each State AIDS Cell must initiate time bound studies covering every district and blocks in the state to collect adequate and authentic information on people's behaviour.

vii. Programme planning should be based on the results of the studies conducted. Further, grassroots level involvement through Panchayati raj institutions should be sought for planning, organising, implementing and evaluating various programmes suiting to local needs.

viii. There should be provision for decentralisation of all activities so that result oriented programmes are developed which only can save the humanity from the jaws of death caused by HIV/AIDS.

9. Blood Safety

With the advent of HIV/AIDS in the country and its unabated spread among all social groups in India, consorted efforts must be made to contain its further spread. For this effective measures in new programming areas such as blood safety, sterilization of skin piercing instruments etc. should be given top priority.

There is shortage of blood in blood banks. Many blood banks function without adhering to the norms and guidelines. Several blood banks are yet to be licensed. Proper equipments are not available in several blood banks. Most of the states and Union Territories (UTs) have not appointed adequate number of staff. Training of blood bank personnel in view of the threat posed by HIV has to be taken up. Adequate testing kits are not supplied. The utilisation of grant released to the states under the blood safety programme has been only to the tune of 15 to 20 per cent.[7]

There is lack of coordination between various responsible agencies like the Ministry of Health & Family Welfare, State Health Ministries, NACO, State AIDS Cells, State FDA(Drug Controller) and other departments. The strategy followed for blood collection is not result oriented. Further, there is no rational use of blood by the physicians. There is shortage of health care professionals in the field of transfusion services.

It is a known fact that transfusion of HIV infected blood is the most efficient means of transmitting HIV infection (about 90 per cent chances). However, estimates show that only about 5 per cent are infected in India through blood transfusion. The Government of India has adopted the recommendation of WHO for testing blood samples with either ELISA or rapid/simple test with unlinked anonymity.

In order to ensure blood safety, increase collection of blood and rational use of blood, a re-thinking is required based on the experience of the strategic plan 1992-97.

Suggestions

i. NACO should take up the full responsibility for the blood safety programme in the country. However, the state AIDS cells should be entrusted with the task of supervising blood safety programme in the state. Recruitment and training of staff, financing the blood banks, providing testing kits and required good quality equipment also should be made the responsibility of the State AIDS Cells.

ii. The State AIDS Cells should adopt a strategy to have blood collection facilities in every district hospitals as well as public health centres within each district.

iii. Blood donation camps must be organised periodically through the Panchayati raj institutions and NGOs in local areas. This will help in creating awareness among the masses about the very concept and need of blood donation as well as precautions required for HIV prevention from blood and blood products. Above all, adequate amount of blood can be collected for local use. However, one should ensure that blood of females particularly from rural areas should not be tapped since nearly 80 per cent rural women are anaemic.

iv. The blood banking system should be expanded with local support. Local support does not mean financial implications on people, but community participation. This will automatically pave the way for eliminating professional blood donors.

v. There are about 162 medical colleges in the country. Each medical college may be entrusted with the responsibility of training blood bank professionals from a fixed number of districts. The districts within state may be distributed among the medical colleges. The staff and students of medical colleges should be involved in the whole exercise. They may also be made responsible for ensuring that the guidelines for blood safety are followed and that good quality testing kits as well as other equipments are available in each centre.

vi. The licensing of blood banks may be done based on the recommendations of NACO. NACO may receive applications from State AIDS Cells for issuing licenses to blood banks. The Medical Colleges may certify whether a centre can be licensed or not. The statute giving autonomy to NACO should clearly spell out all the administrative and intersectoral collaboration required in this regard.

vii. Promoting use of disposable, provision for safely destroying the used disposable, and use of needle destroyers by physicians and para-medical staff should be given sufficient attention under the blood safety programme in order to avoid transmission of HIV via blood.

10. Information, Education and Communication (IEC)

The objectives spelt out in the strategic plan 1992-97 under the IEC component are excellent. However, it is alleged that the efforts made by NACO during the plan period has failed to yield desirable results. To put in brief, the level of awareness, knowledge and understanding about HIV/AIDS among the general population has not improved. The level of knowledge and understanding even among health care providers are limited.

Promotion of desirable practices such as condom use, sterilization of needles and voluntary donation of blood has not made much headway. Some NGOs have succeeded in promoting the use of condoms among sex workers in some of the metros.

In fact, IEC should own the major responsibility for taking the awareness campaign to all nook and corner of the country. However, there was no political will in implementing programmes of IEC. A couple of booklets and manuals with same messages were compiled. The multimedia infrastructure in the country was not fully utilised. There was enough money, but no will on the part of NACO to develop programmes suiting to local needs. As discussed earlier, risk factor oriented approach was not adopted. Some seminars were organized and brochures were developed which was based on risk group or target oriented approach.

Much time was lost in inter-sectoral collaboration initiatives and using trial and error method for developing various programmes. The initiatives provided by the NGOs were far greater than what NACO could achieve during the past five years. There was lack of direction and commitment. Bureaucratic hurdles and vested interests played havoc. There was clear vision, which was evident from the objectives mentioned in strategic plan, but the success rate was limited.

It is time now to learn from the drawbacks and experience of the past. It is time now to develop action plan based on all the four objectives of the IEC component discussed in the previous chapter. Some of the suggestions for meeting the objectives of IEC are given below.

Suggestions

i. NACO has to initiate efforts to decentralise the awareness campaign activities by handing over the full responsibility to the State AIDS Cells. Necessary financial assistance for the programme should be provided well in advance so that programmes are initiated during the first month of every financial year.

ii. Awareness programmes for creating understanding and knowledge about HIV/AIDS/STDs among general population must be given top priority. Each State AIDS Cell will initiate activities suiting to local needs, keeping in view their cultural, religious and traditional practices,

iii. The State AIDS Cell will do everything to reach out to all people within the State through the district and public health centres and by involving Panchayati raj institutions.

iv. The thrust area will now be high risk factor and not high-risk group as the disease has already percolated to all social groups in the country.

v. The programmes will be developed in local languages and dialects.

vi. Every district hospital and public health centres within every district of the state must be provided with hot-line telephone service. Social workers and counsellors may be appointed for helping the clients on phone.

vii. Seminars, conferences, workshops and training programmes should be organised at district level periodically involving people from within the given district. Resource persons could be from medical colleges, State AIDS Cells, academics and other experts involved in HIV/AIDS related activities.

viii. Every effort must be made to use public places within each district like petrol pumps, medical shops, barber shops, beauty parlours, health clinics, post office, railway station, reservation counters, bus terminal, cinema theaters, restaurants and hotels, sports venues, public gatherings like political, religious, educational, social, cultural meets, picnic spots, and tourist spots for the display of AIDS awareness materials like posters, free distribution leaflets, stickers, etc.

ix. Considering the extent of the problem, NACO should do everything to see that AIDS and sex education form part of curriculum at the higher secondary level. For this purpose it may even seek judicial opinion by approaching the Supreme Court, when there is no consensus among bureaucrats and politicians.

x. NACO should also seek the collaboration of the National Open School and the Open Universities in the country to offer programmes of study through distance learning on AIDS and family life education. This is a viable option when a teacher finds it difficult to face students in a face to face interaction in classroom.

xi. Efforts must be made to develop brochures on AIDS education and sex education in vernacular for free distribution through schools and health care centres.

What society needs today is accurate and complete information which most parents are not aware of.

xii. NACO should take steps to initiate action plan for giving short term and long term training to professional social workers and counsellors across the country. Collaboration with the existing schools of social work is one option. The national and state open universities may also be approached for launching similar programmes for the in-service persons. For every 100 students in a school, there should be one social worker/counsellor. Similarly for every 10 hospital beds, at least one social worker should be appointed. We need to have drastic changes if we desire a break through in our efforts in preventing and controlling the spread of HIV/AIDS/STDs in the country.

11. Community Care and Support

People living with HIV are living longer. Therefore, there is more time to intervene medically and psychologically. There is more that can be done behaviourally and socially during the course of disease to maintain health and quality of life.[8]

Survival after the onset of AIDS in developing countries remains short and is estimated to be less than one year. Meanwhile, survival time with AIDS has been increasing in industrialized countries from an average of less than one year to about three years. Longer survival appears to be directly related to routine treatment with antiretroviral drugs, the use of drugs for opportunistic infection and a better overall quality of health care.[9] Although there is treatment available, there is no cure. Therefore, eventually an HIV infected will die of one of the AIDS defining illnesses.

The issues we have to address include: How long an HIV infected will live? Who will take care of the infected? Where can one get treatment? How to finance the treatment? Who will take care of an infected when one develops signs and symptoms of AIDS? Is the country prepared for that day which is already very near? People are dying all over the country due to AIDS. Some are diagnosed, while many die unaware of the illness. There is no provision in the existing strategy to inform the HIV infected his/her status even if diagnosis show that one is HIV positive.

It is better late than never. We have to make all out effort to plan, organise, implement and evaluate community care and support services for the infected and those advancing into AIDS. The strategic plan has already outlined the objectives for community care while drafting the objectives of reduction of impact component. Although hardly anything has been set in motion, every effort must be made to equip every district in the country with technical know how and administrative mechanism to address these issues.

Suggestions

i. NACO as an autonomous body should take initiative in setting up community centres in all the panchayats for taking care of the terminally ill in each locality. Community participation and cooperation may be sought through the Ministry of Rural Development, which may bear the cost of setting up local infrastructures.

ii. Staff, equipments and other expenses including salary etc. should be borne by NACO through the State AIDS Cell.

iii. As far as possible, the community centres may be attached to the primary health centres in the locality.

iv. Every effort must be made to educate the people at the grassroot level about home care of the HIV infected. The task ahead is challenging because of the level of ignorance, illiteracy, poverty along with religious, cultural, and social values and traditional practices.

v. The community care and support services should be attached to medical colleges/district hospitals which in turn may provide health care services. India would need to overhaul its primary health system for it to reach the huge number of people who now live on the fringes of the public health service to address the problem of STDs.[10]

12. Research and Evaluation

If statistics are meant to relate facts, then the figures must be derived carefully and by using the right methodology and epidemiological characteristics of the epidemic.[11] The lackadaisical approach of NACO so far in diagnosing and reporting the prevalence of HIV in the country needs change. Most of the State AIDS Cells are not informing the statistical data on time. There are wide variations in the estimates provided by State AIDS Cells and other agencies and NGOs involved in HIV/AIDS work within a state.

The research studies undertaken are not properly designed and geographically distributed to cover all social groups. Most of the studies commissioned so far are target oriented in selected places. Further the State AIDS Cells hardly play any role in conducting studies on HIV/AIDS its prevalence rate in various communities, the effectiveness of condom programming, IEC, blood safety, STDs and other awareness programmes.

Lessons from several countries show that research studies and evaluation studies of programme implementation go a long way in modifying programme strategies and methods adopted for programme implementation. We in India hardly have any such studies available to quote. Therefore, utmost importance must be given to periodical surveys and evaluation of HIV trends in the country and the effectiveness and accountability of the HIV/AIDS prevention and control programme.

Suggestions

i. Research and evaluation should form an integral part of the HIV/AIDS prevention and control programme for which at least 10 to 20 per cent of the budget estimates should be set aside.

ii. Medical Colleges, University departments, schools of social work and psychology may be given the task of conducting research studies on the prevalence of STDs and behavioural practices of population.

iii. State AIDS Cells should monitor such studies, and the census sample method should be adopted at district level in order to cover all family units within a district. The task seems to be enormous. However, if there is a will, there is a way. One can no longer wait and allow the millions to play with death.

iv. The evaluation of the AIDS prevention and control programme may be given to recognised institutes at the state level like the branches of IMA, VHAI, other state and national institutes of reputation like the Operation Research Group (ORG). However, one agency should not be given more than 2 to 4 districts while efforts must be made to cover every district in the country periodically. Evaluation studies should also cover the functional aspect of State AIDS Cells, district and primary health System responsible for AIDS programme.

v. Adequate financial assistance must be provided through the State AIDS Cells in time to conduct the studies. These studies should be time bound in nature and must be reported to state legislative assemblies and the Parliament.

SUMMARY

In this chapter an effort has been made to present a plan of action for the prevention and control of HIV/AIDS and for the care of those terminally ill with the killer disease. This action plan has been drafted based on the experiences of the National Strategic Plan 1992-97 of NACO. There are twelve major components namely, (1) programme management (2) programme financing (3) inter-sectoral and bilateral collaboration (4) HIV/AIDS surveillance (5) HIV counselling (6) STDs (7) condom programming (8) targeted intervention and high risk factor (9) blood safety (10) IEC (11) community care and support, and (12) research and evaluation. One may call it a Herculean task. Time has run out and we have no choice but embark on this mission with vigor and enthusiasm if we want to save the lives of millions in this country.

REFERENCES

1. Hiroshi Taniguchi. One World, one hope. Integration, Japanese Organization for International Cooperation, in Family Planning, Tokyo, 1996.
2. Andre Picard, "Universal AIDS Fight Urged - World's poor can't Afford Break through, opening conference session told". The Globe and Mail, July 8, 1996.
3. NACO, National AIDS control programme India: Country Scenario update, MHFW, New Delhi, 1995, p.89.
4. Health for the Millions, VHAI, New Delhi, Nov-Dec 1996.
5. S.K. Harikumar, HIV/AIDS control in Kerala: Some reflections: In Health for the Millions, op. cit.
6. *Ibid.*
7. Health for the Millions, op.cit
8. Robert H. Remien, 'Psycho Social Aspects of Counselling': In 1994 National Frontline Forum, NCM publishers, Inc. New York, 1994.
9. UNAIDS, 'The HIV/AIDS situation in Mid 1996 - ,Global and Regional Highlights, UNAIDS Fact Sheet, July 1,1996.
10. John Stackhouse. "Despair Ravages Third World - AIDS treatments are beyond reach', the Globe and Mail, 8 July, 1996.
11. Health for the Millions, op.cit.

7

Curriculum for Life Skill Education

It is a fact that HIV/AIDS has been identified as primarily a sexually transmitted disease. It is also recognized that AIDS and sex education can go a long way in the prevention and control of the further spread of HIV. Very few countries in the world have designed curriculum on sex education. As far as India is concerned, sex education is still in its infancy. This is one of the most controversial topics before the politicians, bureaucrates, parents and teachers in the country while, many adolesents are preoccupied to a greater or lesser degree with ideas, fantasies and desires about sex and sexuality.

In the absence of readily available and reliable information, sex experimentation becomes a common phenomenon among young persons. Some studies have revealed a close correlation between sex ignorance and sex experimentation and delinquency. This perhaps is another way of saying that the uninformed child is much more likely to be involved in sexual experimentation. To such children experimentation or "trial and error" method frequently becomes the option by which they gain their information. Under these circumstances sex often becomes associated with fear, guilt, and suspicion.[1]

Since HIV/AIDS has been identified as a primarily sexually transmitted disease, there has been an expectation that educational institutions should 'do' something about influencing 'high risk' behaviour which the medical profession has not been able to manage. This new challenge requires immediate and effective responses from a socially responsible system of education. It may be noted that to date, no University or Board of school education has come forward to initiate such a programme in the country which may be beneficial to our young people, teachers, health professionals and those interested in acquiring knowledge on the subject.

AIDS, SEX AND FAMILY LIFE EDUCATION

To academics, physicians, religious leaders, parents, school teachers and a man in the street, AIDS and sex education has different meaning and connotation. Some people view the inclusion of AIDS and sex education in school curriculum as an attempt to teach sexual activities and safe sexual practices among school children which are likely to lower their morality. Some others see sex education as an explanation of the anatomy of sex organs. For many other people AIDS and sex education means 'reproduction education' consisting of facts of life in order to prevent unwanted pregnancies, STDs and HIV/AIDS. And still a few others consider AIDS and sex education as teaching "safe sex" practices to the masses. In many circles, reproductive health education, population education and family welfare education are interchangeably used to convey the same meaning.

A meaningful AIDS, sex and family life education programme seeks the development of an individual's sexuality eventually leading to one's personality development and maintaining socially accepted healthy relationship with members of the opposite sex as well as same sex. Therefore, there is no way to provide sex education once and for all. It is a continuing process. Sex education includes "an appreciation for self and the opposite sex, the ability to develop fulfilling personal and family relationship, comfortableness with sexual roles(mother, father, sister, brother, friend, wife, husband),recognition of bodily functions as related to reproduction, an understanding of the part emotions play in sexual behaviour, a maturing of attitudes toward the function of sex in life, the responsibility of being a member of a family and overall, a healthy attitude towards life.[2]

For everyone sex education is a continuing process from birth to adulthood, married life and to old age. In younger days he/she keeps learning about sex and sexuality in peer group, playground, swimming pool, street, social gatherings, media as well as from various circumstances at home: parents, siblings, servants, uncle, aunty, cousin, neighbour etc. This phenomenon is common to all people of all nations. The type of information one receives from these varying circumstances often becomes confusing and disjointed. No one is fully confident in passing on accurate and complete information. The young mind of a person becomes unhappy and disturbed when he/she fails to piece together varying type of information. In course of time one develops a distorted attitude to the subject of sex and sexuality. Eventually adjustment in married life becomes difficult as a result of the negative attitudes formed in younger days. Perhaps there is no better way of drawing undesirable and unhealthy attitude to a subject than by attempting to avoid it. In short, we may say that time is ripe for a sound education on AIDS and sex education in order to help our young people to face the challenges in the present society, in terms of social change as well as changing concept of morality.

With the threat of AIDS looming large and promiscuity being a contributory factor, the view of the National Council of Educational Research and Training(NCERT) that it is not advisable at this stage to make sex education part of school syllabus is amazing. The Ministry of Education, after a prolonged debate on the subject has finally decided not to incorporate sex education in the school cirriculum. The ministry says that academic opinion is not in favour of directly including the subject in the school syllabus.[3]

On the eve of World AIDS Day, WHO published a report in Geneva saying that sex education frequently persuaded young people to delay the start of sexual activity, have fewer partners and to use condoms. In many ways it is youth which is driving this epidemic, said Dr.Michael Merson of WHO's Global Programme on AIDS. We don't want our youth to die of ignorance.[4]

According to a well known Indian sexologist Dr. Prakash Kothari, sexuality is a natural and intrinsic part of an individual's personality and needs to be nurtured and developed like all other facets. This fact is completely ignored by parents and teachers in our society because they are themselves not comfortable and knowledgeable on this subject. Dr. Kothari ridiculed the sexual hypocrisy pervading the present society. On the one hand, the elders discourage the children from any form of sexual expression and encourage them instead to hide their sexuality. On the other hand the television brings in sexual images and messages right inside the drawing room. The sexually mature unmarried youth is caught in a vicious circle, where sexual desire is provoked and aggravated by the influence of the media which necessiates an outlet, the opportunity for which is socially unavailable, leading to a lot of sexual frustration. This frustration Dr. Kothari says, manifests itself in the current social scenario fraught with problems like increasing promiscuity, sexually transmitted diseases, AIDS, sexual crimes and unwanted pregnancies.[5]

The cultural ethos and social taboos in our society have weakened the nerves of our intellectuals and academics to say 'no' to sex education in schools. Whatever be the kind of censorship imposed on the media to preserve the so-called traditional values and morality of our society, we cannot be blind to the fact that our young boys and girls are exposed to all sorts of sex and violence in the satellite television. Since the mid 1980s our children are increasingly being exposed to the world through the expansion of electronic media. Available reports indicate that there is an ever growing increase in sex related violence and crimes in our society.[6] Although no major country wide study has been made on the sexual practices of people in India, particularly that of teenagers, the result of the micro studies conducted by social scientists and physicians provide enough evidence about the active involvement of young boys and girls in sexual activities.

Existing AIDS Education Programme in India

India is still undecided whether to incorporate AIDS and sex education in the school curricula. There are many areas in which the concerns about the AIDS pandemic and its association with the transmission of virus through sexual activities, interact with the fabric of our society. Such interaction becomes particularly intense and conflicting around the issues of AIDS and sex education, subjects that appear erratically in the curricula of our medical sciences, let alone all other disciplines.[7] This is true for the schools, conventional universities and open learning institutions. To date there is no enrichment programme on AIDS or sex education anywhere in the country.

This anomaly in scholarship for creating awareness on AIDS, sex and sexuality through appropriate educational programme cannot be explained by any rational consideration because there are few areas of life that touch everyone so profoundly. Although research on AIDS, sex and sexuality related topics is hardly lacking and intellectuals are well aware of the AIDS threat and consequences of its unchecked spread, no legitimate avenues are made available for the prevention and control of the disease in an intelligent manner.[8]

The UTA programme described in chapter two is now gearing up to reach all major universities and + 2 level schools collaborating with the NSS in the country with technical and financial support from NACO and WHO. They have produced a series of IEC materials for students. The NSS has completed a training module for students on AIDS and sexuality and has begun to implement a national programme through their network. The manual has been translated into 7 languages and is in its fourth edition. NACO has provided intensive technical assistance. The project is currently expecting to train 70,000 student peer educators along with training a permanent core team of 6500 university teachers, says NACO.[9] It may be noted that the above figures of NACO give only a rosy picture while, the ground realities are totally contradicting. Details regarding the actual situation particularly about the extent of knowledge of physicians and other so called experts have been discussed in the preceding two chapters.

The above contradictions in purpose and strategies exacerbate the crisis in a land such as India with its vast population(950 million) and linguistic, communal and geographical differences (with 18 officially recognised languages and 1652 dialectics and 23.5 per cent of her population comprising tribal groups). There are 32 states and union territories and the literacy rate according to 1991 census is 52.1 per cent.[10] It is quite reasonable to argue that the tide of crisis could be stemmed only if AIDS and sex education programmes are launched quickly and efficiently by educational institutions including universities in the country. The impact of the programme will be far greater than one may imagine, since the younger generations can be educated on such delicate and controversial topics through a responsible education system.

RATIONALE

There are several grounds for launching a programme of study on AIDS, sex and family life education. While many generic reasons can be described, there are certain specific rlationale which needs mention. In the following pages, let us briefly list out the generic rationale and specific rationale for offering the proposed programme of study.

(a) Generic Rationale

1. Right to information is a fundamental right. This would mean that the young boys and girls do have the right to accurate and complete information about sex, sexuality, HIV/AIDS/STDs etc.
2. Physical changes during adolescence may trigger confusion in relation to physical and sexual identity. Wanting to appear knowledgeable and experienced often lead to reluctance to show gaps in knowledge by asking questions publicly.
3. The present sex educators in the country are the friends and scores of acquaintance who do not have accurate and complete information on the subject. As a result very often young people receive misguidance in sexual matters.
4. Teenage pregnancies involving school and college going girls are very common particularly in urban centres. This only shows the extent of early involvement of heterosexual activities which has implications as far as the tramission of HIV is concerned.
5. Child marriage is a common phenomenon, particularly in many North Indian states. This practice has been going on from time immemorial. These marriages are performed without the consent of the kids involved. These are performed with social sanction. The law of the land prescribes the age for marriage, 18 for girls and 21 for boys. There is no political will to stop this practice which has many implication in this era of HIV/AIDS.
6. Scores of girl children are offered to the temples across the country as devadasis. The devadasi system is a practice prevalent in India since ancient times when young girls of a certain section of society were trained as skilled courtesans and were initiated into a profession through a ritual in a temple. These young girls are sexually

exploited at tender ages by temple priests and are thrust into motherhood in their early teens.

7. There is widespread child prostitution prevalent in the country. Besides, we have the estimated three million girl children of the prostitutes who are also sexually exploited in the sex market.
8. Sexual exploitation of institutionalised children - both boys and girls is a regular feature in this country. Very often freshers to institutions of higher learning are forced into sexual acts and watching pornographic films and print materials.
9. Sexual violence and scenes from films and TV network often expose the young minds to experimentation and unhealthy practices.
10. For females from many tribal communities particularly along the highways and rural belt prostitution is their traditional occupation. Truck drivers are their regular clients.
11. There are many myths, bias and prejudices within our cultures: having sex with a virgin (often infants) will cure one of STDs/HIV/AIDS; female genital mutilation will preserve sanctity of marriage; an infant has to be married in infancy; eunuchs who abduct and castrate adolescents are godlike persons etc.
12. Kamasutra—the world's first literary classic on sexual matters—was compiled by an Indian sage, Vatsayana in the 4-5th century A.D. based on collections which date as far back as 2000 B.C. The century old sculptures, worship of Phallus and icon of goddess Yonoi etc. are all associated with sex and sexuality which had no taboo attached to them once upon a time.

(b) Specific Rationale

1. Information, Education and Communication(IEC) are important components of the AIDS prevention and control programme in the country .In order to have an effective

and meaningful campaign on the subject, there is a need for professionally trained and skilled personnel from within the country. And professional training requires a purposely planned programme of study prepared by experts which has the approval of a competent authority. (in this case UGC/University/NCERT).

2. There is an urgent need to train and prepare a large contingent of 'Trainers of Trainees' (TOTs). The TOTs will require adequate training on all aspects of the subject. They have to be expert in this field of study in order to be effective in performing their task.
3. At present there is no cure for AIDS available anywhere in the world. There is no vaccine available which can prevent the spread of this pandemic. Even the available treatment is found to be very costly which is beyond the reach of an ordinary citizen. Further there is no chance of providing treatment facilities, care and rehabilitation to the HIV infected in the near future in India. Therefore, the only way to prevent and control the epidemic is through IEC.
4. One of the most common routes of HIV transmission is through causal sex, although many are also getting affected by substance abuse. These are certain behaviroural patterns that pave the way for rapid spread of the HIV virus. Therefore, prevention and control of the further spread of HIV is mainly possible through changes in behavioural patterns. In order to bring about such behavioural changes, people need to be informed and educated. There is a need for providing accurate and complete information which only a well designed and carefully planned curriculum can offer.
5. There is much hue and cry on the existing AIDS awareness programme which solely propagates one message i.e. the use of condoms-an idea copied from the West. There is much resistance to such teachings both from the parents and teachers. What India requires today is to attack the illness through indigenously developed prevention strategies. This would mean that an AIDS, sex and education programme will require adequate in-put in terms of our cultural, social, religious and traditional values.

6. There is resistance to schools going in for sex education in our country. The teachers are not trained for that task. Therefore, there is a need for providing adequate provisions whereby a teacher in a school is able to master himself/ herself on the subject.
7. Till date none of the over 225 Universities and 162 medical colleges in the country offer any programmes of study (Certificate, Diploma or Degree) on AIDS and Sex Education. It is high time that we initiated a programme which is the need of the hour for our school teachers.

THE OBJECTIVES OF AIDS, SEX AND FAMILY LIFE EDUCATION

Given the unabated spread of HIV in the country if we say no to AIDS, sex and family life education in school life, then that component of our growing children's total being will be shortchanged. Various problems such as unwanted pregnancies, teenage pregnancies, mental and emotional disorders among our adolescents, sexual violence, suicides, rape, eve-teasing, intravenous drug abuse, family disorganization, divorce, single parenthood, child abuse, spouse abuse, wife-swapping, incest and STDs/HIV/AIDS will continue to plague our society. It is high time that we embarked on a mission to launch a comprehensive sex education programme for our young boys and girls against which we may have to face the irreparable damages that the rampant consumerism and media can cause to our children particularly in this age of AIDS.

A comprehensive AIDS, sex and family life education programme should aim at several objectives. An attempt has been made to list out some of the broad objectives of all the three components of the proposed programme of study. It may be noted that the objectives spelt out here below are essentially for teachers, trainers of trainees(TOTs) and those interested in acquiring knowledge on the subject. Depending on the circumstances and target groups like adolescents, youth: boys and girls, one may adopt strategies that are convenient. However, the basic information will remain the same while the extent of discussion will depend on the type of participants, for example urban and rural youth.

I Objectives of AIDS Education

An AIDS education programme in the Indian context may aim at the following objectives :

1. AIDS education should aim at providing accurate and complete information on the biology of HIV/AIDS, its nature, history of its development and the various routes of its transmission.
2. AIDS education curriculum should focus on the various types of STDs and the aspects relating to its prevention, control, treatment and cure.
3. AIDS education should help the participants to be familiar with the commonly used drugs, how these drugs are administered into the human body, the consequences of drug addiction, and its implications in relation to HIV/AIDS.
4. AIDS education should help the learner to prepare oneself to make informed decisions about behaviour that protect one from HIV/AIDS/STDs and substance abuse.
5. AIDS education should enable the learner to understand the signs and symptoms of HIV/AIDS/STDs and seek appropriate medical care, counselling and other support services available in the country.
6. AIDS education should help the learner to value one's own health and relationships free from HIV/AIDS/STDs and substance abuse.
7. AIDS Education should aim at enabling the learner to behave personally and socially in ways that eliminate the risk of spreading HIV infection and involving in substance abuse.
8. AIDS education should provide opportunity to the learner to develop positive attitude towards those who are infected with HIV and addicted to drugs. It should seek to eliminate biased information and myths relating to HIV infection.
9. AIDS education should help the learner to increase the level of knowledge about the impact of HIV/AIDS/STDs and substance abuse on the individual, family, peer group, community, society, state and the national economy.

10. AIDS education programme should develop skills in the learner in initiating action oriented programmes for the prevention and control of AIDS and substance abuse; sensitizing people; initiating teaching, research, extension programmes, etc. In the larger interest of the society, the individual learner should be helped to participate in the rehabilitation programmes and in advocacy.

II Objectives of Sex Education

A comprehensive sex education programme should aim at several objectives. Some of these include:

1. Sex education should seek to help the individual learner in the development of one's sexuality in relation to his/her total being and identity. It should focus on the total personality development of the learner.
2. Sex education should provide adequate opportunity to the learner to increase the knowledge in regard to growth and development of a human being from conception, birth, infancy, to old age through various stages of development particularly in terms of social and psychological adjustment.
3. Sex education should enable the learner to acquire accurate and complete information on facts of life including sexual anatomy, reproductive process and safe sex practices in the light of HIV/AIDS/STDs prevention and control.
4. Sex education programme should aim at increasing awareness and insight regarding physical, mental and emotional, social and spiritual aspects of life as they affect the personality of the individual's relationship between people. It should help the learner to respect self as well as others.
5. Sex education should help the learner to imbibe human values. It should help one to become responsible in making decisions. And it should help the individual to recognize behaviours that are exploitative and self obstructive.

6. Sex education should seek to clear myths and misinformation that are shared in peer groups. It should enable the individual to free oneself from all kinds of guilt feelings.
7. Sex education should prepare the child to face the biological changes that would come about as one steps into puberty and adolescence such as menstruation, seminal emissions, change of voice, enlargement of breasts etc.
8. Sex education should enable the learner to become proud of one's sex and yet appreciative of the attributes and capacities of the other sex. It should help the child to nurture a feeling that sex is something beautiful, positive and creative part of life. Sex education should seek the formation of emotionally stable children.
9. Sex education should provide opportunity to the child to develop ethical, social and spiritual values which will serve as a guide to the individual in personal, family and social relationships. It should endeavour to provide sound knowledge not only of the physical aspects of sex behaviour but also its psychological and sociological aspects so that sexual experience will be viewed as part of the total personality of an individual.

III Objectives of Family Life Education

It may be noted that the family has the primary responsibility for providing sound family life education to children although the school and the religion also play important roles. Some of the goals or objectives of family life education described below are also found in the book on sex education and personality development by Anthony A.D'souza.[11] These objectives are to supplement or reinforce the training provided under the AIDS and sex education programme.

1. Family life education should enable the learner to develop a concept of oneself as a person of worth and dignity. It should help one to understand oneself and lead to growth in personal responsibility.
2. Family life education should seek to encourage the development of ethical, social and spiritual values which

will serve as a guide to the individual in personal, family and social relationships. It will also provide opportunity to increase the ability to use the family effectively as a sanctuary of tolerance and understanding.

3. Family life education should enable the learner to develop appreciation of the roles played by family members and recognise the ways in which these roles interact, change and develop. It will also aim at increasing the knowledge of the family and its importance in the development of healthy personalities.
4. Family life education should promote a wholesome understanding of sexual behaviour, develop respect for a mature and responsible sexual life within marriage; provide forum to discuss the personal and social limitations that are inherent in the use of sex for exploitation or of self satisfaction without regard for others or social consequences.
5. Family life education should help the learner in finding solutions to personal and family problems through increased insight into the needs and behaviour of individuals. It should enable the individual to adjust oneself to the changing situation brought about by changes taking place in the society as a result of liberalisation.
6. Family life education should enable the learner to understand the value of money in relation to the expenditure within the family and prepare one to manage the financial aspects of the person as well as of the family. It should also acquaint one with all sorts of resources available within the community and state which will support and strengthen one's family life.
7. Family life education should provide adequate knowledge and understanding about various aspects related to the health and well being of the members of the family particularly in relation to family welfare, HIV/AIDS/STDs etc.
8. Family life education should seek to provide sufficient understanding about the need for taking care of the sick members within the family, particularly those who are terminally ill.

9. Family life education should prepare the learner to face the challenges posed by the HIV/AIDS/STDs and substance abuse. It should help the learner in understanding the what, why and how of the problems associated with those who are infected. It should also enable the learner to provide home care and emotional support to those infected by HIV within the family.

CURRICULUM DEVELOPMENT

When we talk of curriculum development for the AIDS, sex and family life education programme of study, three major issues have to be borne in mind. They are discipline based issues, individual based issues and relevance based issues.[12] We shall briefly describe these three issues in the following paragraphs.

(a) Discipline Based Issues

Different disciplines make different kinds of demand. Although there may be no issues pertaining to practicals, the very choice of curriculum content, methods of presentation and teaching points of view in interpreting the content chosen, etc. will pose a number of pedagogical and ideological problems. For instance, we have to approach subjects like HIV/AIDS/STDs substance abuse, sex and sexuality and family life education with a lot of flexibility and ideological tolerance as we have to maintain a reasonable degree of objectivity. However, the best we could expect from a democratic curriculum is to make provision for presenting a variety of different and even conflicting views on a given subject. A free play of ideas and interpretations would then allow the learner to make informed choice about the approaches, interpretations, views, etc. while learning a subject. If we are aware of these issues, we could easily anticipate the problems related to each subject and think of possible solutions to them in order that effective implementation of the curriculum may be ensured. Over looking will make even the most well intended curriculum ineffective and narrow.[13]

(b) Individual Based Issues

Because of the change in educational thinking, learner autonomy has gained currency. The curriculum for AIDS, sex and family life education has to take into account a variety of individual needs, the different learning styles and the study habits of the learner. It should also allow individualised learning in geographical, sociological and pedagogical terms. Because of the linguistic, communal, cultural and geographical differences, we need to conduct surveys to identify the areas where individual based programme would be feasible.[14] However, given the present system of higher education supported by around 225 universities across the country, this issue can be tackled if each university developed a curriculum based on the broader objectives and contents developed for a national programme for AIDS, sex and family life education. Besides, the open learning institutions like the Indira Gandhi National Open University and State Open Universities may be able to conveniently provide large number of course with flexibility in choice to suit the individuals specific needs.

(c) Relevance Based Issues

Even curriculum which was very useful and effective at one time may become absolutely irrelevant if it does not respond to the new needs of individuals and the society. Sometimes even the most updated and complete curriculum could become irrelevant, if it does not suit the needs of interests of the learners. This is usually seen in combining diverse subjects under a single programme. Suppose one wants to specialise in the area of sex and family life education, but one is asked to do public administration, economics, and philosophy in order to gain a degree in sex and family life education. Unless the need for a particular combination of subjects is proved valid, the curriculum because of its fixed nature may demotivate the learner.[15] Therefore, care has to be taken to provide large number of electives with about 50 per cent of compulsory courses pertaining exclusively to the discipline in which a certificate, diploma or degree is provided. This is a viable option both in the conventional system and distance learning system of education.

Existing Trends in Curriculum Development

The current popular approach to curriculum development in India at the moment is 'top-down'. This is seen in the conventional system, distance education system as well as in correspondence education in the country. The University Grants Commission(UGC) has compiled curriculum for various disciplines based on the syllabus collected from various universities spread across the country. In most cases, either an individual or a group of academics worked on compiling syllabus on project basis. A 'top-down' approach was adopted for the process where learners and community participation was almost nil. In the Indira Gandhi National Open University(IGNOU), New Delhi the largest open university in the Commonwealth, a team of experts in a subject area makes a proposal for launching a programme of study. Administrative bodies such as the planning Board, the Academic Council and the Board of Management subsequently examine and approve the proposal and programmes are launched.

The contents of a course are decided at various levels by the academics in an area. These will be practising teachers either in the conventional or open university system. A subject centered design pays little attention to learner's need and is therefore of little value when the aim is crisis management.[16]

The context here requires a problem centred design for curriculum development and implementation. A problem-centered design tends to focus on the issues of actual life, individuals and society. The learning tasks are pre-planned, but cater for learners needs. They thus focus on both the context and the needs and experiences of learners. Very often this design takes the form of a core-cum-specific needs model in which core takes care of the basic content and specific needs are attended to with the help of need-based courses used as supplements to the core component. I suggest that India needs a "bottom-up model" [17] which would involve the following stages:

1 identification of a target group
2. formation of specific objectives in relation to identified needs
3. selection of content to meet these objectives
4. organisation of content in the form of study units, and
5. selection of learning activities to accompany the content and to fulfill the objectives.

The development of a comprehensive curriculum for AIDS, sex and family life education should encompass areas concerning cultural ethos, social taboos, religious and community attitudes and the behavioural practices of various communities for whom the course is being prepared, It should provide adequate learning experiences which are relevant and acceptable. Such a plan should help promote responsible practices regarding personal, family and community health. Such a bottom-up approach is discussed by Weinstein and Fantini.[18]

IGNOU as a Model: A Case for the Future

Considering the existing network of IGNOU with 17 regional centres, it is appropriate that the preliminary curriculum development meetings be organised on a regional basis. As a prelude to the regional level meetings, the Regional Director, with academic assistance from IGNOU headquarters, would organise state level meetings in regional centres which have more than one state to monitor under their jurisdiction. Prior to the state level meeting, it is essential that feed back from local communities be obtained. The following steps are suggested.

Firstly, public concern must be created about the serious effect of AIDS upon society and the dangers associated with unprotected sexual activities outside marriage. There is already a massive programme of awareness campaign going in the country. An appeal in the form of a letter could be sent to the IGNOU academic counsellors numbering over 10,000 spread across the country. This will help to mould large scale academic opinion. The academic counsellors in turn can influence over 3,94,388 adult learners(as on 1996-97) of IGNOU.[19] The student population on their part will influence the local leaders.

Secondly, the public concern should enable the formation of advisory committees at the study centre level. IGNOU has about 270 study centres[20] proportionately distributed around the country. The local advisory committees should be representative of appropriate community components. If there is likely to be opposition from individuals, informed professionals should counsel these individuals.

Thirdly, the suggestions of local advisory committees should be used as public opinion to gain support from the policy makers and authorities. The academic counsellors and local intellectuals should be motivated to support the programme through local media.

Local community level committees may include academics who are impartial and sensitive to the issues pertinent to the various communities, such as members of non-governmental organisations working in the field of AIDS and family welfare programmes at the grassroots. Representation may also be necessary from high risk groups.

Rigid religious beliefs, social taboos, cultural ethos, negative family attitudes and lack of appropriate communication tools are among the principal obstacles to educating people in rural settings about AIDS, Sex and Family Life Education. In order to overcome these obstacles, AIDS education programme must be specifically targeted on a community basis. Recruiting community leaders from among local residents is an important strategy.[21]

The state level curriculum designing committee may consist of representatives from the local community level committees. This committee will examine the suggestions received from various local committees and prepare a draft after due filtration. The state level committee will consider the needs and attitudes of various communities and high risk groups. The course coordinators from IGNOU headquarters will participate in the state level meetings. This will enable them to be aware of local needs and interests.

The minutes of the state level expert committee meetings on curriculum should be recorded and circulated among the regional level experts for their careful study, and comments. The regional level experts for curriculum designing should be drawn from participants of the state level curriculum development committee. This will enable the curriculum designing committee at the regional level to cater for all special needs and for the attitudes of various communities. The members of the expert committee for curriculum designing at the national level would consist of members drawn from the regional level expert committees. The faculty members coordinating the programme of study at the headquarters would examine and compile the recommendations of the regional level expert committee meetings., The draft programme would then be passed on to the national curriculum development committee on AIDS.

The national curriculum development committee should follow the following steps in developing the actual curriculum: (a) assessment of needs, interests and comprehension abilities of the learner; (b) statement of the problem; (c) organisational framework for developing curriculum; (d) formulation of goals and objectives; (e) selection of courses, block and units; (f) strategy selection, i.e. learning opportunities, experiences, activities, etc. and (g) evaluation component. The broad content areas are given at the end of this chapter.

The national expert committee for curriculum design will prepare the final draft for the programme of study on AIDS, Sex and Family Life Education. It will list the general and specific objectives, give broad content suggestions, make suggestions for learning experiences and evaluation procedures and provide appropriate references for the learner and the academics teaching the courses. The national expert committee will determine the needs, interests and comprehension abilities of learners from various regions, states, communities and high risk groups. Based on this information, the course preparation team will then compose the units.

Preparation of units on content areas such as AIDS, Sex and Family Life Education can be a very difficult task. Disagreements centre on religious belief, public versus private morality[22] and control from policy makers and authorities. Systematic promotion campaigns and academic support should be aimed at ensuring the success of the programme.

Target Group

The target group for the proposed programme of study on AIDS, Sex and Family Life Education may include: students from conventional university system, correspondence education, distance learning mode as well as those from higher secondary schools. Apart from student population, in-service persons such as teacher(university, college and school) physicians, dentists, nurses, para-medicals and medicos, opinion builders, politicians, members of judiciary, media persons, journalists, religious leaders, public officials, persons from personnel and welfare departments of corporate sector, commercial sex workers, truck drivers, drug users, functionaries from NGO and VO (Voluntary Organization) network and social and welfare sector, police and defence personnel and any other persons interested in the subject.

COURSE CONTENTS

Having discussed various aspects involved in the process of curriculum development let us describe in brief course contents for some of the courses. The course contents given below were developed through deliberations held with academics from various disciplines, NGO functionaries working in the field of HIV/AIDS and family welfare programme, school teachers, media persons, religious leaders and representatives from donor agencies. In all, three half-day workshops were held with about 10 to 12 participants in each workshop. A concept paper with some suggested course structure was circulated well in advance. Course structure was given final shape during the workshops.

Although I have suggested 'bottom-up' approach for curriculum development, due to paucity of funds for the purpose of preparing this dissertaiton, the workshop model with 'top-down' approach was adopted. The purpose of this exercise is only to provide some basic structure based on which a comprehensive and need based curriculum may be developed by various universities across the country using bottom-up approach wherever possible. The course contents mentioned below should not be taken as a foolproof document. Depending upon the local needs within a state and religions within a given state, necessary addition and deletions may be made. Similarly only a broad framework is suggested for any programme of study on the proposed discipline. It is hoped that the provision of large number of courses will enable the learner to have choice according to one's requirement.

BASIC COURSES

1. Significance and need for HIV/AIDS/Education

• Definition of HIV/AIDS, types of HIV. • AIDS as a disease. • Signs and symptoms of HIV infection. • Incubation period.

• History of AIDS origin. •Theories of AIDS origin: isolated community theory, green monkey theory, germ warfare theory, and mutation theory. • Types of tests for HIV; ELISA test and Western Blot-test. • False positive and false negative results and implications.

2. HIV Transmission

• Concept clarification and significance. • Principal routes of HIV transmission; HIV and body fluids; sexual activities and target groups: prostitutes and their clients; truck drivers; devadasis; eunuchs; homosexuals; lesbians; street children and institutionalised persons. • Significance of blood products: organ donation; skin piercing needles and equipments. • Target groups: health clinic workers and clients; barbershop, medical laboratories; blood banks; blood donors: professional and voluntary; blood safety programme. • Mother to child transmission: Donor insemination; milk donation and HIV infected infants. • Other target groups: STD patients; intravenous drug abusers; thalassemia patients; haemophiliac patients; tattooing; male and female circumcision; migratory population; tribal groups HIV and substance abuse: commonly used drugs; HIV and STDs; types of STDs; prevention and treatment of STDs.

3. HIV Testing and Treatment Options

• Objectives of HIV surveillance. • Who needs HIV test. • Types of tests for HIV-ers (ELISA, Rapid, Simple tests), Western Blot test. • Development of testing kits - erratic and poor quality testing kits. • HIV surveillance centres and zonal blood testing centres. • HIV reference Centres for confirmatory tests. • Strategies for testing: targeted interventions; compulsory testing and human rights violation. • Sentinel surveillance *Vs* transfussion test - their implications. • Treatment for HIV: Development of drugs, AZT, protease inhibitors, etc. • Alternative treatment - Ayurvedic and Homoeopathic treatment; efforts in development of vaccine; life expectancy; clinical trails. • Confidentiality, moral struggle and ethical dilemmas.

4. Social Aspects of HIV/AIDS

• AIDS scenario: Global, Regional and National. • Trends in HIV infection in various States and UTs. • HIV and poverty. • High risk groups in India: • prostitutes and their children; • child prostitutes; • homosexuals, lesibans and eunuchs; • thalassemia and haemophilia patients; • intravenous drug users; • prisoners, persons in armed forces; police; • health care providers; • blood banks; sperm banks; milk banks; organ banks; • tattooing and body piercing instruments; barber shops; • HIV and women. • HIV and children. • HIV and its implications on family. • HIV *Vs.* social, cultural, religious and traditional values. • Impact of HIV on national and global economy.

5. HIV Prevention and Control

• National AIDS control programme: strategies and progress. • Programme management : objectives and strategies. • Inter-sectoral collaboration; collaboration with government of India, States and UTs, Bilateral agencies: UNAIDS, WHO, UNICEF, UNESCO, UNFPA UNDP; Bilateral donor agencies: SIDA, USAID, NORAD, ODA(UK): European Community; NGOs and Corporate sector. HIV/AIDS surveillance: strategies and case management. • Sexually Transmitted Diseases: policy and strategies • Condom programming. • Targeted interventions. • Blood safety programme: objectives and strategies. • Information, Education and Communication(IEC). • Reduction of impact: home care, counselling strategies. • HIV programme financing and strategic plan 1992-97. • Monitoring, Evaluation and Research.

. AIDS, Law and Human Rights

Meaning of law and meaning of Constitution. • Human Rights nd Human Rights Commission. • Universal declaration of human ghts. • Rule of law and judiciary as a regulatory mechanism. • IDS and national laws; constitutional provisions. • The Indian enal code, criminal procedure Code and AIDS. • Law of Torts nd medical jurisprudence. • Torts and AIDS. • Consumer protection ct. 1986. • The Dentists Act 1949. • The code of Medical Ethics Indian Medical Council Act 1956. • Lessons from the AIDS revention bill 1989. • The Drugs and Cosmetics(1st Amendment

Rules) 1993. • The Delhi Artificial Insemination(Human) Act 1995. • New Delhi Declaration and Action Plan for HIV/AIDS 1995. • Censorship laws, obscenity laws, right to information. • Termination of pregnancy; compulsory testing; legal aids and access to law.

7. HIV, Substance Abuse and STDs

• Link between HIV, STDs and substance abuse. • Type of STDs; commonly used drugs. • STDs and gender perspective. • Policy and strategy development for STD. • Treatment options in STDs. • Programme management and case management in STDs. • Why people use drugs. • Extent of prevalence of STDs. • Extent of prevalence of substance abuse and target groups. • Treatment options and de-addiction programme. • Condom programme: strategies and target groups.

8. Family Life Education and HIV

• Concept, meaning and scope of family life education. • Significance and need of family life education in the light of HIV/AIDS. • Methods of imparting family life education at various development stages. • Role of home, school and religion in family life education. • Development of personality and moral values in life. • Importance of family life education in individual, family and community. • Objectives of family life education.

9. Sex Education and HIV

• Concept, meaning and scope of sex education. • Importance and need of sex education in the light of HIV/AIDS/STDs. • Changes in moral life, social change; liberalisation and changing concept of gender roles. • Rational for sex, sexuality and sex education. • Sex and society; sex and religion; sex and culture; sex and traditional values. • Forms of sexual control; public resistance. • Objectives of Sex education. • Role of home and school in sex education; when to start sex education.

10. Facts of Life: Physiological Components

• Human sexuality: concept clarification. • Organisation of male and female reproductive system: objectives and purpose.

• The male reproductive system: scrotum and testes, sperm and penis, *vas deferens*, bladder, prostrate gland and urethra, night emissions/wet dreams. • The female reproductive system: clitoris, labia majora, labia minora, female urethra, skene's and bartholin's glands, hymem, and bartholin's glands, hymen, vagina, anus, cervix, uterus, ovary, fallopian tubes, breasts. • Menstrual Cycle and onset of puberty. • Role of sex hormones: estrogens and progesterone. • Masturbation, guilt feeling and release of sexual tension. • Common concerns about sex, sexuality and HIV/AIDS/STDs. • Removal of misconceptions and beliefs. • Pregnancey: signs of pregnancy and health care. • Maternal fears, physical and emotional care of the child in the womb. • Child bearing and preparing for child birth.

11. Marriage, Partnership and Parenthood

• Concept clarification, preparation for marriage • Marriage in a changing society • Changing social scene and changing role of women; marriage; and career. • Meaning of marriage and choosing life partner. • Religious, cultural and social values in family life. • Achieving harmony; learning to give and take. • Sexual adjustment; quarrel and trust. • Planning for a family and becoming parents. • Family planning and spacing : Need for family planning. • Caring of Children and Economic Independence. • Partnership and home making: sharing burden and responsibility. • Family welfare programme of government and religious restrictions. • Methods of family planning: advantages and disadvantages. • Medical termination of pregnancy etc. medical, legal, social, and emotional aspects, and religious attitudes.

12. Human Growth, Maturity and Self-control

• Biological, social, psychological and development aspects of various stages of human growth. • Conception, infancy, babyhood, childhood, adolescent, adulthood, aging and death. • Youth, love and awakening of sexual interests. • Ethical values and personal behaviour. • Sex and self control; pre-marital chastity; responsible sexual behaviour. • Arranged marriage *Vs* love marriage; mature relationship and religious attitudes. • Adjustment and maladjustment; confusion about sex and false attitudes to sex.

• Early years of marriage; life along with offspring. • Role of husband, wife, parents, grand parents. • Separation, divorce, responsibility of children, religious and legal restrictions.

13. HIV/AIDS and Social Life

• Nature of social relationships in social institutions: Religion, marriage and family. • Changing features in the family in relation to HIV/AIDS. Means and agencies of social control in society that have a bearing on the spread and check on HIV/AIDS/STDs. • Importance of culture, norms and the forces that contribute their degradation in ethical and moral terms. • Modernisation and industrialisation process as factors responsible for the erosion or degradaton of values and ethics in society. • Low standards of living, illiteracy, lack of awareness, poor health and hygiene and their implication on HIV. • Links between economic pressures, migration, unplanned growth of urban centres, development of slums and implication for the prevention and control of HIV/AIDS/STDs. • Low status of women in Indian society and family. • Women tending to become passive victims of exploitation and their vulnerality to HIV/AIDS/STDs.

14. HIV/AIDS and Family Counselling

Meaning, goals and nature of counselling. • Types and dimensions of counselling. • Models and process in counselling; approaches in counselling. • Principles in counselling; its techniques and skills. • Factors influencing counselling; social, emotional, religious, gender, age, etc., their relationship in counselling. • Group counselling; referral services; professional ethics and legal aspects involved in counselling. • HIV/AIDS/STDs counselling and guidance : pre-test counselling and post-test counselling; substance abuse, sexual violence; family crisis, breakdown in marriage; separation; sudden death etc., • Family counselling; preparation for marrigae; partnership, adjustment, love, patience, compromise, counselling for family planning. • Sex education counselling: removing misconceptions and beliefs; counselling for behavioural defects; counselling against fears and anxieties. • Existing trends in counselling services in India.

15. Health and Social Aspects of HIV/AIDS/STDs

• Concept of health and health care and rehabilitation services in the context of terminal illness like HIV/AIDS. • Facts affecting health and health care system in India. • National Health Policy, Health Planning and Health programmes in five year plans. • Establishment of National AIDS Control Programme by Government of India. • National strategic plan 1992-97 for prevention and control of HIV/AIDS in India. • District and primary health centre: organisation and functions. • Concept of public health; programmes; community diagnosis; community treatment and care. • Health education—meaning, importance, components of health education. • Concept of the patient as a person; social and psychological factors involved in HIV/AIDS/STDs; home care and rehabilitation. • Cultural and social response to HIV/AIDS. • Levels of prevention and control: Role of social worker in health care team; role of national and international agencies in health care and promotion.

ELECTIVES

1. Population dynamics and Family planning.
2. Human growth and development.
3. Substance Abuse, HIV/AIDS/STDs: prevention and control.
4. Health Education and Population education.
5. HIV and women.
6. HIV and children.
7. Health care system and services in India.
8. Communication theories and their application in the field of health.
9. Medical information for HIV/AIDS workers.
10. Health and socio economic development.
11. Home care and coping with terminal illness.
12. Social security and health insurance.
13. Implications of AIDS on economy, culture, religion, social, moral and traditional values.
14. Education for awareness and-strategies of social change.
15. Psychiatric information for health workers.
16. Dynamics of human behaviour.
17. Preventive and correctional law.
18. Policy formulation and programme implementation.

During the second half of the twentieth century (just after independence), teachers were busy imparting knowledge and information on good character which included responsibility, courage, fairness, honesty, respect and self control. Modesty and sexual morality were also taught to youth as values. Abstinence until marriage is still the expected standard of behaviour for youth from good families and most of the young people in rural India. Character based sex education or life skill education will go a long way in helping young people to understand the moral dimensions of sexual conduct. Once the core ethical values such as respect, responsibility and self-control with regard to sex and sexuality can be incorporated in the exiting curriculum, society can expect drastic changes in the attitudes and behaviours of young people in lifestyles to a great extent. In order to meaningfully impart life skill education in the context of HIV/ADIS, sex and sexuality, we need to teach the young about honesty, respect, courage, self-discipline, justice, humility, responsibility and Kindness.

Life skill education should also include activity oriented methods to make the learner to be aware about one-self; cultivation of empathy; learning to cope with emotions and stress; learning to take appropriate decisions and solving problems; inculcating creative thinking; acquiring effective communication skills; and maintaining good interpersonal relationship with people of the same sex as well as that of the opposite sex.

Methods that could be adopted for imparting life skill education could include group work, sharing of experiences, quizzes, puppet shows, organizing literacy activities such as debates, essay writing, inter-school competitions, story writing, development of posters and poems which are culture specific.

SUMMARY

For the first time an attempt has been made towards developing a curriculum for AIDS, sex and family life education by involving academics, physicians and NGOs involved in HIV related activities. Through a series of three workshops, course structure for 15 basic courses have been developed. Further a list of as many as 18 electives have been provided which may be adopted by universities and other institutions of higher education in the country. This chapter has also described the details of existing AIDS education programme in the country the generic and specific rationale and objectives of the proposed programme of study on AIDS, sex and family life education. It has also suggested the replacement of the "top down approach" by "bottom-up approach" for curriculum development.

REFERENCES

1. Anthony A D'Souza, Sex education and personality development. Indian Social Institute, New Delhi. 1979, p. 117.

2. Anspaugh, J.David and Ezell, O.Gene, Teaching Today's Health (3ed edition) Merril Publishing Company, Columbus, 1983, pp. 309-334.
3. Sabina Inderjit, No to sex education in school, TOI, New Delhi, 21 Sept. 1994.
4. WHO Call for more sex education, TOI New Delhi, 1 December, 1994. (The report is quoted from a Geneva publication by AP)
5. Dr. Prakash Kothari in his draft proposal on the "National Sexual Health Education Programmes", released at the Valedictory function of the third Asian Conference of Sexology, held in New Delhi, Hindustan Times, New Delhi, 1 December, 1994.
6. Gracious Thomas, AIDS and Family Education, Rawat Publication. Jaipur, 1995, pp. 167-195.
7. Gracious Thomas and V. Ranga, Prevention and Control of AIDS through distance education. In One World, many voices (conference paper) 17 World Conference for Distance Education, Birmingham, 26-30 June, 1995.
8. Gracious Thomas, concept paper (unpublished) : submitted for the establishment of a Teaching, Research and Extension Centre for AIDS programme' at Utkal University. Bhubaneswar, 1996.
9. NACO, National AIDS Control Programme India : Country Scenario up date, MHFW, Government of India, December 1995, pp. 73-74.
10. Manorama, India and the states : principal languages. The Manorama Year Book, Malayala Manorama, Kottayam, 1994.
11. Anthony A. D'souza, op. cit., pp. 84-85.
12. IGNOU, Curriculum Development for Distance Education. Learning Transactions and Improvements, ES-316, Block 3,IGNOU, New Delhi, 1993, pp. 64-66.
13. *Ibid.*
14. *Ibid.*
15. *Ibid.*
16. Gracious Thomas and V. Ranga, *op. cit.*
17. Tabu, H. Curriculum Development: Theory and Practice, (1962) in : Ornstein, C. and Hunkins, P. Curriculum : foundations, Principles and Issues, New Jersey, Prentice Hall. 1986.
18. Weinstein, G. and Fantini, M. Towards, Humanistic Education: A Curriculum of affect, New York, Praeger, 1970
19. Data available with the Planning Division, Indira Gandhi National Open University (IGNOU), New Delhi, August 1997
20. IGNOU Profile 1997. IGNOU Printing and Publication Division, New Delhi, 1997.
21. Hultz Bot, Educating people in non-urban settings : Using local "leaders" to help overcome obstacles. Highlights from the 2nd international counterpart forum at the IXth International Conference on AIDS, International Counterpart Reporter, 1993.
22. Anspaugh, J. David, and Ezell, O. Gene, *op. cit.*

Bibliography

Abu Baker, Dato Suleiman. 1991. An overview of the HIV/AIDS situation in Malaysia. Paper presented at the National Seminar on AIDS. December 3—5, 1991, Kuala Lumpur, Malaysia.

Ahmed P.I.(ed) 1992. Living and dying with AIDS, New York: Plenum Press.

Altman, D. 1986. AIDS in the mind of America. New York: Anchor Press/ Doubleday.

Anderson, R. and MAY, R. Ploting the spread of AIDS. New Scientist. March 1987, Volume 26. pp. 54—57.

Anspaugh. David. J. and Ezell. Gene 0. 1983. Teaching today's health (3rd ediction). Columbus: Merril Publishing company.

Asian Development Bank. 1992. The economic impact of AIDS in Asia. Manila: Asian Development Outlook.

Anon. 2002. AIDS Stigma forms an Insidious Barrier to Prevention / care: HIV Experts describe Problem in India: Aids Alert, 17: pp. 111-113.

APAC-VHS. 2004. *HIV Risk Behaviour Surveillance Survey in Tamil Nadu —Wave VIII*. Chennai: APAC-VHS.

Barnett. T. and P. Blaikie. 1992. AIDS in Africa: Its present and future impact. London: Bellhaven.

Bhagbanprakash(ed). 1994. AIDS education for student youth: A training manual. New Delhi: National Service Scheme, Department of youth Affairs and Sports, Ministry of Human Resource Development, Govt. of India.

Bloom, David. E. and Lyons, Joyce, V. (eds). Economic Implications of AIDS in Asia. New Delhi: UNDP.

Bloom D. and G. Carliner, 1988. The economic impacts of AIDS in the United States. Science 239:604—10

Bremner, Jeni and Hillin, Anthony. 1993 Sexuality, young people and care. London: CCETSW.

Burns, Jo. and Wright, Cathie. 1993. A trainer's guide to workshops on young people and sexuality in the context of HIV/AIDS. London: HMSO Publications.

Bate, S.C. 2002a. Good News for AIDS Myths in *Missionalia*, 30:1 (April) 93-108.

Callen. M. 1991. Surviving AIDS. New York: Harper Collins.

Chela, C.M., I.D. Campbell, and Z. Siankanga. 1989. Clinical care as part of integrated AIDS management in a Zambian rural community. AIDS care 1(3) 319—325.

Cohen F.L., Durham J.D. (eds). 1993. Women, children and HIV/AIDS. New York: Springer publishing.

Coombs, R.H. (ed). 1988. The family context of adolescents drug use. New York: Harrington Park Press.

Choo, S. and D. Chand. 1990. Report on HIV high risk group population. Seoul: Korea Institute of Health and Social Affairs.

Coleman, G. 1992. *Human Sexuality*. N.Y.: Alba House.

Directorate General of Health Services. 1990. Medium team plan for the prevention and control of AIDS in India, New Delhi: Ministry of Health & Family Welfare in cooperation with WHO.

D'souza, Anthony. A. 1975. Happiness in marriage. New Delhi: Indian Social Institute.

D'souza, Anthony. A. 1979. Sex education and personality development. New Delhi: Indian Social Institute.

Dunlop, D. 1987. The economic impacts of the disease AIDS: an analysis of the costs of the disease and a proposed study strategy in poor countries. Bostan, Massachusetts: Abt Associates.

De Guzman, A. 2001. Reducing Social Vulnerability to HIV/AIDS: Models of Care and their Impact in Resource-Poor Settings. *AIDS Care*, 13(5): 663-675.

Eastwood, A., and Maynard. 1988. Treating AIDS patients: Is it ethical to be efficient? Paper presented at the first international conference on the global impact of AIDS. London, March.

Fee E.. Fox D.M. (eds). 1992. AIDS: The making of a chronic disease. Berkeley: University of California Press.

Fernando, M.D. 1993. AIDS and Intravenous Drug Use: The influence of morality, politics, social science, and race in the making of Tragedy. Westport, Conn: Praeger Press.

Fisher D.G. (ed). 1990. AIDS and Alcohol/Drug Abuse. New York: Harrington Park Press.

Fox, D., and E. Thomas. 1987. AIDS cost analysis and social policy. Law medicine and Health care 15:185—211.

Friedlander, Walter, A. 1964. Concepts and methods of social work. New Delhi: Prentice Hall of India.

Frumkin, Lyn and Leonard John. 1994. Questions and Answers on AIDS. Los Angeles: PMIC.

Farmer, P., et al., 2001. Community-based Approaches to HIV Treatment in Resource Poor Settings. *Lancet*, 358: 404-409.

Gani A., and F. Jalal. 1992. Indonesia: Economic Implications of HIV/AIDS. Paper presented at the regional consultations on economic implications of HIV/AIDS, organized by UNDP. May 25—28, 1992. Bangalore, India.

Gillespie, S. 1989. Potential impact of AIDS on farming systems: a case study from Rwanda. Land use policy 6: 301—12.

Gingburg H.M. 1984. Intravenous drug users and AIDS. Public Health Report. 1984, pp. 206—212.

Glick, Robert. A. (ed). 1993. Law, ethics and HIV New Delhi: UNDP.

Geodert J.J., and Blattner. W.A. 1985. The epidemiology of AIDS and related conditions. In, De Vita V.T.(ed). AIDS: Etiology, diagnosis, treatment and prevention. Philadelphia: Lippincott.

Gordon, G. and Klouda. A. 1988. Talking AIDS — a guide for community workers. London and Basingstoke: Macmillan publishers.

Griffin, Charles. C. 1990. Health Financing in Asia. Report No. 8553—ASI. Washington, D.C: World Bank.

Grugni, Anthony. 1994. Sex education. Bombay: Better yourself books.

Gaie, J.B.R. 2002. Moral issues and Responsibilities regarding HIV/AIDS in *Missionalia*, 30:2 (August) 265-287.

Hardy, A., Rauch, K., Echenberg, D., Morgan, W., and Curran, J. 1986. The economic impact of first 10,000 cases of AIDS in the U.S. Journal of the American Medical Association 255(2).

Hayzer, Noeleen. 1986. Working women in South—East Asia. In Development, Subordination and Emancipation. Philadelphia: Open University Press.

Huber J.T.(ed). 1992. How to find information about AIDS. Binghamton. N.Y: Harrington Park Press.

Hubley, John., Choudhury Shankar and Chandramouli, V. 1995. The AIDS handbook: a guide to the understanding of AIDS and HIV. Bombay: Popular Prakashan Private Limited.

Huddart. Jenny, and Lyons, Joyce. V. 1992. NGO response to H1V/AIDS in Asia: Case studies. New Delhi: UNDP.

Hsiung, P.C. and Thomas, V. 2001 Coping Strategies of People with HIV/ AIDS in Negative Health Care Experiences: *AIDS Care*, 13(6): 749-762.

ILO. 2000. *HIV/AIDS: A threat to decent work, productivity and development*, Document for discussion at the Special High-Level Meeting on HIV/AIDS and the World of Work. Geneva.

ILO. 2001. *Report of the Tripartite Meeting of Experts on HIV/AIDS and the World of Work*. Geneva.

Jeffers, James R. 1991. Economic analysis for the AIDS surveillance and education project. Manila, Philippines: Philipine Department of Health.

Jejeebhoy, S.J. 1998. Adolescent Sexual and Reproductive Behaviour: A Reveiw of the Evidence from India. *Social Science Medicine*, 46(10): 1275-1290.

Kapoor, Indira. 1991. Training in AIDS/HIV Counselling in India. In Indian Journal of Social Work. Bombay: Tata Institute of social Science. November 1991.

Kapoor, Promilla. 1994. The Indian call girls. New Delhi: Orient paperbooks.

Katchadourian, Herant. 1972. Human sexuality: sense and nonsense. Stanford, California: Stanford Alumini Association.

Korshed. M. Parvi. 1992. Challenge of AIDS. New Delhi: National Book Trust, India.

Kristol, I. 1992. AIDS and false innocence. The wall street journal, August 7—8.

Kubler, Ross. E. 1993. AIDS: The ultimate challenge. New York: Macmillan Publishing co.

Kumio, I. 1998. Report on one AIDS risk group. MPH thesis. School of public health, Yonsei University, Korea.

Leukefeld. C.G., Battjes R.J. and Amsel. A. (eds). 1990. AIDS and intravenours drug use. Future directions for community—based prevention research. New York: Gordon Press.

Lewis, Gwyneth., Joel, Finlay., and Roy, Widdus. 1991. AIDS programme in transition. World Health Forum 12: 297—306.

Lynch. V.J., Lloyd, G.A., and Fimbres M.F. (eds). 1993. The changing face of AIDS: Implications for Social Work practice. Westport, Conn: Auburn House Press.

Lyons, Joyce. V., and Morita, Karen. Y. 1993. Promoting NGO/Business sector partnerships for AIDS prevention: consultation proceedings and manual. New Delhi: UNDP.

Mane, Purnima, and Mitra, Shubhada. A. 1992. AIDS prevention—the socio—cultural context in India. Bombay: Tata Institute of Social Science.

Manorma. 1994. India and the States: principle languages. In Manorama year book. Kottayam: Malayala Manorama.

Mathew, N.M.(ed). 1996. Health for the Millions. New Delhi: VHAI (Nov.—Dec. 1996).

Maurus, J. 1992. A woman's guide to a happy home. Bombay: Better yourself books.

McBride, D. 1991. From T.B. to AIDS: Epidemics among urban blacks since 1900. New York: University of New York Press.

McDonald, H. 1992. AIDS in Asia: The Africa Syndrome. Far Eastern Economic Review. February 20: 28—29.

Monette. P. 1990. Borrowed time: An AIDS Memoir. New York. Avon.

Muecke, Marjorie. A. 1990. The AIDS prevention dilema in Thailand. Asian and pacific population forum 4(4): 1—28.

Mulleady G. 1992. Counselling drug users about HIV and AIDS. Cambridge, Mass: Blackwell Scientific publications.

Myers. C., and H. Henn. 1988. Potential impact of AIDS in Africa. In Robert, I Rothberg. (ed). Africa in the 1990s. Algonac, Michigan: Reference Publications.

Mukhopadhyay, Swapna et al. 2000. *Gender dimensions of HIV/AIDS: A Community-based study in Delhi*. New Delhi: Institute of Social Studies Trust.

NACO, 1994. AIDS education in shcools; A Training package. New Delhi: National AIDS control Organisation, MHFW, Govt. of India.

NACO. 1995. National AIDS Control Programme India—country scenario update. New Delhi: NACO. MHFW, Govt. of India (Dec. 1995).

NACO. 2000-2001. *Combating HIV/AIDS in India*, National AIDS Control Organization. Ministry of Health and Family Welfare, GOI.

Nataraj, S. 1990. Indian prostitutes highlight AIDS dilemmas, Development forum (UNDP) XVIII (6) 1, 16.

National Institute of Mental Health. 1986. Coping with AIDS. Rockville: U.S. Department of Health and Human Services.

Panos Dossier. 1990. The 3rd epidemic—repercussions of the fears of AIDS. London: The Panos Institute.

Panos Dossier. 1990. Triple Jeopardy—women & AIDS London: The Panos Institute.

Preble, E.A. 1990. Impact of HIV/AIDS on African children. Social Science and Medicine 31(6): 671—680.

Priya, R. 1998. Rethinking AIDS in Women and the RHC Package. *Some Epidemiological and Social Considerations*. New Delhi: Centre of Social Medicine and Community Health.

Randall R.C. 1991. Marijuana & AIDS: Pot, Politics & PWAs in America. Washington, D.C: Galen Press.

Remien, Robert. H. 1994. Psychological aspects of counselling. In 1994 National HIV Frontline Forum. New York: NCM Publishers.

Remien R.H., Rabkin R.G., Kotoff L. and Williams J.B.W 1992. Coping strategies and health beliefs of AIDS long—term survivors. Psychol Health 6:335—345.

Ramachandran R., et al. 2003. Seroprevalence of human immunodeficiency virus (HIV) infection among tuberculosis patients in Tamil Nadu. *Indian Journal of Medical Research*, 118: 147-151.

Sabatier, Reena. 1998. Blaming Others: Prejudice, race and worldwide AIDS. London: The Panos Institute. Shilts, Randy. 1987. And the band played on. New York: ST. Martin's Press.

Seigel, Larry. 1988. AIDS and substance abuse. New York: Harrington Park Press.

Shepard, D. 1990. Cost of AIDS in a developing area: Indirect and direct cost of AIDS in Puerto Rico. In Economic Aspects of AIDS and HIV infection, pp. 226—237. Berlin and New York: Springer—Verleg.

Sircar, Debashree, De., and Tewari. H.R. 1996. Migration mobility and HIV infection. In Social Action, New Delhi Indian Social Institute (Oct/Dec. 1996)

Soda, K. 1991. Epidemiology and control of HIV/AIDS in Japan. In current and Future Dimensions of HIV/AIDS Pandemic. A capsule summary. Geneva: Global programme on AIDS. WHO.

Sen, S. 2003. High HIV Prevalence States: An Analysis of the HIV/AIDS Scenario. *Health for the Millions*, 28(6): 28-30.

Sharma, D.C. 2004. Indian Health Groups Demand Right to Health. *The Lancet*, 363(9415): 1123.

Smith–Fawzi M.C. et al. 2003. Prevalence and Risk Factors of STDs in Rural Haitri: Implications for Policy and Programming in Resource-poor Settings. International Journal of STDs and AIDS.

Swaminathan, S. et al. 2000. Risk of development of tuberculosis in HIV infected patients. *International Journal of Tuberculosis and Lung Disease*, 4: 839-44.

Saayman, W. 1999. AIDS-still posing an unanswered question: in *Missionalia*, 27:2 (August) 208-219.

Taba, H. 1962. Curriculum development. Theory and practice. In Ornstein. C., and Hunkins.p 1986. Curriculum Foundations, principles and issues. New Jersey: Prentice Hall.

Thampu, Valson. 1994. The dream and the dragon... The truth about substance abuse. New Delhi: TRACI.

Taniguchi, Hiroshi (ed). 1996. Integration. Tokyo: Japanese Organisation for International cooperation in family planning. (Winter 1996).

Temoshok. L., and Baum. A. (eds). 992. Psychosocial perspective on AIDS. Etiology, prevention and treatment. Hillstate. N.J: Lawrence Erlbaum Associate.

Thomas, Gracious. 1994. AIDS in India: Myth and Reality. New Delhi and Jaipur: Rawat Publications.

Thomas. Gracious. 1995. AIDS and Family Education. New Delhi and Jaipur: Rawat Publications.

Thomas, Gracious. 1995. AIDS in India: Need for social work intervention. In contemporary social work. Lucknow: Department of Social Work, Lucknow University (oct. 1995).

Thomas, Gracious, and Ranga V. 1995. Prevention and control of AIDS through distance education. In one world many voices: Quality in open and distance learning. Sewart David (ed). Birmigham U.K. 26—30 June 1995. 17th World conference for distance education. The Open University.

Thomas Gracious. 1997 (third impression: 2000) Prevention of AIDS: In search of answers. New Delhi: Shipra publications.

Thomas, Gracious., Sinha. N.P. and Thomas, Johnson K. 1997. AIDS Social Work and Law. New Delhi and Jaipur: Rawat publications.

Thomas, Gracious and Pereira, George, 1999 HIV and Pastoral Care, New Delhi, CBCI Health Commission.

Thomas, Gracious, 1999 HIV/AIDS Ki Rokdham: Patiya Pusthak. New Delhi, CBCI Health Commission.

Thomas, Gracious, 1999, Prevention of HIV/AIDS: A textbook for schools, New Delhi, CBCI Health Commission.

Thomas, Gracious, 1999, HIV/AIDS Prevention Guide for students, New Delhi, IGNOU.

The World Bank. 1998. *Confronting AIDS: Public Priorities in a Global Epidemic*. New York: Oxford University Press. 103-71.

TNSACS. 2004. *Annual Report: 2002-2003*. Tamil Nadu State AIDS Control Society, Government of Tamil Nadu.

Tripathy S., et al. 2002. Sentinel surveillance for HIV infection in tuberculosis patients in India. *Indian Journal of Tuberculosis*, 49: 17-20.

UNAIDS. 1996. The HIV/AIDS Situation in mid 1996—global and regional highlights. UNAIDS fact sheet. July 1, 1996.

Vasadevaiah, V. 1997. HIV infection among tuberculosis patients. *Indian Journal of Tuberculosis*, 44:97-8.

Giri, V.V. National Labour Institute. 1999. *Prevention of HIV/AIDS at the Workplace* (Draft). Noida: VVGNLI.

Weinstein, G. and Fantini. M. 1970. Towards humanistic education: Curriculum of affect. New York: Praeger.

Williams, G. 1993. Community responses to HIV and AIDS; Experiences from India and Thailand. New Delhi: UNDP.

Wing. C. 1991. A Family guide to HIV and AIDS in Malaysia and Singapore. Malaysia: Southbound.

Wing, C., and Chowdhury. S. 1994. A family guide to HIV and AIDS in India. Bombay: Popula Prakashan.

WHO. 1992. AIDS global situation. New Delhi, India: Southeast Asia Regional Office.

WHO. 1992. AIDS prevention: What MCH/FP service providers need to know. New Delhi: WHO Regional Office for South—East Asia.

WHO. 1994. Carrying out HIV sentinal surveillance: A guide for programme managers. New Delhi: WHO Regional Office for South—East Asia.

WHO. 1994. HIV testing policies and guidelines. New Delhi : WHO Regional Office for South—East Asia.

World Bank. 1990. Uganda: Economic impact of AIDS—Study outline. Washington. D.C: Eastern Africa Department, Human Resources Division.

Wojcicki, J.M. and Malala, J. 2001. Condom use, power and HIV/AIDS risk: sex-workers bargain for survival in Hillbrow/Jourbert Park/Berea, Johannesburg. *Social Science and Medicine*, 53: 99-121.

APPENDICES

Appendix — I

National AIDS Prevention and Control Policy*

1. INTRODUCTION

1.1 In India the Human Immunodeficiency Virus/Acquired Immunodeficiency Syndrome (HIV/AIDS) epidemic is now 15 years old. Within this short period it has emerged as one of the most serious public health problems in the country. The initial cases of HIV/AIDS were reported among commercial sex workers in Mumbai and Chennai and injecting drug users in the north-eastern State of Manipur.

The infection has since then spread rapidly in the areas adjoining these epicenters and by 1996 Maharashtra, Tamil Nadu and Manipur together accounted for 77 per cent of the total AIDS cases with Maharashtra reporting almost half the number of cases in the country. Even though the officially reported cases of HIV infections and full-blown AIDS cases are in thousands only, it was realised that there is a wide gap between the reported and estimated figures because of the absence of epidemiological data in major parts of the country. The latest estimate for the HIV/AIDS infected adult population in the country is 3.8 million in 2000. The overall prevalence in the country is still, however, very low, a rate much lower than many other countries in the Asia region.

Adults HIV Prevalence Rate (15-49 Years) in Some Selected Countries in Asia

Cambodia	2.77
Myanmar	1.99
Thailand	1.85
India	0.75
Malaysia	0.36
Nepal	0.30
Vietnam	0.29
Pakistan	0.10
Indonesia	0.09
Sri Lanka	0.07
China	0.08
Bhutan	0.01

Source: National AIDS Control Organization, Ministry of Health and Family Welfare, Govt. of India (naco.nic.in)

1.2 The available surveillance data clearly indicates that HIV is prevalent in almost all parts of the country. In the recent years it has spread from urban to rural areas and from individuals practising risk behaviour to the general population. Studies indicate that more and more women attending ante-natal clinics are testing HIV-positive thereby increasing the risk of perinatal transmission. About 85 per cent of the infections occur from the sexual route (both heterosexual and homosexual), about 4 per cent through blood transfusion and another 8% through injecting drug use. About 89% of the reported cases are occurring in sexually active and economically productive age group of 18-49 years. One in every 4 cases reported is a woman. The attributable factors for such rapid spread of the epidemic across the country today are labour migration and mobility in search of employment from economically backward to more advanced regions, low literacy levels leading to low awareness among the potential high risk groups, gender disparity, sexually transmitted infections and reproductive tract infections both among men and women. The social stigma attached to sexually transmitted infections also holds good for HIV/AIDS, even in a much more serious manner. The effects of stigma are devastating. Discrimination against People Living With HIV/AIDS denies them access to treatment, services and support and hinders effective responses. It creates a climate in which decisive action from the government may be side stepped. There have been cases of refusal of treatment and other services to AIDS patients in hospitals and nursing homes both in Government and private sectors. This has compounded the misery of the AIDS patients. More often it is mistaken to be a contagious disease and patients are isolated in the wards creating a scare among the general patients. In the workplace there are cases of discrimination leading, on some occasions, to loss of employment. The active part played by some non-Governmental organisations in bringing out public interest litigations against such cases of discrimination and the judicial pronouncements by courts in support of the rights of such people has partly helped in alleviating the misery of the affected persons. People Living With HIV/AIDS have provided the best response to the stigma and the denial that shroud the epidemic. They bring faces and voices to the realities. Only clear and candid information about how HIV is and is not transmitted will alleviate unnecessary fear and discrimination. Efforts need to be made to train all medical and Para medical health care workers to create a congenial environment where HIV/AIDS patients are admitted and treated without any fear and scare. The treatment options are still in the initial trial stage and are prohibitively expensive. While there is no vaccine in sight, multi-drug anti retroviral therapy, popularly known as 'cocktail therapy', is not a cure to the disease and may help only in prolonging the life of the patient. Standardisation of treatment regimens for these drugs is still evolving and there are fears of patients developing drug resistance and side effects if the therapy is not administered under proper medical supervision. There are instances of quacks taking advantage of the situation and promising cures and defrauding unsuspecting people who are infected with the virus of large sums of money.

1.3 Transmission of the disease through blood, though limited to 4% of the cases down from 8% in 1992, is also a serious issue as unsuspecting population can get infected through this route if safe blood is not ensured. Existence of a large number of small and medium blood banks, many of them in the private sector, also compounds the problem. The Supreme Court directive of May, 1996 has helped in phasing out unlicensed blood banks by May, 1997 and professional blood donors by December, 1997. Mandatory testing of blood for HIV along with Syphilis, Malaria Hepatitis B and C has helped in checking transmission of HIV virus through blood transfusion.

1.4 Transmission among injecting drug users is also one of the major causes for the spread of HIV/AIDS in the country. Even though the cases are more prevalent in the north-eastern States, incidence of HIV through injecting drug use is evident from many parts of the country, specially the urban areas.

1.5 Harm reduction programmes which involve exchange of syringes and needles, coupled with peer education, community outreach, access to health services and a range of treatment modalities from abstinence to oral drug substitution have been adopted by other countries to effectively reduce transmission of HIV through injecting drug use. In India the harm-reduction approach is yet to find wider acceptability because of ethical and moral considerations. Although transmission of HIV through use of needles, razors and other cutting instruments in beauty parlors, hair-cutting saloons and dental clinics is insignificant, lack of hygienic practices in majority of these establishments also poses a health risk to the unsuspecting general population who visit these places every day. There is an urgent need to bring these establishments to acceptable standards of hygiene to minimise and almost eliminate the chances of HIV transmission through the use of needles and sharp cutting instruments.

1.6 With a high prevalence of TB infection in India the problem of HIV/TB co-infection also poses a major challenge. Nearly 60% of the AIDS cases are reported to be opportunistic TB infection cases. Treatment of TB among the HIV-infected persons is a new challenge to the National TB Control Programme which has now adopted Directly Observed Treatment Short-course (DOTS) strategy for control of TB infection. Some of the drugs which are recommended for TB treatment pose complications in cases of HIV-infected persons and had to be withdrawn in areas of high HIV prevalence. At the same time looking for HIV among TB infected persons will also cause the problem of scaring away a large number of TB infected cases in the country from seeking treatment under the DOTS strategy. There is no risk of any TB patient getting infected with HIV unless he or she practises high risk behaviour or gets infected from transfusion of HIV-infected blood.

1.7 HIV/AIDS is not a disease which spreads randomly and is transmitted as a consequence of a specific behavioural pattern and has strong socio-economic implications. It not only costs huge sums of money in terms of controlling the opportunistic infections such as TB, Pneumonia and cryptococcal meningitis, but seriously affects individuals in their prime productive years causing serious economic loss to them and their families.

Economic Impact

The effects of the epidemic radiate from the household across society. In Cote d'lvoire, urban households that have lost at least one family member to AIDS have seen their income drop by 52-67%, while their expenditure soared four fold. To cope up, they have to cut their food consumption by about 41%. Rural households facing similar predicaments in Thailand are seeing their agricultural outputs shrinking by half. In 15% of the cases, children are removed from schools to take care of family members who are ill and to regain lost income.

Some companies in Africa have already felt the impact of HIV on their bottom line. Managers at one sugar estate in Kenya said they could count the cost of HIV infection in a number of ways: absenteeism, lower productivity (a 50% drop in the ratio of processed sugar recovered from raw cane between 1993 and 1997) and higher overtime costs for workers obliged to work longer hours to fill in for sick colleagues. Direct cash costs related to HIV infection have risen dramatically in the same company: spending on funerals rose fivefold between 1989 and 1997, while health costs rocketed up by more than 10-fold over the same period, reaching KSh 19.4 million (US$ 325000) in 1997. The company estimated that at least three-quarters of all illness is related to HIV infection. Indeed, illness and death have jumped from last to first place in the list of reasons for people leaving a company, while old-age retirement slipped from the leading cause of employee drop-out in the 1980s to just 2% by 1997.

1.8 While addressing the problem of HIV/AIDS among the economically productive and sexually active sections of population, specific emphasis needs to be given not only to high risk groups like commercial sex workers and injecting drug users, but also to specific groups in general population like students, youth, migrant workers in urban and rural areas, women and children. Migration of economically productive sections of population from rural to urban areas in search of employment is a common phenomenon all over the country. Most of the migrant labour are in the unorganised sector, are highly mobile and live in unhygienic conditions in urban slums. Long working hours, relative isolation from the family and geographical social mobility may foster casual sexual relationships and make them highly vulnerable to STDs/HIV/AIDS. All these aspects provide an unusual challenge of spread of HIV infection through various routes which comes with its long period of invisibility and subsequent manifestation through opportunistic infections. In India with a large population and population density, low literacy levels and consequent low levels of awareness, HIV/AIDS is one of the most challenging public health problems ever faced by the country.

2. RESPONSE

2.1 Soon after reporting of the first HIV/AIDS case in the country, the Government recognised the seriousness of the problem and took a series of important measures to tackle the epidemic. A high-powered National AIDS Committee was constituted in 1986 itself and a National AIDS Control Programme was launched a year later. In the initial years the programme focussed on generation of public awareness through mass communication programmes, introduction of blood screening for transfusion purposes and conducting surveillance activities in the epicentres of the epidemic. In 1992 the Government formulated a multi-sectoral strategy for the prevention and control of AIDS in India. It is implemented through the National AIDS Control Organisation at the national level and State AIDS Cells at the State/UT levels. The programme concentrated on the following areas which conform to the global AIDS prevention and control strategy:

(i) Programme Management
(ii) Surveillance and research
(iii) Information, Education and Communication including social mobilization through Non-Governmental Organisations (NGOs)
(iv) Control of Sexually Transmitted Diseases
(v) Condom Programming
(vi) Blood Safety; and
(vii) Reduction of impact.

2.2 Eight years into the programme, the Government can look back with a measure of satisfaction for its success in important areas like generation of awareness about HIV/AIDS among the urban and rural population of the country. Awareness levels which were almost insignificant at the beginning of the epidemic have substantially increased in urban areas even though the level of awareness in rural areas continues to remain low. The Behavioural Surveillance Survey (BSS) carried out by Government of India in 2000-01 general population in various states clearly indicated that the overall awareness about HIV/AIDS among people in reproductive age group (15-49 years) was 76.1%; males –82.4% and females-70%. In the urban areas, 89.4% respondents had heard of HIV/AIDS as against 77.3% in rural areas. However, the lowest awareness rates were recorded among rural women in Bihar (21.5%), Gujarat (25%), Uttar Pradesh (27.6%), Madhya Pradesh (32.3.%) and West Bengal (38.6%). More than half of the respondents in the country (57%) were aware that having one faithful and uninfected partner could prevent transmission of HIV/AIDS. Some very successful intervention programmes among the high risk groups like commercial sex workers in the Sonagachi area of Calcutta, men having sex with men in Chennai and injecting drug users in Manipur were carried out through the dedicated involvement of non-Governmental organisations. Emphasis has been laid on control of STDs by strengthening STDs clinics at the district level by early diagnosis and proper management of STDs. Availability of good quality condoms through social marketing has made a significant increase in the last three years.

2.3 Several important actions have been taken to ensure blood safety by modernisation and strengthening of blood banks, introduction of licensing system for blood banks and gradual phasing out of professional blood donors. Introduction of component separation facilities has also helped in proper clinical use of blood for transfusion. The percentage of infections occurring through blood transfusion has reduced from 8% in 1994 to 3- 4% in 2001.

2.4 HIV/AIDS is not merely a public health challenge, it is also a political and social challenge. Behaviour change will not occur without a significant change in the social and political environment. Unequal gender and power relations, taboos in frank and open communication about sexual health and stigma and discrimination are particularly significant obstacles to an effective response. The economic impact of AIDS epidemic needs to be acknowledged. The largest economic cost of a death due to HIV/AIDS is usually lost income as those who die from AIDS are generally younger and in their most productive years.

2.5 There are still many gaps left in the programme and many lessons have been learnt. The inexorable spread of the disease from the initial epicenters to the rest of the country underscores the immediate need to have a paradigm shift in the response against HIV/AIDS at all levels making it imperative to formulate a comprehensive national policy on HIV/AIDS in order to cope effectively with the changed nature of the HIV/AIDS problem. The entire programme of prevention and control of HIV/AIDS needs to adopt a more holistic approach looking at AIDS as a developmental problem and not as a mere public health issue.

3. OBJECTIVES AND GOALS

The general objective of the policy is to prevent the epidemic from spreading further and to reduce the impact of the epidemic not only upon the infected persons but upon the health and socio-economic status of the general population at all levels. The policy envisages effective containment of the infection levels of HIV/AIDS in the general population in order to achieve zero-level of new infections by 2007. The specific objectives of the policy are:

(i) to reiterate strongly the Government's firm commitment to prevent the spread of HIV infection and reduce personal and social impact.

(ii) to generate a feeling of ownership among all the participants both at the Government and non-Government levels, like the Central Ministries and agencies of the Government of India, State Governments, city corporations, industrial undertakings in public and private sectors, panchayat institutions and local bodies to make it a truly national effort

(iii) To create an enabling socio-economic environment for prevention of HIV/AIDS, to provide care and support to people living with HIV/AIDS and to ensure protection/promotion of their human rights including right to access health care system, right to education, employment and privacy to mobilise support of a large number of NGOs/Community Based Organisations (CBOs) for an enlarged community initiative for prevention and alleviation of the HIV/AIDS problem.

(iv) To decentralise HIV/AIDS control programme to the field level with adequate financial and administrative delegation of responsibilities.

(v) To strengthen programme management capabilities at the State Governments, municipal corporations, panchayat institutions and leading NGOs participating in the programme.

(vi) To bring in horizontal integration at the implementation level with other national programmes like Reproductive and Child Health, TB Control, Integrated Child Development Scheme and with the primary health care system.

(vii) To prevent women, children and other socially weak groups from becoming vulnerable to HIV infection by improving health education, legal status and economic prospects.

(viii) To provide adequate and equitable provision of health care to the HIV-infected people and to draw attention to the compelling public health rationale for overcoming stigmatisation, discrimination and seclusion in society

(ix) To constantly interact with international and bilateral agencies for support and cooperation in the field of research in vaccines, drugs, emerging systems of health care and other financial and managerial inputs.

(x) To ensure availability of adequate and safe blood and blood products for the general population through promotion of voluntary blood donation in the country.

(xi) To promote better understanding of HIV infection among people, especially students, youth and other sexually active sections to generate greater awareness about the nature of its transmission and to adopt safe behavioural practices for prevention.

4. STRATEGY

4.1 The national AIDS control policy principally aims at the following strategy for prevention and control of the disease:-

I. Prevention of further spread of the disease by
   (i) making the people aware of its implications and provide them with the necessary tools for protecting themselves.
   (ii) controlling STDs among vulnerable sections together with promotion of condom use as a preventive measure
   (iii) ensuring availability of safe blood and blood products; and
   (iv) reinforcing the traditional Indian moral values among youth and other impressionable groups of population.

II. To create an enabling socio-economic environment so that all sections of population can protect themselves from the infection and families and communities can provide care and support to people living with HIV/AIDS.

III. Improving services for the care of people living with AIDS in times of sickness both in hospitals and at homes through community healthcare.

5. POLICY INITIATIVES

One of the biggest lessons learnt globally as well in the country is that national responses should not wait for HIV/AIDS cases to soar. Policies should not wait at a time when crucial prevention and care information and services are needed. HIV is particularly fuelled by situations of injustice and poverty and its impact is felt beyond health sectors. Another important lesson learnt is that a multi sectoral response must be designed in the context of the overall development strategy to ensure its sustainability and effectiveness. A substantial component of AIDS prevention and care relies on strong public health infrastructure in order to mount a more effective health sector response to AIDS. They include early diagnosis and treatment of sexually transmitted infections using the syndromic approach, blood transfusion safety, epidemiological surveillance and research and a continuum of HIV/AIDS care linking health institutions, community and home. It can only be achieved if the programme is decentralized and owned up completely by States/UTs for implementation. NGO's and private sector have an equally critical role to play in an effective response. The challenge is to identify appropriate, locally relevant interventions and experienced community based organisations to work with poor and marginalized populations who are particularly vulnerable to HIV infections. HIV/AIDS control programme however well planned and designed at the central level remains ineffective unless they reach out where people live, work, study and access health and other welfare services including information services.

For this purpose the policy recognizes the following issues as critical for bringing in a paradigm shift in the response to HIV/AIDS at all levels both within and outside Government.

5.1 Programme Management

5.1.1 AIDS control programme has hitherto been seen as a public health matter dealt by the Ministry of Health and Family Welfare. However, because of the behavioral nature and the strong socio-economic implications, the disease requires to be treated as a developmental issue which impinges on various economic and social sectors of Governmental and non-Governmental activity. As economically productive sections of the population are the most susceptible to the disease, participation of Ministries like Railways, Surface Transport, Heavy Industry, Steel, Coal, Youth affairs & Sports and other public sector undertakings employing large workforce require to be actively involved in the programme. Organised and unorganised sector of industry needs to be mobilised for taking care of the health of the productive sections of their workforce. Ministries like Social Justice & Empowerment, Women and Child Welfare, Human Resource Development, etc. should devise and own up the HIV/AIDS control programmes within their own sectoral jurisdiction. There should be strong budgetary and managerial support to these sectoral programmes from within these Ministries.

5.1.2 The State Governments at their levels should develop strong ownership of the HIV/AIDS prevention and control programme. As the prevalence of the disease and its implications vary from State to State, the State Governments should devise their own strategies and action programmes for tackling the disease keeping the national objectives in view. For smooth flow of funds to the programme and for greater functional autonomy, the State Governments have already adopted the Society model by forming State AIDS Control Societies with proper representation from NGOs, experts in the field and organisations of people living with HIV/AIDS. The Societies are provided with adequate number of technical and managerial personnel for effective management of the programme. As high prevalence of the disease is directly related to the degree of urbanisation and consequent high risk behaviour among groups like commercial sex workers, drug users, and men having sex with men, the municipal corporations of large metropolitan cities should be encouraged to draw up their own programme strategy for AIDS prevention and control. Direct funding of programmes undertaken by the municipal corporations can go a long way in reducing the administrative bottlenecks and help in effective control of the disease.

5.1.3 As HIV/AIDS is relatively new to the country, there has been no effective field organisation at the district or sub-district level to tackle the problem. In diseases like leprosy, TB, etc. the district level Societies play a very active role in implementing the programmes and receive funds directly from the national programmes. There is an urgent need to use this infrastructure at the district level for prevention and control of HIV/AIDS. This will not only help in quick channelisation of funds but bring in participation of elected representatives of the people from the 3-tier panchayati raj system and urban municipalities. The district administration headed by the District Magistrate/Collector and the Chief Medical Officer of Health should be able to provide the necessary administrative and technical infrastructure for supporting the programme. Amalgamation of State and District level Societies formed for various disease control programmes will bring in synergy in efforts at disease control, and ensures optimal resource utilization.

5.2 Advocacy and Social Mobilisation

5.2.1 In spite of the strong IEC campaign on HIV/AIDS, there is still inadequate understanding of the serious implications of the disease among the legislators, political and social and religious leaders, bureaucracy, media, leaders of trade and industry and professional agencies not to speak of the medical and paramedical personnel engaged in health care delivery system. A strong advocacy campaign needs to be launched at all levels for these opinion leaders, policy makers and service providers to make them understand and motivated about the need for immediate prevention of the disease and also for adopting a humane approach towards those who have already been infected with HIV/AIDS. The Government emphasises the need to start advocacy from the topmost level and spread it down throughout the country.

5.2.2 There is still a serious information gap about the causes of spread of the disease even among a large number of medical and paramedical personnel both within the Government and outside. This occasionally leads to discrimination of HIV/AIDS-infected persons in hospitals, dispensaries, workplaces and the community at large. There is a strong need for advocacy at all levels to eliminate such discrimination and hostility against HIV/AIDS-infected people.

5.2.3 In educational institutions AIDS education should be imparted through curricular and extracurricular approach. The programme of AIDS education in schools and the 'Universities Talk AIDS' (UTA) programme should have universal applicability throughout the country in order to mobilise large sections of the student community to bring in awareness among themselves and as peer educators to the rest of the community. Non-student youth should also be addressed through the large network of youth organizations, sports clubs, National Service Scheme (NSS) and Nehru Yuvak Kendras spread across the country. AIDS prevention education should also be integrated into the programmes of workers education and schemes of social development.

5.2.4 Electronic and print media has almost reached universal coverage for dissemination of information in India. The impressive rise in the levels of awareness about HIV/AIDS in the general community can be partly attributed o the electronic media which has taken this message right up to the village level. While there is general awareness about the disease, specific aspects like mode of transmission, method of protecting oneself from getting infected, etc. are still not known to a large section of the population. There is therefore an urgent need to generate appropriate programmes which lays stress on interpersonal communication for targeted groups like students, youth, women, migrant workers and children. The electronic media should evolve a well-coordinated media policy for dissemination of information on all aspects of HIV/AIDS including reinforcement of positive cultural and social values like love, warmth and affection within the family. The newspapers, magazines and other print media should be used for conducting campaigns for social mobilisation to generate awareness about prevention and for sharing information and expertise. The media should in general play a positive role in generating an enabling environment for AIDS prevention and control and care of the HIV-infected people. The best communication talents available in Government and private sector should be utilised in designing these media campaigns which should be developed in local languages and ethos. Media campaigns in rural areas should lay emphasis on local traditions and cultures and should be conducted through folk dances, jatras, puppet shows, street plays, etc. The Family Health Awareness Campaigns which lay stress on community mobilisation for awareness generation and utilisation of primary health care services for control of STDs/RTISs should be conducted at frequent intervals throughout the country.

5.2.5 The corporate sector should be encouraged to undertake AIDS prevention activities including provision of services for their employees both at the workplace and outside as a part of their social responsibility. Industrial units in organised sector should evolve workplace intervention programmes for industrial workers with the active involvement and participation of trade unions. The intervention programmes should have all the important components of the prevention and control strategy for HIV/AIDS. The large network of ESI hospitals and dispensaries under the Employees State Insurance Scheme should be effectively used to spread the message of prevention of the disease and providing service to HIV/AIDS infected workers and their families.

5.2.6 Because of faster economic development in certain regions of the country in the last few decades, there has been significant migration of population from rural to urban areas, both inter-State and intra-State. Migration of rural population in search of employment has also led to increase in the number of slums with poor public health infrastructure in urban and semi-urban areas. Migration is mostly single with the workers living alone in substandard living conditions. The separation from families for long periods also result in high risk behaviour among these migrant workers. These workers, after they get infected with HIV, do also infect their unsuspecting housewives when they go home for vacation or for agricultural operations. The problem therefore has to be addressed both at the place of origin and the place of migration. The problem of these migrant workers needs special IEC and intervention programmes for provision of services like STDs clinics, condom distribution centres and access to health care. All these measures should be able to increase the awareness levels of the general population both in urban & rural areas to more than 90% in the next five years.

5.3 Participation of NGOs/CBOs

5.3.1 Non-Governmental organisations have made significant contribution in the health sector by their innovative approach in the areas of public health, family welfare and in arresting the spread of communicable diseases. It is essential to continue to encourage the involvement of the voluntary sector in HIV/AIDS. The National AIDS Control Programme has recognised the importance of NGOs participation in the Programme for providing community support to people living with HIV/AIDS and their families and for providing the required care and counselling. NGOs bring with them their experience of community level work in enhancing people's participation by adopting an interpersonal approach with sensitivity and thus benefit the HIV/AIDS programme immensely.

5.3.2 Government commits itself to large-scale involvement and participation of NGOs/CBOs in NACP in the following manner:

(i) Involvement of NGOs at the policy making level through regular interaction and adequate representation in national and State level bodies.

(ii) Extending their participation to new areas like provision of medical facilities including home-based care, opening of community care centres, etc. apart from the conventional areas of awareness, counselling and targeted interventions among risk groups.

(iii) Greater efforts to undertake training and capacity building programmes for the NGOs to empower them to take up these additional responsibilities.

(iv) Periodical updating of guidelines issued by NACO for involvement of NGOs to facilitate greater participation of NGOs and for better accountability.

Encourage networking among NGOs to avoid duplication of efforts in some of the areas. Efforts will be made to identify nodal NGOs in different States for coordinating the work of all the NGOs working in that State. State Governments also need to address the problem of motivation among Government officials towards involvement of NGOs in the programme.

5.4 Control of Sexually Transmitted Diseases (STDs)

5.4.1 The large prevalence of STDs in Indian population is cause for concern as presence of STDs, specially with ulcer or discharge, facilitates transmission of HIV infection. The risk of transmission is 8 to 10 times higher in case of persons with STDs compared with others. As the risk behaviour of persons with STDs and HIV is the same, Government attaches top priority to the prevention and control of STDs as a strategy for controlling the spread of HIV/AIDS in the country. The following approach will be adopted by the Government for STDs control:

(i) Management of STDs through syndromic approach (management of sexual transmitted diseases based on specific symptoms and signs and not dependent on laboratory investigations) would be incorporated into the general health service. Once the STDs case management is integrated in peripheral health system, unnecessary referral can be avoided leaving the specialised services free for management of complicated cases, operational research (the systematic study, by observations and experiment, of the working of a system, e.g. health services with a view to improvement.) and supervision of sites where STDs patients are treated.

(ii) STDs among women though highly prevalent, are suppressed because of the social stigma attached to the disease. It has therefore been decided to integrate services for treatment of reproductive tract infections (RTIs) and sexually transmitted diseases (STDs) at all levels of health care. Department of Family Welfare and NACO should coordinate their activities for an effective implementation of such integration. STDs Clinics at district/block/First Referral Unit (FRU) level would function as referral centres for treatment of STDs referred from peripheries. STDs clinics in all district hospitals, medical colleges and other centres would be strengthened by providing technical support equipment, reagents and drugs. A massive orientation-training programme would be undertaken to train all the medical and paramedical workers engaged in providing STDs/RTIs services through a syndromic approach. All STDs clinics would also provide counselling services and good quality condoms to the STDs patients. Services of NGOs would be utilised for providing such counselling services at the STDs clinics.

5.5 Use of Condoms as a HIV/AIDS Prevention Measure

5.5.1 Condoms were advocated earlier as a safe method of population control under the Family Welfare Programme. Use of condoms now assumes special significance in the AIDS-related scenario, as it is the only effective method of prevention of HIV/AIDS through the sexual route apart from total abstinence. Government feels that there should be no moral, ethical or religious inhibition towards propagating the use of condoms amongst sexually active people specially those who practise high-risk behaviour.

5.5.2 The Government has adopted a conscious policy of use of condoms through the social marketing and community-based distribution system. The social marketing strategy has helped in increasing the use of condoms in the country at large. There is greater need to ensure availability of condoms at places and times where they are needed. Hospitals, STDs clinics, counselling centres, nursing homes and even private clinics of medical practitioners should have adequate supply of condoms for use of the patients. General availability of condoms in the community drug stores, important road and railway junctions, public places, luxury hotels, etc. should also be ensured for use among sexually active people. This will help in achieving the twin purposes of control and prevention of HIV and for promoting the small family norm. Government would promote development of culturally acceptable information packages about the efficacy of condoms to achieve both these objectives.

5.5.3 While ensuring availability of condoms, it is equally necessary to see that the quality and reliability is also guaranteed. 'Condom' has recently been included in Schedule 'R' of the Drugs and Cosmetics Act for ensuring adequate quality control in their manufacture and distribution. There are adequate numbers of manufacturers both in the public and private sectors in the country to take care of the increased demand for condoms in the community.

5.6 HIV Testing

5.6.1 There is an active debate in the country on the issue of mandatory testing of people suspected of carrying HIV infection. Considerable thought has been given to this issue. The Government feels that there is no public health rationale for mandatory testing of a person for HIV/AIDS. On the other hand, such an approach could be counter-productive as it may scare away a large number of suspected cases from getting detected and treated. HIV testing carried out on a voluntary basis with appropriate pre-test and post-test counseling is considered to be a better strategy and is in line with the WHO guidelines on HIV testing. Government of India has earlier issued a comprehensive HIV testing policy and the following issues are reiterated here:

(i) No individual should be made to undergo a mandatory testing for HIV.

(ii) No mandatory HIV testing should be imposed as a precondition for employment or for providing health care facilities during employment. However, in the case of Armed Forces, before employment, HIV screening may be carried out voluntarily with pre-test and post-test counselling and the results may be kept confidential.

(iii) Adequate voluntary testing facilities with pre-test and post-test counselling should be made available throughout the country in a phased manner. There should be at least one HIV testing centre in each district in the country with proper counselling facilities.

(iv) In case a person likes to get the HIV status verified through testing, all necessary facilities should be given to that person and results should be kept strictly confidential. Such results should be given out to the person and with his consent to the members of his family. Disclosure of the HIV status to the spouse or sexual partner of the person should invariably be done by the attending physician with proper counselling. However, the person should also be encouraged to share this information with the family for getting proper home-based care and emotional support from the family members.

(v) In case of marriage, if one of the partners insists on a test to check the HIV status of the other partner, such tests should be carried out by the contracting party to the satisfaction of the person concerned.

5.6.2 The HIV testing policy adopted is found to be appropriate for different types of testing done under the programme. At present people are tested for:

(a) Screening in blood banks
(b) epidemiological surveys; and
(c) confirmatory testing for clinical management and voluntary testing.

In the case of screening for blood donation, a single test of ERS (ELISA/Rapid/Simple) is conducted to eliminate HIV sero-reactive blood. In the case of epidemiological surveys, two tests either with ELISA, or Rapid or Simple will be done. In both these cases the testing is unlinked and anonymous. In the case of diagnosis of clinically suspected cases and for voluntary testing, the testing will be done with 3 ERS using HIV kits with different antigens. HIV testing under these conditions will be carried out with proper pre-testing and post-testing counselling with informed consent of the individual and with proper follow up facilities.

5.6.3 In case of HIV testing facilities in the private sector hospitals, clinics, nursing homes and diagnostic centres, the State Governments should adopt legislative and other measures to ensure that these testing centres conform to the national policy and guidelines relating to HIV testing.

5.7 Counselling

Counselling services for suspected cases of HIV infection and for people living with HIV/AIDS (PLWHAs) should be expanded to increase their reach to those who need them. All hospitals, HIV testing centres, blood banks, STDs Clinics and organisations formed by PLWHAs should have counselling services manned by trained and professional counsellors. Government will extend all necessary help to create necessary infrastructure for establishment of these centres and in training counsellors in large numbers to man these counselling centres. Group counselling among PLWHAs which has proved to be very effective will be encouraged by giving necessary financial and other incentives.

5.8 Care and support for People Living With HIV/AIDS (PLWHAs)

5.8.1 With the spread of the infection across the country, there will be a sharp increase in the number of HIV-infected persons in the society who may belong to different social and economic strata. Apart from providing counselling before declaring the HIV status, the Government would try to ensure the social and economic well being of these people by ensuring (a) protection of their right to privacy and other human rights, and (b) proper care and support in the hospitals and in the community.

5.8.2 The HIV-positive person should be guaranteed equal rights to education and employment as other members of the society. HIV status of a person should be kept confidential and should not in any way affect the rights of the person to employment, his or her position at the workplace, marital relationship and other fundamental rights.

5.8.3 HIV-positive women should have complete choice in making decisions regarding pregnancy and childbirth. There should be no forcible abortion or even sterilisation on the ground of HIV status of women. Proper counselling should be given to the pregnant women for enabling her to take an appropriate decision either to go ahead with or terminate the pregnancy. The prophylaxis for prevention of mother to child transmission will be introduced to cover all infected mothers as a part of the National programme. This facility will be entirely voluntary on the basis of informed consent.

5.8.4 The Government would actively encourage and support formation of self-help groups among the HIV-infected persons for group counselling, home care and support of their members and their families. Social action through participation of NGOs would be encouraged and supported for this purpose.

5.8.5 As regards the treatment care and support for PLWHAs, the policy is to build up a continuum of comprehensive care comprising of clinical management, nursing care, access to drugs, counselling and psychosocial support through home-based care without any discrimination. Resources from Government and private sectors will be mobilised for this purpose.

5.8.6 Government has initiated intensive advocacy and sensitisation among doctors, nurses and other paramedical workers so that PLWHAs are not discriminated, stigmatised or denied of services. Government expresses serious concern at instances of denial of medical treatment by doctors in their clinics, nursing homes and in hospitals which causes enhanced stigmatisation to the PLWHAs. With updated knowledge available on the risks or absence of risk of HIV transmission, such denial of medical care to needy victims is inappropriate and regrettable. The Government would expect the health service sector to display necessary concern for the welfare of the community of PLWHAs and ensure proper medical care and attention. The professional organisations of medical and paramedical health workers should disseminate information about HIV/AIDS to their members up to the field level. Training of health care personnel in diagnosis, rational treatment and for follow up of HIV-related illness should continue with greater vigour.

An efficient referral system would be established starting from testing centres and counseling sites to hospitals or clinics, community-based services and home-based care. PLWHAs would be given adequate information for home care in the form of books and documents to enable them to lead a healthier life and to promote self-help.

5.8.7 Clinical management of HIV/AIDS requires strict enforcement of biosafety and infection control measures in the hospitals as per the universal safety precaution guidelines. Treatment of AIDS cases do not require any specialised equipment than what is necessary for treatment of the opportunistic infections arising out of HIV/AIDS. Government would ensure adequate supply of essential drugs for treatment of these opportunistic infections. Adequate facilities would also be created for proper disposal of plastic and other wastes and injecting needles used for treatment of HIV-infected persons.

5.8.8. Although, HIV/AIDS still defies a cure, infection can no longer be equated with imminent death. Advances in management of opportunistic infections, and the development of effective anti-retroviral therapies mean that the illness associated with HIV infection can be treated. People Living With HIV/AIDS can now live longer and better quality of lives. Government at present provides financial support to States/UTs for the treatment of opportunistic infections in all public sector hospitals. But ante-retroviral therapies are not supported by the Govt. in the programme because of their prohibitive costs on account of indefinite period of treatment and other supportive investigations required for monitoring the progress of the disease. Govt. as a matter of policy has been progressively reducing the excise and custom duties on Anti Retroviral Drugs to make them available to PLWAs at reasonable price. Govt. would review its policy on ante-retroviral therapies from time to time in order to asses their affordability and provision under the National AIDS Control Programme.

5.9 Surveillance

5.9.1 To adopt the right strategy for prevention and control of HIV/AIDS/STDs, it is necessary to build up a proper system of surveillance to assess the magnitude of HIV infections in the community. The surveillance system would include:

(a) HIV Sentinel Surveillance
(b) AIDS Case Surveillance
(c) STDs Surveillance; and
(d) Behavioral Surveillance.

(a) **HIV Sentinel Surveillance:** The Government would enlarge and refine the present surveillance system for obtaining data on HIV infections in high risk as well as low risk groups of population in rural and urban areas for monitoring the trends of the epidemic. An in-built quality control mechanism will be evolved and adopted in order to have reliable and good quality data. Government is aware of the inadequacy of comprehensive epidemiological data on the prevalence of HIV/AIDS in India which will be addressed through a proper and consistent sentinel surveillance mechanism.

(b) **AIDS Case Surveillance:** To assess the incidence of AIDS cases in the country, information will be collected from all hospitals having trained Physicians with standard AIDS case definition in Indian context. Efforts will be made to evolve a proper reporting system so that most of the AIDS cases are reported from public and private institutions and health care providers.

(c) **STDs Surveillance:** Although National Venereal Disease Control Programme was in place since early 1950s with institutional surveillance system, it remained patchy and incomplete. Due to close link of STDs with HIV/AIDS, there is a need to strengthen this system to know the incidence and prevalence of various STDs. Government would establish etiological-based surveillance system through all STDs clinics while syndromic–based surveillance system will be established through peripheral health institutions in a phased manner.

(d) **Behavioral Surveillance:** To assess the changing pattern of behaviour in different risk groups of population behavioral sentinel surveillance will be instituted initially on pilot basis which will be expanded as per the needs of the programme from time to time.

5.10 HIV and Injecting Drug Use

The problem of injecting drug use through needles has emerged as a serious problem firstly in Manipur and other North-Eastern States and in metropolitan cities like Mumbai, Chennai, Calcutta and Delhi. The problem of HIV/AIDS has added a new dimension as sharing of injection equipment for narcotic drug use is one of the most efficient routes of HIV transmission and is considered to be much more risky than unprotected sexual contact. While most of Injecting Drug Users (IDUs) are male, their female partners are not known to be in the habit of injecting drug use. The latter therefore suffer the risk of sexual transmission from HIV-infected IDUs without their knowledge. It has also been noticed that majority of the IDUs are youth in their most productive age group of 15-25. Government therefore considers it as a serious issue and is committed to adopt appropriate strategies for preventing the risk of transmission through injecting drug use.

The Risk of Transmission of HIV Through Different Modes

Route	Efficiency (%)
Sexual	0.01 to 1
Transfusion of blood/blood products	>90
Sharing of needles/syringes	3-5
Percutaneous exposure	0.4
Muco-cutaneous exposure	0.05
Mother to child transmission	25-30

The most important strategy to combat the problem of intravenous drug use and its serious consequences in transmission of HIV/AIDS would be the 'Harm Minimisation' approach which is now being accepted world wide as an effective preventive mechanism. Harm minimization aims to reduce the adverse social and economic consequences and health hazards by minimizing or reducing the intake of drugs leading to gradual elimination of their use. Harm minimization in the context of Intra Venous (IV) drug use would require not only appropriate health education, improvement in treatment services but in most practical terms, providing of bleach powder, syringes and needles for the safety of the individual. An appropriate Needle Exchange Programme with proper supervision by trained doctors/counsellors, etc. will be required. Government will encourage NGOs working in the drug de-addiction programmes to take up harm minimization as a part of the HIV/AIDS control strategy in areas, which have a large number of drug addicts. Greater convergence will be brought about between the NGOs based programmes for drug de-addiction and the hospital-based de-addiction programmes run by the Government.

5.11 Safety of Blood and Blood Products

5.11.1 To minimise the risk of transmission of HIV infection through blood and blood products, Government has taken a series of measures:

(i) The Drugs and Cosmetics Rules provide mandatory testing of blood for HIV in addition to other blood-transmissible diseases namely Hepatitis B Surface Antigen, Hepatitis 'C', Malaria and Syphilis.

(ii) Under Supreme Court directives, licensing of blood banks is mandatory and operation of unlicensed blood banks has been banned.

(iii) The system of collection of blood from paid donors has been phased out completely. To ensure availability of blood, Government has undertaken large scale mobilisation efforts to increase voluntary blood donation through involvement of governmental and non-governmental agencies.

(iv) Government would ensure establishment of adequate blood banking services at the State/District levels including provision of trained manpower.

(v) To ensure proper clinical use of blood, more blood component separation facilities would be established in the country which would improve availability of adequate blood components and their use instead of whole blood.

(vi) Government has set up National and State Blood Transfusion Councils to oversee blood transfusion services as autonomous bodies. The facility of 100% tax exemption for contributions to these Councils has also been given. These Councils will play a very important role in augmenting blood transfusion services in the country and to ensure safe blood to the people. To ensure generation of adequate medical and para medical personnel specialised in blood banks, States are required to upgrade blood banks located in medical colleges and to be named as Department of Transfusion Medicine.

5.11.2 With the modernisation of blood bank services, it is expected that the demand for blood and blood components will be fully met through a modernised and efficient network of blood banks in the public, private and voluntary sectors thus minimising the risk of HIV transmission through blood.

5.11.3.1 A comprehensive National Blood Policy encompassing all the aspects of the operation of blood banks including voluntary blood donation programme and appropriate clinical use of blood and blood products has been prepared and annexed with this document.

5.12 Research and Development

5.12.1 The research and development efforts in the field of HIV/AIDS have hitherto been very limited in the country. Government recognises the need to encourage and support research and development in the following areas:

(i) The Government will look out for collaborative research with scientific groups in developed countries for development of vaccines suitable for the strains of HIV prevalent in India. Development and trials of each vaccines will be subject to standard ethical guidelines developed and adopted by the Indian Council of Medical Research.

(ii) In the last few years a number of anti-retroviral drugs were introduced in USA and other developed countries which help in reducing the viral load in the body of the infected person and thus ensure greater longevity. The efficacy of anti-retrovirals like Azidothymidine (AZT) and Nevirapine in reduction of HIV transmission from mother to child has also been recently proved in drug trials in USA and Thailand. Pilot studies have been conducted in established medical institutions in India on efficacy of AZT and Nevarapine prophylaxis on HIV-positive pregnant women.

(iii) As regards use of antiretroviral drugs for clinical use, it is recognised that these drugs are not only extremely expensive even by the standards of developed countries, but also result in adverse side effects and drug resistance in case of improper use. There is however a great need to indigenise the technology for manufacture of these drugs which will result in their cheaper availability to the HIV-infected people. Government would pursue all available means to encourage indigenous drug manufacturers to take up manufacture of antiretroviral drugs within the country.

(iv) For creating epidemiological data base on HIV/AIDS and other related subjects, Government would identify the institutions to pursue cohort and cross sectional studies.

(v) Government would also encourage indigenisation of the HIV-related equipment like test kits which will help in reducing the cost of service to a considerable extent.

5.13 Indigenous Systems of Medicine (ISM)

5.13.1 There is an urgent need to look for a cost-effective alternatives to antiretroviral drugs in the indigenous system of medicine like Ayurveda, Unani and Siddha apart from Homoeopathy. Some of the medicines in these systems have the potential of reducing the viral load in the body of the patient thus ensuring a healthier and longer life with the infection. The Government has sponsored research projects in Homoeopathic and Siddha systems of medicines and is receiving encouraging response. It will pursue a policy of sponsoring research in ISM and Homoeopathy for development of drugs which can serve the purpose of anti-retrovirals, but at a much lesser cost.

5.13.2 At the same time it is necessary to be vigilant against unscrupulous persons claiming a cure for HIV/AIDS by magic remedies. Any medicine or system of treatment which cannot stand the test of scrutiny by professional organisations like the Ayurveda Council or the Homoeopathic Council cannot be accepted as a drug or a system of treatment in the country. The Drugs and Magic Remedies Act requires amendment to stringently deal with cases of unscrupulous persons taking advantage of the misery of HIV-infected persons and defrauding them of huge sums of money. A massive awareness campaign has also been launched to make people aware of the dangers of such medication by unqualified persons indulging in quackery.

5.14 Bilateral and International Cooperation

5.14.1 Government notes with satisfaction the active support provided by international agencies of the UN system and bilateral agencies from different countries in the developed world to its HIV/AIDS control efforts. The World Bank has participated in funding a major part of the national AIDS control programme during the last five years and has since expanded its funding in the second phase. The UN organisations which are constituent units of the UNAIDS Theme Group have all done work in India on various social & economic sectoral programmes. These organisations will have to take a relook at their programmes and priorities in the context of the increasing prevalence of HIV/AIDS among the economically productive and socially exploited sections of the population. The Joint United Nations programme on HIV/AIDS known as UNAIDS is expected to assume a larger role both in terms of providing financial as well as technical expertise to the programme. Government's policy is to promote international cooperation to ensure optimal utilisation of resources to avoid unproductive duplication of efforts. Bilateral cooperation which has been developed with countries like USA, UK, and others will be extended further to take up specific intervention programmes where the technical and managerial input from these countries can be put to optimum use. Government will promote mutual information sharing with these countries and the neighboring countries in the South Asia region on their national AIDS control plans. Cross country issues like drug use, labour migration, trafficking among women & children, etc. could be the common ground for regional cooperation among the neighbouring countries. Government would also be actively looking for technical inputs for development of vaccines, drugs and equipment for prevention and control of HIV/AIDS and would explore bilateral and multilateral collaboration towards this end.

6. HIV/AIDS AND HUMAN RIGHTS

The wide spread abuse of human rights and fundamental freedom associated with HIV/AIDS has emerged as a serious issue in all parts of the world in the wake of the epidemic. Discrimination against people living with HIV/AIDS denies their rights to access health care, information and other social and economic rights granted by the constitution to its citizen. The protection of human rights is essential to safeguard human dignity in the context of

HIV/AIDS. Public health interest does not conflict with human rights. On the contrary, it has been recognised that when human rights are protected, fewer people become infected and those living with HIV/AIDS and their families can better cope with HIV/AIDS. Government recognises that without the protection of human rights of people, who are vulnerable and afflicted with HIV/AIDS, the response to HIV/AIDS epidemic will remain incomplete. Government will adopt the following measures to implement an effective rights based response:

(i) Government will review and reform criminal laws and correctional system to ensure that they are consistent with international human rights obligations and are not misused in the context of HIV/AIDS or targeted against vulnerable groups.

(ii) Government will strengthen anti-discrimination and other protective laws that protect vulnerable groups, people living with HIV/AIDS and people with disabilities from discrimination in both the public and private sectors, ensure privacy, confidentiality and ethics in research involving human subjects, emphasize education and conciliation and provide for speedy and effective administrative and civil remedies.

(iii) Government will ensure widespread availability of qualitative prevention measures and services, adequate HIV prevention and care information and services.

(iv) Government will ensure support service that will educate people affected by HIV/AIDS about their rights, provide legal services to enforce these rights and develop expertise on HIV related legal issues.

(v) Government will promote wide distribution of creative, education, training and media programmes explicitly designed to change attitudes of community towards discrimination and stigmatization associated with HIV/AIDS.

(vi) Government in collaboration with and through the community will promote a supportive and enabling environment for women, children and other vulnerable groups by addressing underlying prejudices and inequalities through community dialogue, specially designed social and health services and support to community groups.

(vii) Government will co-operate through all relevant programmes and agencies of the United Nations System, including UNAIDS, to share knowledge and experience concerning HIV related human rights issues and would ensure effective mechanisms to protect human rights in the context of HIV/AIDS at international level.

7. IMPLEMENTATION STRATEGY

7.1 The success of any implementation strategy for the prevention and control of HIV/AIDS would depend largely on the commitment of the political, administrative and community leaders and their sensitization on the potential risks and consequences of a widespread HIV/AIDS epidemic in the country. HIV/AIDS therefore, should not be treated as a mere public health programme alone but must be viewed as a developmental issue to which a multisectoral response should be evolved.

7.2 The implementation strategy would, therefore, be mainly based on securing the involvment and participation of all sectors both in the Government and outside to integrate HIV/AIDS prevention and control activities in their ongoing programmes. In particular, the social sector Ministries such as Human Resource Development, Youth affairs, Women & Child development, Rural Development and large employer Ministries such as Defence, Railways, Steel Mines etc. must be involved in undertaking focused programmes on HIV/AIDS prevention and control. The involvement of the political leadership, particularly, the elected representatives of the three tier Panchayat system, the district administration and public health service providers, is critical in creating a conducive environment to reduce social stigma and discrimination and enable greater access to services. Since the socio-economic impact of a widespread epidemic can be severe in the employment sector, the involvement of industry and business is important. This should be facilitated through the formation of business coalitions at the national and State level.

7.3 For effective interventions it is necessary to empower the state Governments by decentralizing the entire delivery system to the State and district levels through autonomous State AIDS Control societies. While HIV/AIDS should have strong focus and identity as a line programme at the state level, it is necessary to integrate this into the general health care system at the district level and below. To ensure that the public health system as well as private health care providers are responsive and sensitized to the issue, intensive training programmes must be undertaken not only to create awareness but to also provide clinical care and treatment of HIV/AIDS cases in hospitals and community settings.

7.4 In India, majority of the population is still not infected with HIV. Prevention strategies must continue to be given primary focus through awareness campaigns and counselling facilities, which will lead to behavioral change. With the increase in awareness levels in the community, the demand for voluntary counselling and testing services would rise. Voluntary counselling and testing services must be set up in hospitals at various levels as part of the diagnostic facilities as this provides an entry point for prevention and care. Specific groups like students, out of school youth, sexual partners or migrant workers need specially packaged awareness programmes on the risk and vulnerability to HIV/AIDS.

7.5 As socially marginalized sections like commercial sex workers, injecting drug users, street children, men having sex with men, etc. are not normally accessible through the traditional Government machinery, involvement of non-Governmental organizations and CBOs should be secured to effectively reach these populations through a holistic approach of targeted intervention programmes. These programmes should aim at prevention and control of sexually transmitted diseases, deliver relevant IEC messages which are in the local idiom and are interactive in nature, promote condom use for effective prevention of the spread of HIV/AIDS and create an enabling environment that reduces vulnerability of these groups. NGOs and charitable organizations should also be actively involved in organizing low cost care and support systems and outreach for people living with HIV/AIDS.

7.6 The programme should proactively promote formation of self help groups for PLWHAs and support drop-in centers where PLWHAs can get together and discuss their common problems.

7.7 With such a large decentralized programme in operation, it is essential to evolve a strong monitoring mechanism at every level to periodically monitor implementation of targeted intervention projects, care and support programmes, family health awareness campaigns, etc which are implemented by the State AIDS Control Societies. Periodic external evaluation should be a part of the monitoring and evaluation strategy to test effectiveness of the programme in controlling the spread of the infection.

8. CONCLUSION

Just as the HIV infection is transcending the boundaries of high risk groups and spreading into the general populace, prevention and care programmes have also reached a critical phase. Government of India is fully committed to prevent the spread of HIV/AIDS at the initial stage itself before it emerges into a catastrophic epidemic. Government of India looks at HIV/AIDS prevention and control as a developmental issue with deep socio-economic implications. It touches all sections of the population, both infected and affected, irrespective of their regional, economic or social status. By following a concerted policy and an action plan that emerges out of it, Government hopes to control the epidemic and slow down its spread in the general population within the shortest possible time. All participating agencies in the Governmental and non-Governmental sectors, international and bilateral agencies, would need to adopt policies and programmes in conformity with this national policy in their effort to prevent and control HIV/AIDS in India.

Appendix — II

National Blood Policy*

INTRODUCTION

A well organised Blood Transfusion Service (BTS) is a vital component of any health care delivery system. An integrated strategy for Blood Safety is required for elimination of transfusion transmitted infections and for provision of safe and adequate blood transfusion services to the people. The main component of an integrated strategy include collection of blood only from voluntary, non-remunerated blood donors, screening for all transfusion transmitted infections and reduction of unnecessary transfusion.

The Blood Transfusion Service in the country is highly decentralised and lacks many vital resources like manpower, adequate infrastructure and financial base. The main issue, which plagues blood banking system in the country, is fragmented management. The standards vary from State to State, cities to cities and centre to centre in the same city. In spite of hospital based system, many large hospitals and nursing homes do not have their own blood banks and this has led to proliferation of stand-alone private blood banks.

The blood component production/availability and utilisation is extremely limited. There is shortage of trained health-care professionals in the field of transfusion medicine.

For quality, safety and efficacy of blood and blood products, well-equipped blood centres with adequate infrastructure and trained manpower is an essential requirement. For effective clinical use of blood, it is necessary to train clinical staff. To attain maximum safety, the requirements of good manufacturing practices and implementation of quality system moving towards total quality management, have posed a challenge to the organisation and management of blood transfusion service.

Thus, a need for modification and change in the blood transfusion service has necessitated formulation of a National Blood Policy and development of a National Blood Programme which will also ensure implementation of the directives of Supreme Court of India - 1996.

MISSION STATEMENT

The policy aims to ensure easily accessible and adequate supply of safe and quality blood and blood components collected/procured from a voluntary non-remunerated regular blood donor in well equipped premises, which is free

---

Source: National AIDS Control Organization, Ministry of Health and Family Welfare. Govt. of India, (naco.nic.in).

from transfusion transmitted infections, and is stored and transported under optimum conditions. Transfusion under supervision of trained personnel for all who need it irrespective of their economic or social status through comprehensive, efficient and a total quality management approach will be ensured under the policy.

OBJECTIVES OF THE POLICY

To achieve the above aim, the following objectives are drawn:

1. To reiterate firmly the Govt. commitment to provide safe and adequate quantity of blood, blood components and blood products.
2. To make available adequate resources to develop and re-organise the blood transfusion services in the entire country.
3. To make latest technology available for operating the blood transfusion services and ensure its functioning in an updated manner.
4. To launch extensive awareness programmes for donor information, education, motivation, recruitment and retention in order to ensure adequate availability of safe blood.
5. To encourage appropriate clinical use of blood and blood products.
6. To strengthen the manpower through human resource development.
7. To encourage Research & Development in the field of Transfusion Medicine and related technology.
8. To take adequate regulatory and legislative steps for monitoring and evaluation of blood transfusion services and to take steps to eliminate profiteering in blood banks.

Objective 1

To reiterate firmly the Govt. commitment to provide safe and adequate quantity of blood, blood components and blood products.

Strategy

1.1 A national blood transfusion Programme shall be developed to ensure establishment of non-profit integrated National and State Blood Transfusion Services in the country.

1.1.1 National Blood Transfusion Council (NBTC) shall be the policy formulating apex body in relation to all matters pertaining to operation of blood centres. National AIDS Control Organisation (NACO) shall allocate a budget to NBTC for strengthening Blood Transfusion Service.

1.1.2 State/UT Blood Transfusion Councils shall be responsible for implementation of the Blood Programme at State/UT level, as per the recommendations of the National Blood Transfusion Council.

1.1.3 Mechanisms for better co-ordination between NBTC and SBTCs shall be developed by the NBTC.

1.1.4 Mechanisms shall be developed to monitor and periodically evaluate the implementation of the National Blood Programme in the country.

1.1.5 The enforcement of the blood and blood products standards shall be the responsibility of Drugs Controller General India) as per Drugs and Cosmetics Act/Rules, with assistance from identified experts.

1.1.6 NBTC shall ensure involvement of other Ministries and other health programmes for various activities related to Blood transfusion services.

1.2 Trading in blood i.e. Sale & purchase of blood shall be prohibited.

1.2.1 The practice of replacement donors shall be gradually phased out in a time bound programme to achieve 100% voluntary non-remunerated blood donation programme.

1.2.1.1 State/UT Blood Transfusion Councils shall develop an action plan to ensure phasing out of replacement donors.

1.3 The following chain of Transfusion Services shall be promoted for making available of safe blood to the people.

1.3.1 State Blood Transfusion Councils shall organise the blood transfusion service through the network of Regional Blood Centres and Satellite Centres and other Government, Indian Red Cross Society & NGO run blood centres and monitor their functioning. All Regional Centres shall be assigned an area around in which the other blood banks and hospitals which are linked to the regional centre will be assisted for any requirement and shall be audited by the Regional Centre. It will also help the State Blood Transfusion Council in collecting the data from this region.

1.3.2 The Regional Centres shall be autonomous for their day to day functioning and shall be guided by recommendations of the State/UT Blood Transfusion Councils. The Regional Centre shall act as a referral centre for the region assigned to it.

1.3.3 NBTC shall develop the guidelines to define NGO run blood centres so as to avoid profiteering in blood banking.

1.4 Due to the special requirement of Armed Forces in remote border areas, necessary amendments shall be made in the Drugs & Cosmetics Act/ Rules to provide special licences to small garrison units. These units shall also be responsible for the civilian blood needs of the region.

Objective 2

To make available adequate resources to develop and re-organise the blood transfusion service in the entire country.

Strategy

2.1 National & State/UT Blood Transfusion Councils shall be supported strengthened financially by pooling resources from various existin programmes and if possible by raising funds from international/bilatera agencies.

2.2 Efforts shall be directed to make the blood transfusion service viab through non-profit recovery system.

2.2.1. National Blood Transfusion Council shall provide guidelines f ensuring non-profit cost recovery as well as subsidised system.

2.2.2. Efforts shall be made to raise funds for the blood transfusion service for making it self-sufficient.

2.2.3. The mechanism shall be introduced in government sector to route the amounts received through cost recovery of blood/blood components to the blood banks for improving their services.

Objective 3

To make latest technology available for operating the blood transfusion services and ensure its functioning in an updated manner.

Strategy

3.1 Minimum standards for testing, processing and storage shall be set and ensured.

3.1.1. Standards, Drugs & Cosmetics Act/Rules and Indian Pharmacopoeia shall be updated as and when necessary.

3.1.2. All mandatory tests as laid down under provisions of Drugs & Cosmetics Act/Rules shall be enforced.

3.1.3. Inspectorate of Drugs Controller of India and State FDA shall be strengthened to ensure effective monitoring.

3.1.4. A vigilance cell shall be created under Central/State Licensing Authorities.

3.2. A Quality System Scheme shall be introduced in all blood centres.

3.2.1. Quality Assurance Manager shall be designated at each Regional Blood Centre/any blood centre collecting more than 15,000 units per year to ensure quality control of Blood & its components in the region assigned. He shall be exclusively responsible for quality assurance only.

3.2.2 Every blood centre shall introduce an internal audit system to be followed by corrective actions to reduce variations in Standard Operating Procedures (SOPs) as a part of continuous improvement programme.

3.2.3. Regular workshops on the subject of quality assurance shall be conducted to update the personnel working in blood centres.

3.2.4. Regular proficiency testing of personnel shall be introduced in all the blood centres.

3.3. An External Quality Assessment Scheme (EQAS) through the referral laboratories approved by the National Blood Transfusion Council shall be introduced to assist participating centres in achieving higher standards and uniformity.

3.3.1. Reference centres shall be identified in each State/UT for implementation of EQAS. All blood centres shall be linked to these reference centres for EQAS.

3.3.2. NBTC shall identify a centre of national repute for quality control of indigenous as well as imported consumables, reagents and plasma products.

3.4. Efforts shall be made towards indigenisation of kits, equipment and consumables used in blood banks.

3.5. Use of automation shall be encouraged to manage higher workload with increased efficiency.

3.6. A mechanism for transfer of technology shall be developed to ensure the availability of state-of-the-art technology from out side India.

3.7. Each blood centre shall develop its own Standard Operating Procedures on various aspects of Blood Banking.

3.7.1. Generic Standard Operating Procedures shall be developed by the National Blood Transfusion Council as guidelines for the blood centres.

3.8. All blood centres shall adhere to bio-safety guidelines as provided in the Ministry of Health & Family Welfare manual "Hospital-acquired Infections: Guidelines for Control" and disposal of bio-hazardous waste as per the provisions of the existing Biomedical Wastes (Management & Handling) Rules - 1996 under the Environmental Protection Act - 1986.

Objective 4

To launch extensive awareness programmes for blood banking services including donor motivation, so as to ensure adequate availability of safe blood.

Strategy

4.1 Efforts shall be directed towards recruitment and retention of voluntary, non-remunerated blood donors through education and awareness programmes.

4.1.1 There shall not be any coercion in enrolling replacement blood donors.

4.1.2 The replacement donors shall be encouraged to become regular voluntary blood donors.

4.1.3 Activities of NGOs shall be encouraged to increase awareness about blood donation amongst masses.

4.1.4. All blood banks shall have donor recruitment officer/donor organiser.

4.1.5. Each blood centre shall create and update a blood donor's directory which shall be kept confidential.

4.1.6. In order to increase the donor base specific IEC campaigns shall be launched to involve youth in blood donation activities.

4.2. Enrolment of safe donors shall be ensured.

4.2.1Rigid adherence to donor screening guidelines shall be enforced.

4.2.2 At blood donation camps, appropriate attention shall be paid on donor enrolment and screening in accordance with national standards instead of number of units collected.

4.2.3 A Counselor in each blood centre shall be appointed for pre and post donation counseling.

4.2.4 Result seeking donors shall be referred to a Blood Testing Centre (BTC) for post donation information and counseling.

4.3 State/UT Blood Transfusion Councils shall recognise the services of regular voluntary non-remunerated blood donors and donor organisers appropriately.

4.4 National/State/UT Blood Transfusion Councils shall develop and launch an IEC campaign using all channels of communication including mass-media for promotion of voluntary blood donation and generation of awareness regarding dangers of blood from paid donors and procurement of blood from unauthorised blood banks/laboratories.

4.5 National/State/UT blood transfusion councils shall involve other departments/sectors for promoting voluntary blood donations.

Objective 5

To encourage appropriate clinical use of blood and blood products.

Strategy

5.1 Blood shall be used only when necessary. Blood and blood products shall be transfused only to treat conditions leading to significant morbidity and mortality that cannot be prevented or treated effectively by other means.

5.2 National Guidelines on **"Clinical use of Blood"** shall be made available and updated as required from time to time.

5.3 Effective and efficient clinical use of blood shall be promoted in accordance with guidelines.

5.3.1 State/UT Governments shall ensure that the Hospital Transfusion Committees are established in all hospitals to guide, monitor and audit clinical use of blood.

5.3.2 Wherever appropriate, use of plasma expanders shall be promoted to minimise the use of blood.

5.3.3 Alternative strategies to minimise the need for transfusion shall be promoted.

5.4 Education and training in effective clinical use of blood shall be organised.

5.4.1 Medical Council of India shall be requested to take following initiatives:

5.4.1.1 To introduce Transfusion Medicine as a subject at undergraduate and all post graduate medical courses.

5.4.1.2 To introduce posting for at least 15 days in the department of transfusion medicine during internship.

5.4.1.3 To include Transfusion Medicine as one of the subjects in calculating credit hours for the renewal of medical registration by Medical Council of India, if it is introduced.

5.4.2 CME and workshops shall be organised by State Blood Transfusion Councils in collaboration with professional bodies at regular intervals for all clinicians working in private as well public sector in their States.

5.5 Blood and its components shall be prescribed only by a medical practitioner registered as per the provisions of Medical Council Act - 1956.

5.6 Availability of blood components shall be ensured through the network of regional centres, satellite centres and other blood centres by creating adequate number of blood component separation units.

5.7 Appropriate steps shall be taken to increase the availability of plasma fractions as per the need of the country through expanding the capacity of existing centre and establishing new centres in the country.

5.8 Adequate facilities for transporting blood and blood products including proper cold-chain maintenance shall be made available to ensure appropriate management of blood supply.

5.9 Guidelines for management of blood supply during natural and man made disasters shall be made available.

Objective 6

To strengthen the manpower through Human Resource Development.

Strategy

6.1 Transfusion Medicine shall be treated as a speciality.

6.1.1 A separate Department of Transfusion Medicine shall be established in Medical Colleges.

6.1.2 Medical Colleges/Universities in all States shall be encouraged to start PG degree (MD in transfusion medicine) and diploma courses in Transfusion Medicine.

6.1.3 PG courses for technical training in transfusion medicine (PhD/ MSc) shall also be encouraged.

6.2 In all the existing courses for nurses, technicians and pharmacists, Transfusion Medicine shall be incorporated as one of the subjects.

6.3 In-service training programmes shall be organised for all categories of personnel working in blood centres as well as drug inspectors and other officers from regulatory agencies.

6.4 Appropriate modules for training of Donor Organisers/Donor Recruitment Officers shall be developed to facilitate regular and uniform training programmes to be conducted in all States

6.4.1 Persons appointed as Donor Organisers/Donor Recruitment Officers shall undergo training for Donor Motivation and Recruitment organised by State Blood Transfusion Councils.

6.5 Short orientation training cum advocacy programmes on donor motivation and recruitment shall be organised for Community Based Organisations (CBOs)/NGOs who wish to participate in Voluntary Blood Donor Recruitment Programme.

6.6 Inter-country and intra-country exchange for training and experience of personnel associated with blood centres shall be encouraged to improve quality of Blood Transfusion Service.

6.7 States/UTs shall create a separate cadre and opportunities for promotions for suitably trained medical and para medical personnel working in blood transfusion services.

Objective 7

To encourage Research & Development in the field of Transfusion Medicine and related technology.

Strategy

7.1 A corpus of funds shall be made available to NBTC/SBTCs to facilitate research in transfusion medicine and technology related to blood banking.

7.2 A technical resource core group at national level shall be created to co-ordinate research and development in the country. This group shall be responsible for recommending implementation of new technologies and procedures in coordination with DC(I).

7.3 Multi-centric research initiatives on issues related to Blood Transfusion shall be encouraged.

7.4 To take appropriate decisions and/or introduction of policy initiatives on the basis of factual information, operational research on various aspects such as various aspects of Transfusion Transmissible Diseases, Knowledge, Attitude and Practices (KAP) among donors, clinical use of blood, need assessment etc shall be promoted.

7.5 Computer based information and management systems shall be developed which can be used by all the centres regularly to facilitate networking.

Objective 8

To take adequate legislative and educational steps to eliminate profiteering in blood banks.

Strategy

8.1 For grant/renewal of blood bank licenses including plan of a blood bank, a committee, comprising of members from State/UT Blood Transfusion Councils including Transfusion Medicine expert, Central & State/UT FDAs shall be constituted which will scrutinise all applications as per the guidelines provided by Drugs Controller General India).

8.2 Fresh licenses to stand-alone blood banks in private sector shall not be granted. Renewal of such blood banks shall be subjected to thorough scrutiny and shall not be renewed in case of non-compliance of any condition of licence.

8.3 All State/UT Blood Transfusion Councils shall develop a State Action Plan for the State/UT Blood Transfusion Service where in Regional Blood Transfusion Centres shall be identified. These centres shall be from Government, Indian Red Cross Society or other NGO run blood banks of repute. Approved regional blood centres/government blood centres/Indian red cross blood centres shall be permitted to supply blood and blood products to satellite centres which are approved by the committee as described in para 8.1. The Regional Centre shall be responsible for transportation, storage, cross-matching and distribution of blood and blood products through satellite centres.

8.4 A separate blood bank cell shall be created under a senior officer not below the rank of DDC(I) in the office of the DC(I) at the headquarter. State/UT Drugs Control Department shall create such similar cells with the trained officers including inspectors for proper inspection and enforcement.

8.5 As a deterrent to paid blood donors who operate in the disguise of replacement donors, institutions who prescribe blood for transfusion shall be made responsible for procurement of blood for their patients through their affiliation with licensed blood centres.

8.6 States/UTs shall enact rules for registration of nursing homes wherein provisions for affiliation with a licensed blood bank for procurement of blood for their patients shall be incorporated.

8.7 The existing provisions of drugs & Cosmetics Rules will be periodically reviewed to introduce stringent penalties for unauthorised/irregular practices in blood banking system.

Glossary on HIV/AIDS

AIDS: An acronym from the abbreviation AIDS. A shortening of the full form, Acquired Immune Deficiency Syndrome. A group of symptoms and signs caused by the Human Immune Deficiency Virus (HIV)

AIDS Test: The HIV antibody test. A laboratory test done on a small sample of person's blood to detect the presence or absence of HIV antibodies. These antibodies indicate, whether an individual has been exposed to the virus or not.

Anemia: A condition marked by a low number of red blood cells and associated with weakness and fatigue.

Antibodies: Substances produced by white blood cells in response to antigens. They fight off bacteria, viruses and other organisms, which attack our bodies and cause disease. In the case of HIV, antibodies produced by the body are not effective in neutralizing the virus. These antibodies serve as markers for the presence of or exposure to HIV.

Antibody Positive: Means a person has been exposed to HIV and that his immune system has developed antibodies to it. An HIV antibody test will give a positive result for the presence of HIV antibodies. The person may look and feel perfectly well but is potentially infectious and can pass the virus on to others.

Anus: The external opening of the bowel.

ARC: AIDS-Related Complex/Condition. A term for the possible combination of conditions experienced by people with symptomatic HIV infection.

Artificial Insemination: The introduction of semen into the vagina or uterus to induce pregnancy by non-sexual means.

B Cell: A lymphocyte, which matures in the bone marrow, and produces antibodies to pathogens.

Bacteria: Often called germs, these are single-cell organisms, visible only under a microscope. They can usually be treated with antibiotics.

Bi-Sexual: People who engage in sexual activities with people of both sexes.

Blood Count: The number of red and white blood cells in the bloodstream.

Carrier: A person who appears well but is capable of transmitting an infection to another person. Carriers have no outward signs or symptoms of the disease they are carrying.

CD4 Cell: A type of lymphocyte crucial to the normal function of the immune system. Also known as T4 cells, CD4+lymphocytes and T-helper lymphocytes; they are the principal target cells for HIV infection.

Cerebrospinal Fluid (CSF): The fluid found within the cavities of the brain Fluid and surrounding both the brain and the spinal cord.

Chancroid: Chancroid is an STD transmitted through sexual contact. This disease is very common among men who have frequent contact with prostitutes. Usually within about seven days of the exposure, the symptoms start appearing. Painful and open sores on the genitals accompanied by swollen tender lymph nodes in the groin are the common symptoms. In women the symptoms are less noticeable. The common symptoms that appear in women include painful urination, painful defecation, painful intercourse, rectal bleeding and vaginal discharge.

Client: The person seeking or receiving HIV counseling and or testing. In the case of a child or other person unable to consent to testing on his/her own behalf, the client is the parent or other adult with the ethical and legal competence to do so.

Clotting Factors: Proteins essential to blood coagulation found in the bloodstream; absence of these proteins leads to prolonged, sometimes pathological bleeding as in hemophilia.

Condoms: Condom is a sheath used to cover the penis during sexual intercourse. In India it is propagated as a method of Family Planning. This is an artificial way to avoid pregnancy. Now a days, lot of publicity is given for using Condoms against HIV infection.

Counseling: A confidential dialogue between a client and a counselor (usually professionally trained) aimed at enabling the client to cope with stress and take personal decisions related to HIV/AIDS.

Dementia: The last stage of AIDS infection. A progressive impairment of intellectual function with marked compromise in at least three of the following areas of mental function: language, visuospat

ELISA: Enzyme-linked immunosorbent assay, a test employed to detect the presence of HIV antibody.

Factor VIII: That factor in the blood, which is essential to clotting. People with hemophilia type A have a Factor VIII deficiency and people with severe hemophilia require frequent Factor VIII replacement with specially prepared blood products.

Genital Herpes: Genital herpes is a painful STD, which has no known cure as yet. It is a contagious viral infection and affects millions each year.

Genital Warts: Genital Warts are caused by certain types of HPV. Genital warts are contagious and are spread by sexual contact. The warts usually occur within three months of exposure.

Gonorrhea: A sexually transmitted disease causing inflammation most often in the genitourinary tract.

GUD: Genital Ulcer Disease.

Hemophilia: An inherited condition, which mainly affects men. The condition involves a reduced capacity for the blood to clot due to a deficiency of Factor VIII. Consequently, an otherwise minor accident can be dangerous because the person continues to bleed. Most bleeding occurs internally.

Hepatitis: There are several types of hepatitis virus, which can cause disease in humans. Infection with any hepatitis virus can result in a mild illness that is often undetectable. However, more severe forms of illness, even death, may result in some cases. Chronic infection with hepatitis B virus also exposes the individual to a higher risk of developing liver cancer.

The three types of hepatitis virus are transmitted differently.

*Type A through the fecal-oral route.

*Type B through sexual intercourse by the introduction of infected seminal fluids, blood and blood products, and sharing of needles and syringes.

*Non A Non B, and Type B, through infected blood and blood products.

Herpes: There are two major types of herpes simplex virus (Types I and II) in humans. Some herpes viruses cause cold sores and some cause genital herpes. Genital herpes is a common opportunistic infection in people with AIDS.

HIV: Human Immunodeficiency Virus. The virus which causes AIDS and renders the human immune system deficient and unable to resist opportunistic infections.

Homosexuality: A broad category, which refers to the general phenomenon of sexual relationship between persons of the same sex. The Catholic Church does not approve of this type of relationship, which is unnatural.

Human Papillomavirus: Human Papillomavirus (HPV) is one of the common STDs that affect men and women. It is reported that there are over 60 types of HPV. Like many STDs, most HPV infections often do cause visible symptoms.

Immune Deficiency: When a person's immune system cannot satisfactorily protect the body, resulting in an increased susceptibility to various infections.

Immune System: The body's defense system against attack by bacteria, viruses, harmful food substances and some proteins. It consists of cells, which, among other things, produce circulating substances called antibodies. Antibodies can recognize materials or agents as foreign and then attempt to neutralise or eliminate them without injury to the host's tissues.

Immune-deficiency: Any decrement in the ability of the immune system to respond appropriately to foreign substances or organisms.

Infectious: A person is infectious, when he/she has been infected with a pathogen, like HIV, and is capable of transmitting that pathogen to another person. In all categories of HIV infection a person is considered infectious for life.

Incubation Period: The time between infection with a disease-causing organism and the onset of the visible signs and symptoms of the disease.

Infection: The invasion of a host by organisms such as viruses, fungi, protozoa, or bacteria with consequent disease.

Intravenous (IV): Injected or delivered through a needle into a vein.

IV Needles: Intra-venous needles. Needles used to inject drugs directly into the bloodstream. They are inserted into veins.

IVDU: Intro-venous drug user, self-injects substances directly into veins.

Lesbian: Refers to women who involve in sexual relationship with other women. The Catholic Church does not approve of same sex relationship, which is un-natural in itself.

Lymph Glands: These are small nodes, which usually contain large numbers of white-bodied cells. Agents of infection may be gathered around these areas so they become battlegrounds. Infections can therefore cause swelling of these glands.

Lymphocytes: A class of white blood cells responsible for regulation of the immune system. Divided into B-cells (which produce antibodies) and T-Cells.

Monogamous: Relationship exclusively between two people of the opposite sex. The most ideal way of life approved by social norms. The Catholic Church approves only a monogamous marital life.

Opportunistic Infections: Organisms, which cause infection in individuals with an impaired immune system.

Pandemic: An epidemic over a wide geographic area, usually worldwide.

Parasite: An organism that lives solely in/on another. Lice, mites and fungi and all parasites which may live in/or, humans and in doing so sometimes cause disease.

Pathogen: A living microorganism or virus capable of producing a disease.

PGL: Persistently enlarged lymph glands.

Pneumocystis: One of the opportunistic Carinii Pneumonia (PCP) infections seen in immune suppressed people. It is caused by a very common airborne organism, which is normally destroyed by healthy immune systems. It is one of the most common opportunistic infection seen in people with AIDS.

Pneumonia: A type of inflammation of the lungs usually associated with infection with a microorganism.

Post-test Counseling: Dialogue between a client and a counselor aimed at discussing the HIV test result and providing appropriate information, support and referral, and at encouraging risk-reduction behaviour to those testing positive. In case the test results are negative, the client is encouraged to keep off from all types of high-risk behaviours.

Pregnancy: In relation to AIDS, pregnancy is considered unwise for a woman who is HIV antibody positive. Pregnancy may hasten development of the disease. The baby of a HIV antibody positive mother can be infected with HIV in the womb, or during birth.

Pre-natal: Existing or occurring before birth.

Pre-test Counseling: Dialogue between a client and a care provider aimed at discussing the HIV test and the possible implications of knowing one's HIV Sero status, which leads to an informed decision to take or not take the test.

Protein: Molecules found in all forms of life that are the principal components of all tissues.

Public Lice: Public Lice are parasites, which often spread by sexual contacts. One must be extremely careful to avoid handling and touching the clothing and bedding of an infected person. People who visit red light districts for sex as well as those who go to brothels are likely to get infected with these tiny insects. These lice are visible to the naked eye. They are pinhead size, oval in shape and appear reddish-brown when full with the blood of the host.

Retrovirus: Retroviruses are a class of viruses characterized by their ability to convert RNA to DNA during replication in the host cell (instead of the reverse as in most other pathogenic viruses). To do this, it requires an enzyme called reverse transcripts. HIV belongs to this group of viruses.

Reverse: An enzyme, which HIV uses to replicate itself.

Risk group: A group of individuals sharing a common behaviour or characteristic placing them at a risk for HIV infection that is higher than the general population.

RNA: Ribonucleic Acid. Genetic material inside a cell.

Scabies: Scabies are usually transmitted through sexual contact. However, it is also transmitted through contact with sheets, towels and furniture being used by those already infected. The scabies mite cause intense itching. Apart from genitals, the areas most affected include hands (especially between fingers), wrists, elbows and lower abdomen.

Sero-conversion: When an individual, who is HIV antibody negative becomes HIV antibody positive after exposure to the virus i.e. blood serum has converted from negative to positive. During this process the person may suffer an acute illness. In the case of HIV infection the symptoms may be those of flu and/or swollen glands. Sometimes no symptoms are experienced.

STD: An abbreviation of the term Sexually Transmissible Disease. Any disease which may be passed on sexually.

Sero-positivity: Synonymous with antibody positively.

Sero-negativity: The absence of antibodies directed against HIV and indicative of no infection, synonymous with antibody negativity.

Syndrome: A set of symptoms and signs resulting from a single cause, or so commonly occurring together that a definite pattern is apparent.

Syphilis: Syphilis is an STD caused by bacterium called Trephonema Palladium. This bacterium can move throughout the body, damaging many organs in course of time. Physicians describe the course of this disease by dividing it into four stages-primary, secondary, latent and tertiary. A person who is infected may infect others during the first two stages and during the latent stage if he/she does not get treatment. These three stages usually last one to two years. However, during the tertiary stage, untreated syphilis, although not contagious, can cause serious abnormalities, mental disorders, blindness, other neurological problems and death.

Tattooing: Tattooing the body with various figures of animals or plants or with scrolls has been in use from the most ancient times. It is a process by which a permanent coloured mark, design or emblem is made on the body by the introduction of pigment through ruptures in the skin.

Thalassemia: A hereditary disease, widespread in the Mediterranean countries, Asia and Africa, in which there is an abnormality in the protein part of the hemoglobin molecule. The affected red cells cannot function normally leading to anemia. Other symptoms include enlargement of the spleen and abnormalities of the bone marrow. Patients with this major disease are treated with repeated blood transfusions.

T-Helper Cells: Also called T4 cells. This is one type of white blood cell or lymphocyte that helps in defending against the disease by initiating antibody production. In people with AIDS, T-helper cells are so depleted that the immune system no longer fights off disease and opportunistic infections can occur.

Transmission: The spread of infectious pathogens from one person to another. The most common methods of HIV transmission are by allowing infected blood, semen and vaginal fluid into the body during sex and by allowing infected blood into the body by sharing IVDU equipment.

Trichomoniasis: Trichomoniasis is another STD that often develops without any symptoms. If symptoms occur, they usually appear within 4 to 20 days of exposure. In some cases symptoms may occur years after infection. In women some of the symptoms that can be noticed include a heavy, yellow-green or gray vaginal discharge, discomfort during intercourse, vaginal odor, and painful urination. Irritation and itching of the female genital area and lower abdominal pain are other symptoms. In men, the symptoms include a thin, whitish discharge from the penis and painful urination. However, most men may not show any symptoms.

Vaccine: A substance, which contains antigen of an organism. In the vaccinated person it stimulates active immunity and future protection against infection by that organism.

Virus: An extremely small organism visible only through an electron microscope. Viruses cause a wide variety of diseases in humans. They do not respond to treatment with antibiotics.

Western blot: A test to diagnose HIV infection through detection of antibodies against the virus.

Window Period: The period of time when a person may be infected with HIV, but before antibodies have been formed. This period is usually two to three weeks and is rarely longer than three months. The virus is in the blood and may be detected by an antigen test, but an antibody test will be negative.